OUR PATHWAY OF BEING

Our Pathway of Being

Jenny Masefield

JANUS PUBLISHING COMPANY
London, England

First published in Great Britain 2010
by Janus Publishing Company Ltd,
105-107 Gloucester Place,
London W1U 6BY

www.januspublishing.co.uk

British Library Cataloguing-in-Publication Data
A catalogue record for this book is available from the British Library

ISBN 978-1-85756-614-7

Cover Design: Janus Publishing

Printed and bound in Great Britain

This book is dedicated to you as you
turn the pages to widen your search.

Contents

Acknowledgements	ix
The Guide to Our Pathway	xi
Foreword by David Lorimer	xv
1. Moving Through Life's Momentum	1
2. The Rounds of our Returning	19
3. Karma, and its Consequence	41
4. Chosen Lives in Childhood	59
5. Spirits and Inspiration	79
6. Mediums and their Messages	103
7. Possession, Depossession	129
8. Withdrawal from the Body	151
9. Tasting Death and Dying	177
10. To Judgement and Connection	197
11. Extensions of Existence	221
12. The Ultimate Expression	247
The Sources of Information	271
Index of Authors, Titles and source codes	291
Bibliography	303

Acknowledgements

I would like to acknowledge and thank every author and publisher whose work has contributed to *Our Pathway of Being*. The details of the authors' names, the publishers, and the titles – numbering one hundred and twenty four books – are given in the Bibliography.

The Guide to Our Pathway

Our Pathway of Being is written as a philosophical and thought-provoking exploration of our lives, both before and beyond death. It examines many interrelated concepts and life-experiences in a way that opens a path through the varied realms of our existence.

- Chapter 1. MOVING THROUGH LIFE'S MOMENTUM questions the meaning of life and consciousness, and explores some related concepts of eternal life, pre-existence and reincarnation.

- Chapter 2. THE ROUNDS OF OUR RETURNING looks at the subject of reincarnation in greater depth, and studies its wide acceptance by Christian philosophers before the questionable 6th century anathemas. The chapter moves on through Eastern and modern philosophies, and finds that many people have had memories of living in the past.

- Chapter 3. KARMA, AND ITS CONSEQUENCE discovers some research that suggests that our lives are affected by preceding lives. It studies the concepts of karma, the development of evil and the counteractive force of better choices within free will, our spiritual development through many lives, our pre-selection of the karmic conditions and relationships for the present life, and the emotions of rebirth.

- Chapter 4. CHOSEN LIVES IN CHILDHOOD explores the experiences and frustrations of our return to earth-life. It discusses the ideas that learning is often a recollection of previous knowledge, that our inborn talents are the fruit of our efforts in the past, that our unexpected attitudes to life have been inherited from our past, and that children may retain an awareness of spirit beings.

- Chapter 5. SPIRITS AND INSPIRATION touches on our fear of ghosts, and moves on to consider some helpful spirit communications that have been received through dreams. It studies our subconscious and conscious interactions with spirit influences, the possible origin of true inspiration, our intuitive relationships with spirit guides, and furthering this contact through good mediums.

- Chapter 6. MEDIUMS AND THEIR MESSAGES explores various forms of mediumship, the growth of Western Spiritualism, the development of communication between spirits and people, fraudulent practices, and the contrast between contrived human efforts and the quality of most spirit communications. It gives the examples of a medium's development and a spirit's purpose in returning to work within the earth planes.

- Chapter 7. POSSESSION, DEPOSSESSION describes the risk of possession that is taken by those who communicate with unknown spirits. It discusses the lifestyles that can invite possession, the motives of possessing spirits and the view that some of these spirits had once had good intentions, depossession and the freedom experienced when a possessing spirit leaves the victim's body.

- Chapter 8. WITHDRAWAL FROM THE BODY suggests that the spirit of a living person can withdraw from its sleeping body, and techniques that enable people to leave their bodies at will, despite their tenuous connection with the body until the release of death. It studies some spontaneous out of body experiences, including those that occur when life becomes unbearable or preceding death; and it examines some views on suffering and death, the atonement of sins and the karmic view of our own salvation.

- Chapter 9. TASTING DEATH AND DYING explores the levels of near death experiences, and the first stages of the life reviews that show how our private thoughts and actions have affected others. It discusses the suppression of bad near death experiences and the subsequent transformation of character that may follow these experiences; and it studies some medical research that confirms the accuracy of the subject's observations and deathbed visions, and some spirit communications that describe death as passing on within a continuing life.

- Chapter 10. TO JUDGEMENT AND CONNECTION studies some accounts of violent deaths, and deaths caused by long illness, as described by the surviving spirits whose personalities are unchanged, and who are with their 'dead' relatives and friends. It studies some life reviews which include self-judgement and a profound empathy with those who were affected by the recent life, and this increases our understanding of the karma of our interconnected lives, the development of individual failing and evil, and the importance of free will in our spiritual evolution. The chapter then describes the guidance of higher beings during these reviews, adding their understanding of the recent life, and hope and strength for the future.

- Chapter 11. EXTENSIONS OF EXISTENCE studies the early levels of the afterlife, and suggests that these planes are energised by thought. It describes the period of rest and recovery, which is followed by the choice of staying on in the higher planes or preparing to return to earth for further development. The chapter then explores the experiences of those who stay on, and their development through working in creative ways and in teaching, healing and caring for the incoming souls from earth. It describes the depth of evil in some of these souls, their initial selection of the hell levels, and the efforts of advanced souls in helping them rise to higher levels. It then describes the increasing connection between the advanced souls and their group-souls, and the extraordinary interactions of their consciousness in sharing knowledge, experience and inspiration in the higher levels and rising towards the overall unity – the consciousness and mystery of God.

- Chapter 12. THE ULTIMATE EXPRESSION explores the concept of God as the Whole that includes all – as Brahman includes all Atman – and describes creation as the unfolding of part of the Divine, the

Mystery of Being lying within and beyond the matter-energy of physics. It studies the belief that a purpose of this universe is that of 'becoming' through the kingdoms of creation at all levels of evolving consciousness, developing through the shared lower levels of consciousness, then through our apparent individuality as humans, and then merging with the higher levels of increasing consciousness. This chapter finally describes the great cosmological force of universal karma, the concepts of oscillating universes, the endless days and nights of Brahma, and the word – the end of the path – God.

What is this life that we are living?
What is death – when we are dying?

Preface: 1. I think ... that although it is very difficult if not impossible in this life to achieve certainty about these questions, at the same time it is utterly feeble not to use every effort in testing the available theories, or to leave off before we have considered them in every way. [1]

Preface: 2. In religion and spirituality, in every human science, and in psychical research, we stand on the shoulders of others in order to try to see further than they have been able to do. If that is what I have done, I shall be satisfied, and if others can use what I have written in such a way as sets their own thoughts into motion, I shall be even more gratified. [2]

The original English or American English spelling has been retained in the quotations in this book.

Pre: 1. Plato: *The Last Days of Socrates.* pp.138-9. *(see Bibliography)*
[Plato. Greek philosopher; 5/4th C. BC.] Source C-a.

Pre: 2. Perry, Archdeacon Michael: *Psychic Studies: A Christian's View.* p.16.
[English theologian; 20th C.]

Foreword

by David Lorimer

The unexamined life not worth living – Socrates.

The 17th century French writer and scientist, Blaise Pascal, famously argued that it was worth betting on the exercise of God and immortality. If he was wrong, he would know nothing about it. If, however, he was right, then he would have lived his life according to higher principles, which would benefit others as well as himself. We all know that we will die someday, but very few of us are curious about the possible continuation of our existence. It is as if we knew we were going on a journey but had no interest in finding out about the country of our destination We make plans for our holidays, but do not think it worth researching our potential post-mortem itinerary.

Nor do we receive much encouragement in this respect either from our society or from science. Modern society is concerned primarily with the acquisition of material goods, while science insists that consciousness is a by-product of brain processes. On this basis, death spells the extinction of consciousness and personality. However, many anomalous experiences point towards a different conclusion, namely that the death of the physical body is a gateway to a new form of existence. In other words, death is not so much an extinction as a transition. I have spent many years pondering the themes that constitute the chapters of Jenny Masefield's book, *Our Pathway of Being.*

Jenny represents the serious seeker of spiritual knowledge while acting as a guide to the reader throughout the book. Hence the alternation between her own reflections and the extracts that build up the overall picture. She poses the very questions that readers themselves will want to explore and answers them through the texts selected from a wide variety of sources. The sources themselves are indexed under headings and include all the main religious traditions of the world as well as Rosicrucian philosophy, Theosophy, mediumship and psychical research. This means that the book draws on an unsusual range of teachings, and that these teachings are juxtaposed in interesting ways. Thus an extract from the Bhagavad Gita might be followed by one from 'Seth', a personality channelled by Jane Roberts developing the same point. The bibliographical references are then listed at the end of the book.

The structure of the book enables the reader to examine all the main elements of the perennial philosophy: the nature of consciousness, reincarnation, karma, spirits, mediums, possession, out of body and near death experiences, descriptions of bodily death, life review, post-mortem communications and descriptions of corresponding states of consciousness. Finally, the relationship between the individual mind and universal consciousness. The reader is gradually able to construct a coherent picture of life, and one that certainly corresponds closely with my own understanding of the same material. A number of key case histories are chosen to illuminate the argument: they are not the subject of critical analysis as the author's object is rather to convey her insights and reflections to the reader, who can then research particular themes more deeply.

The final chapter takes the reader into the heart of the mystery of the conscious Cosmos. Paul Brunton reminds us that "Looked at from the outside, the universe comes forth out of nothingness and passes away into nothingness. But looked at from inside, there has always been an internal hidden reality in its background. This reality is Mind. The world is only its manifestation".[1] The science of the last three centuries has given us a detailed picture of what the world looks like from the outside. The new science of consciousness is beginning to enable us to

1. Brunton, Dr Paul: *The Wisdom of the Overself*. p. 40.

understand how the world looks from the inside as well. Here it can join forces with the mystics, who are the specialist explorers of the dimensions of inner space. Jenny quotes Elisabeth Haich in this respect: "there is only one eternal being – only one God. In everything alive there lives this one single being, there lives this one single God. God is the indivisible unity, he is present everywhere, he fills the entire universe. The whole universe lives because God animates it with his own eternal being!"[2] God is the ultimate source of life and consciousness, of which the physical Cosmos is a manifestation and expression.

Our Pathway of Being is the distillation of a lifetime's reading and reflection. Readers will find between the covers of a single book an immense wealth of wisdom about the nature and purpose of human existence. As far as I can tell, it is a reliable map of the spiritual territory in which we already exist and which will open up new vistas when we make a transition into another dimension of existence. As such, it not only sheds light on our current situation, but also on our long-term prospects and the evolution of consciousness. It is a Michelin guide for the ultimate journey of life.

David Lorimer

Programme Director of the Scientific and Medical Network, and Chairman of the International Association for the Near-Death Studies (UK)

---

2. Haich, Elisabeth: *Initiation*. p. 174.

1

Moving Through Life's Momentum

"Day by day, week by week and year by year we live in this tumble of time that just goes on and on. We all go on until we die," I said to myself. "Yes, we just keep going on – whatever we believe, or have believed, or will believe – until we die. But is that really the end? Or does death lead on, somehow, to something else? I used to think so, but my ideas were too woolly to be called 'Belief'. 'Faith' would be a better word. Or 'Hope'. But if we could go on to something after dying, it seems logical to ask if we could have come from something before living in this life. –

"So what is dying, really? Come to that, what is living? –

"And what exactly are we living for? –

"Oh! I'm getting nowhere with all this wondering," I said with some frustration, "but I really must find out!" So I turned to search the libraries, and there, in the potent stillness of the British Library, and in the London College of Psychic Studies, and in between the dim stacks of the Harvard Libraries I opened up the tomes and found others who were with me in my questioning.

1:1. Albert Schweitzer, for example, had struggled to understand the 'whys' and 'wherefores' of his life. I knew that he had been a man of many talents as he was a famous doctor who had worked for years in Africa, and a gifted musician and, not least, a philosopher; so I thought his autobiography would help me. But I found it ponderous, till it caught my interest when he described a journey up a West African river to get to his mission hospital.

Schweitzer had failed to find a good boat for this trip, so he boarded a barge that would be towed behind a decrepit steamer. He had also failed to take enough provisions – but the local passengers were kind, and shared the food from their cooking pots. This was fortunate as the journey of a hundred and sixty miles would be difficult; the river was lower than usual, and the captain had to search for the safer channels between the shifting sandbanks. But Schweitzer was quite unconcerned and retreated into the privacy of his philosophical ruminations – as he explains in his autobiography, saying, "Lost in thought I sat on the deck of the barge, struggling to find the elementary and universal conception of the ethical, which I had not discovered in any philosophy."[1]

1:2. Schweitzer was not happy at this time. He was a German, and the terrible war – the First World War – was spreading inexorably through Europe. Schweitzer's concern was that the war was, in reality, the result of a serious breakdown in ethical and social values, and he felt that the guiding concept of the Europeans – their 'world-view' – had lost its great strength, and adds:

> It had become clear to me that, like so many other people, I had clung to that world-view from inner necessity. ... Only if it offers itself to us as something desired from the depth of thought can it become spiritually our own.

Now 'the depth of thought' was Schweitzer's métier, and he was convinced that he could discover some truth or revelation that would counter the decline of the traditional 'world-view'. But in this instance he describes his increasing frustration:

> Without the least success I let my thought be concentrated ... on the real nature of world – and life-affirmation and of ethics, and on the question of what they have in common. I was wandering about in a thicket in which no path was to be found. I was leaning with all my might against an iron door which would not yield.
>
> All that I had learnt from philosophy about ethics left me in the lurch. The conceptions of the Good which it had offered were all so lifeless, so unelemental, so narrow, and

---

1:1. Schweitzer, Dr Albert: *My Life and Thought.* p. 185.
[German missionary doctor/philosopher; 19/20th C.]

so destitute of content. ... [Then] late on the third day, at the very moment when, at sunset, we were making our way through a herd of hippopotamuses, there flashed upon my mind, unforeseen and unsought, the phrase, 'Reverence for life'. The iron door had yielded: the path in the thicket had become visible. Now I had found my way. ...

What is 'Reverence for Life', and how does it arise in us?

If man wishes to reach clear notions about himself and his relation to the world, he must ever again and again be looking away from the manifold, which is the product of his thought and knowledge, and reflect upon the first, the most immediate, and the continually given fact of his own consciousness. Only if he starts from this can he arrive at a thinking world-view. ... The beginning of thought, a beginning which continually repeats itself, is that man does not simply accept his existence as something given, but experiences it as something unfathomably mysterious. Life-affirmation is the spiritual act in which he ceases to live unreflectively and begins to devote himself to his life with reverence, in order to raise it to its true value.[2]

Schweitzer then gave me a vital lead to Descartes, saying:

1:3. Descartes makes thinking start from the sentence "I think; so I must exist" (*Cogito, ergo sum*), and with his beginning thus chosen he finds himself irretrievably on the road to the abstract.[3]

Now Descartes was a French philosopher who had lived in the 16th and 17th centuries, and I turned to his work with some hesitation as Schweitzer's philosophy had been heavy. But Descartes' argument was charming:

1:4. All that up to the present time I have accepted as most true and certain I have learned either from the senses

---

1:2. Ibid. pp.183-187.
1:3. Ibid. p. 186.

> or through the senses; but it is sometimes proved to me that these senses are deceptive.

Descartes developed his theme, explaining that he knew he was working while sitting in a dressing gown in front of his fire; but he also knew that he often slept:

> How often it has happened to me that in the night I dreamt that I found myself in this particular place, that I was dressed and seated near the fire, whilst in reality I was lying undressed in bed! At this moment it does indeed seem to me that it is with eyes awake that I am looking at this paper; that this head which I move is not asleep, that it is deliberately and of set purpose that I extend my hand and perceive it. ... [Yet] I have in sleep been deceived by similar illusions, and in dwelling carefully on this reflection I see so manifestly that there are no certain indications by which we may clearly distinguish wakefulness from sleep that I am lost in astonishment. And my astonishment is such that it is almost capable of persuading me now that I dream.[4]
>
> 1:5. What, then, can be esteemed as true? Perhaps nothing at all, unless that there is nothing in the world that is certain. But how can I know that there is not something different? ... Is there not some God, or some other being by whatever name we call it, who puts these reflections into my mind? That is not necessary, for is it not possible that I am capable of producing them myself? ... I hesitate, for what follows from that? Am I so dependent on body and senses that I cannot exist without these? ... Not at all: of a surety I myself exist since I ... think that I am something. So that after having reflected well, and carefully examined all things, we must come to the definite conclusion that the proposition: *I am, I exist*, is necessarily true each time that I pronounce it, or that I mentally conceive it.[5]

1:4. Descartes, René: *The Philosophical Works of Descartes*. pp. 145-146. [French philosopher; 16/17th C.]

1:5. Ibid. pp. 149-150.

At this point a third writer, Dr Paul Brunton, joins the discussion:

> 1:6. What is it in us that is conscious? ... Is it the brain? Pah! – a lump of mere flesh not much different from what we can buy in any butcher's shop. The notion that consciousness is an emanation kindled in the cells of the cerebral cortex in the brain is a mistaken one. Out of this superficial notion are born most of our metaphysical illusions ...

Metaphysics and oriental philosophy seemed to be the main subjects in Brunton's work, and I was interested to see that he was a prolific writer from his line of titles on the library shelf. But I should not digress, as Brunton rushes on with his argument that 'consciousness' cannot possibly be 'kindled' in the brain:

> By *brain* is meant that touchable and seeable portion of the human body canopied by the bony skull and filled with winding convolutions of grey and white substance, which anatomists handle in the dissecting room. By *consciousness* is meant the sum total of the changing series of sense-impressions, perceptions, thoughts, feelings, images, intuitions, ideas and memories which we know directly as our own and which cannot be got at by any dissection with a surgical knife.

Brunton then explains that consciousness, with its extraordinary range of ethereal qualities and attributes, is such that it must have had its origins from beyond the bounds of our material limitation.[6]

And these ideas are taken even further by a cleric of the Anglican Church, Michael Perry, who says:

> 1:7. I think most Christians believe that the brain doesn't so much *create* consciousness as act as a kind of receiver or filter for it. There is something – let's call it the 'essential self' for lack of a better term, though many Christians

---

1:6. Brunton, Dr Paul: *The Wisdom of the Overself*. pp. 89-91.
[British writer on acient philosophy; 19/20th C.] Source A-d.

would be traditional and call it the 'soul' – which uses the human brain in order to come to consciousness in this material world of ours.

If the 'brain is damaged' or dysfunctional – Perry continues – the 'soul' is unable to express itself in the normal way. One can understand this by comparing the brain to a 'television set' and the soul to an incoming 'programme' from the transmitting station. If the set is faulty or badly tuned it will not receive the programme properly, though the programme is still being transmitted from the station. And this leads Perry to the intriguing question as to whether our own 'normal' brains could, in fact, be limiting us in some way:

> If our brains were perfect instruments, might we perhaps be aware of abilities, consciousness, powers, which at present transcend even our wildest dreams? ... There *are* people about who have strange sensitivities which the rest of us can hardly guess at – people of intuition, of psychic awareness, people with healing powers. ... Perhaps they are indicators that it is possible – and will be possible, after this earthly life of ours is over – for the soul to work, not through a physical brain or a material body, but in another way altogether.[7]

Now this idea intrigued me, as I had been looking through a biography on Emanuel Swedenborg – who was an unusual man of intuition and psychic awareness, and a man who knew something of life after death. He had been an extraordinary mystic and a renowned scientist in the 17th and 18th centuries, and I felt that there was a lot to be learnt from his views. But at this early stage of my work I was interested in Swedenborg's analysis of the soul–body relationship – as he says:

> 1:8. Whoever duly considers the subject can know that ... all rational life that appears in the body belongs to the soul,

---

1:7. Perry, Archdeacon M: *Phschic Studies: A Christian's View.* pp. 207-208. [English theologian; 20th C.]

> and nothing of it to the body; for the body, as said above, is material, and the material, which is the property of the body, is added to and, as it were, almost adjoined to the spirit, in order that the spirit of man may be able to live and perform uses in the natural world, all things of which are material. ... And because the material does not live but only the spiritual, it can be established that whatever lives in man is his spirit, and that the body merely serves it, just as what is instrumental serves a moving living force. An instrument is said indeed to act, to move, or to strike; but to believe that these are acts of the instrument, and not of him who acts, moves, or strikes by means of the instrument, is a fallacy.
>
> As everything in the body that lives, and that acts and feels from that life, belongs exclusively to the spirit, and nothing of it to the body, it follows that the spirit is the man himself. ... In consequence, when the body is separated from its spirit, which is what is called dying, man continues to be a man and to live.[8]
>
> 1:9. All this has been said to convince the rational man that viewed in himself man is a spirit, and that the corporeal part that is added to the spirit to enable it to perform its functions in the natural and material world is not the man, but only an instrument of his spirit.[9]

I liked reading Swedenborg; his writing was somewhat slow and solid but his deductions were so logical. And the American Theosophist, William Judge, supports his views on the relative unimportance of the physical body, saying:

> 1:10. The body is considered by the Masters of Wisdom to be the most transitory, impermanent, and illusionary of the whole series of constituents in man. Not for a moment is it the same. Ever changing, in motion ... in every part, it is in fact never complete or finished though tangible. The

1:8. Swedenborg, Emanuel: *Heaven and Hell.* paras. 432-433. [Swedish scientist/mystic; 17/18th C.] Source J-a.

1:9. Ibid. para. 435.

> ancients clearly perceived this, for they elaborated a doctrine called Nitya Pralaya, or the continual change in material things, the continual destruction. This is known now to science in the doctrine that the body undergoes complete alteration and renovation. ... [At the end of our days] it is not the same body it was in the beginning. It has changed ...[10]

Shankara's classic, *The Crest Jewel of Wisdom*, now lay before me. Shankara was possibly the greatest of the Indian Brahmins, and is thought to have lived in the 5th century BC; yet despite all the trials of time, his arguments are still valid:

> 1:11. The food-formed vesture is this body, which comes into being through food, which lives by food, which perishes without food.
>
> It is formed of cuticle, skin, flesh, blood, bone, water; this is not worthy to be the Self, eternally pure. ... For the Self is the witness of all changes of form; ... [it] is the Life, because its power is indestructible; it is controller, not controlled.
>
> Since the Self is witness of the body, its character, its acts, its states, ... the Self must be of other nature than the body.[11]
>
> 1:12. Therefore, O thou mind deluded, put away the thought that this body is the Self.[12]

So what exactly is 'the Self'?

I was really intrigued; but when a friend suggested that a *Seth* book would help me, I opened the volume with some doubt as the cover explained that Seth – a "personality no longer focused in physical reality" – had dictated his book through an entranced Jane Roberts. Despite my cautious approach, however, Seth joined the discussion as his argument was fascinating:

1:10. Judge, William: *The Ocean of Theosophy*. p. 36.
[American Theosophist; 19th C.] Source 1-a.

1:11. Shankara, Acharya: *The Crest Jewel of Wisdom*. p. 29.
[Hindu teacher; c. 5th C. BC.] Source A-c.

1:12. Ibid. p. 32.

> 1:13. If you could travel within your body, you could not find where your identity resides, yet you say, "This is my body," and, "This is my name."
>
> If you cannot be found, even by yourself, within your body, then where is this identity of yours that claims to hold the cells and organs as its own? Your identity obviously has some connection with your body, since you have no trouble distinguishing your body from someone else's, and you certainly have no trouble distinguishing between your body and the chair, say, upon which you may sit.
>
> In a large manner, the identity of the soul can be seen from the same viewpoint. It knows who it is, and is far more certain of its identity, indeed, than your physical self is of its identity.[13]

The Sufi teacher, Hazrat Inayat Khan, also wrote on this theme – saying that when he was young he had struggled and struggled to find his own soul, till he recognised it in the simplest way:

> 1:14. I realized that that in me which believed and that in me which wondered, that which persevered in me, and that which found, and that which was found at last, was no other than my soul.[14]
>
> 1:15. That which holds the conception of 'I', a living entity, is not the body but the soul deluded by the body. The soul thinks that it is the body; it thinks that it walks, sits, lies down when the body does, but it does not really do any of these things. A little indisposition of the body makes it think, 'I am ill'. A slight offence makes it dejected. A little praise makes it think itself in heaven. In reality it is not in heaven nor on earth, it is where it is: ... for the body is nothing but a covering put over our soul.[15]

1:13. In Roberts, Jane: *Seth Speaks*. p. 98.
[Seth: Spirit teacher, through medium, Jane Roberts; 20th C.]

1:14. Khan, Hazrat Inayat: *The Sufi Message*: Vol. 5. p. 137.
[Indian Sufi teacher, 19/20th C.] Source E-b.

1:15. Ibid. p. 41.

1:16. Paul Brunton extends these views, explaining that our thoughts and emotions may be active in the self, but they do not form the whole self.

There is, in addition, a 'sense of awareness' that lies within and beyond all we do, think and feel. This sense of awareness does not change, despite the to-ing and fro-ing of our thoughts and actions; it coordinates and maintains our individual self; it is the mystical but consistent watcher that is within each one of us, yet stands above the dealings of our hectic lives:

> It is our truest deepest self because it alone outlives unchanged the surface self of changing personality. Thus the witness-self walks through this world *incognito.* ... But the man who has come to genuine self-knowledge knows what he really is *over* and above ... [the] embodied individual; hence he may aptly adopt the expressive term 'Overself' when referring to it. Theologians probably mean this when they speak of the 'soul'.[16]

And Hazrat Inayat Khan comments:

> 1:17. The soul has no birth, no death, no beginning, no end. ... It has been always, and always it will be. This is the very being of man.[17]
>
> 1:18. [For] the soul is alive, it is the spirit of eternal Being.[18]

1:19. Now the *Bhagavad Gita* – which is recommended as being the best-loved Hindu classic – agrees that there is an especially vital and eternal element within our being. "Oh, this really does describe the soul," I thought, as I read these simple but beautiful words:

1:16. Brunton, Dr Paul: *The Wisdom of the Overself.* pp. 120-121.
[British writer on ancient philosophy; 19/20thC.] Source A-d.

1:17. Khan, Hazrat Inayat: *The Sufi Message.* Vol. 5. p. 237.
[Indian Sufi teacher; 19/20th C.] Source E-b.

1:18. Ibid. p. 239.

Unborn, undying,
Never ceasing,
Never beginning,
Deathless, birthless,
Unchanging for ever,
How can It die
The death of the body?

Knowing It birthless,
Knowing It deathless,
Knowing It endless,
For ever unchanging. ...

Innermost element,
Everywhere, always,
Being of beings,
Changeless, eternal,
For ever and ever.[19]

There are other poets who are calling from the past – as in this ancient script from Egypt:

> 1:20. Thou art from old, O Soul of man, yea, thou art from everlasting.[20]

And from Proverbs, one of the Judaic books in the Old Testament:

> 1:21. I was set up from everlasting, from the beginning, or ever the earth was.
> When there were no depths, I was brought forth; when there were no fountains abounding with water.

1:19. *Bhagavad, Gita: The Song of God.* pp. 41-42.
[Krishna's teaching; pre-5th C. BC.] Source A-b.
1:20. In Head, Joseph and Cranston, Sylvia: *Reincarnation.* p. 557.
[Egyptian hermetic fragment; a few C. BC.] Source F-a.

Before the mountains were settled, before the hills was I brought forth:

While as yet he had not made the earth, nor the fields, nor the highest part of the dust of the world.

When he prepared the heavens, I was there: when he set a compass upon the face of the depth:

When he established the clouds above: when he strengthened the fountains of the deep:

When he gave to the sea his decree, that the waters should not pass his commandment: when he appointed the foundations of the earth:

Then I was by him, as one brought up with him: and I was daily his delight, rejoicing always before him.[21]

These concepts are found in many traditions, as in this North American Indian legend:

1:22. At the beginning, all things were in the mind of [God]. ... All creatures, including man, were spirits. They moved about in space between the earth and the stars. ... They were seeking a place where they could come into a bodily existence. They ascended to the sun, but the sun was not fitted for their abode. They moved on to the moon and found that it also was not good for their home. Then they descended to the earth. ... The hosts of spirits descended and became flesh and blood.[22]

And Edgar Cayce takes up the theme:

1:23. We were all created in the beginning as spiritual beings, children of God, born of His desire for companionship, with the potential to become co-creators with Him. As souls, we were given minds with which to

---

1:21. *Holy Bible.* Proverbs. Ch. 8. vs. 23-30.

[Ancient Judaic scripture in the *Holy Bible;* c. 6th C. BC.] Source D-a.

1:22. Seton, Ernest Thompson: *Gospel of the Redman.* pp. 73-74.

[American Indian teaching; compiled in the 19th C.] Source G-a.

> build, wills with which to choose, and access to the Spirit, the one great force of the universe.

Edgar Cayce, who was described as the greatest American mystic in the mid-20th century, believed that we then became proud, self-centred and "rebellious"; and this led to our descent. We explored the cosmos "as a wave of souls" and when we reached the earth we "were attracted to, and projected our consciousness into an ongoing evolutionary development of life". The earth, of course, was part of God's great creation; but in projecting ourselves into its dimensions, we restricted ourselves:

> Our *entrapment* in the earth was not at all due to the evil nature of the flesh but rather to the limiting effect of our own thought forms and desire patterns. Imagine a swimmer who ties a rock around his waist so that he may walk on the ocean floor. He struggles to the surface for a breath but is drawn down again by the weight. There is nothing evil about experiencing the ocean floor but the rock about his waist draws him away from his true source of life. He is no longer free. The rocks about our waists are our own thought forms and desire patterns. Even after death, they may focus our consciousness away from an awareness of our oneness with God and draw us back again into the earth experience.[23]

Plotinus – who was a Roman philosopher in the 3rd century – held a similar view, saying –

> 1:24. ... the soul, though of divine origin, and proceeding from the regions on high, becomes merged in the dark receptacle of the body; ... it descends hither through a certain voluntary inclination.[24]

1:23. In Puryear, Herbert: *The Edgar Cayce Primer*. pp. 19-20.
[Cayce, Edgar. American healer; 19/20th C.]
1:24. Plotinus: *Five Books of Plotinus*. p. 273.
[Roman philospher; 3rd C.] Source C-b.

> 1:25. Yet our souls are able alternately to rise from hence, carrying back with them an experience of what they have known and suffered in their fallen state; from whence they will learn how blessed it is to abide in the intelligible world, and, by a comparison, as it were, of contraries, will more plainly perceive the excellence of a superior state.[25]

Plotinus's words reminded me of the spirit, Seth – the 'personality no longer focused in physical reality' – who had inspired Jane Roberts to write *Seth Speaks.* "I suppose he could be a soul who has risen from our 'fallen state'," I said to myself, less doubtfully. But Seth's philosophy had intrigued me, despite my early scepticism; so I searched the shelves and found a book that claimed to contain teaching from another spirit, Silver Birch. It looked quite interesting, and I turned the pages – and read:

> 1:26. You are an eternal spirit, part of the life force that sustains the whole universe ... [and] transcends all material conceptions. It transcends all physical limitations. It is greater than anything you can conceive.
>
> You are indeed mighty atoms – infinite, yet expressing yourselves in a finite manner. Within you there is a power that one day bursts all its bonds and insists that it shall express itself in a body more fitting to its reality. That you call death. ... But death has no power over life; death cannot touch life; death cannot destroy life; ... death is but a stepping-stone, a door through which you enter into the larger freedom of the realms of the spirit.[26]

The Greek philosopher, Euripedes, wrote in the 5th century BC:

> 1:27. Who knows if to be alive is not really to die, and if dying does not count in the nether world as being alive?

1:25. Ibid. pp. 279-280.

1:26. In Ortzen, Tony (Ed.): *Siver Birch Companion.* pp. 28-29.
[Silver Birch: Spirit teacher, through medium, Barbanell; 20th C.]

> Who knows if this experience that we call dying is not really living, and if living is not really dying?[27]

And the Irish poet, W.B. Yeats, adds:

> 1:28. Many times man lives and dies
> Between his two eternities.[28]

The mystic healer, Edgar Cayce, takes this even further – saying:

> 1:29. It is not all of life to live, nor all of death to die; for one is the birth of the other when viewed from the whole or the center, and is but the experience of the entity in its transitions to and from the universal center from which all radiation takes place.[29]

Paul Brunton now returns to guide our views:

> 1:30. Nature circles infinitely. If she destroys it is only that she may create afresh. This is true of every part of her domain, whether in the life and fate of human beings or whether among the lands and waters of the globe.

And Brunton quotes from an ancient Egyptian transcript that says: "Nothing in the world perishes and death is not the destruction but only the change and transformation of things." He develops this theme by explaining that it is a misconception to view death as the end of life. Life is indestructible and carries on without any interruption, flowing through all its countless forms of being. Life is a stable 'principle', a force that is within and supportive of all created forms. The life-force is vast and eternal:

1:27. In Lorimer, David: *Survival?* p. 270.
[Euripedes: Greek philospher; 5th C. BC.]
1:28. Yeats, William Butler: *The Collected Poems of W.B. Yeats*. p. 398.
[Irish poet; 19/20th C.]
1:29. In Cerminara, Dr Gina: *Many Mansions*. p. 290.
[Cayce, Edgar: American healer; 19/20th C.]

> It does not die with these forms but, like an everflowing river bearing all things uninterruptedly along its surface, bears them along without a break in its own existence ... Thus the very idea of immortality arises for us because there actually exists an immortal principle within us.[30]

1:31. Now the writer, Elisabeth Haich, had recognised her immortality when she was very young. She had just been told about death, and she went straight to a mirror and stared into it, trying to see her inner self - her *real* self - which, she knew, would live beyond her death:

> I wanted to see where this 'I' was that was thinking things and did not want to die. I kept looking into the mirror, moving closer and closer until my nose touched the glass. I looked into my own eyes from as near as I could get. I wanted to see this 'I'! Even though there was a black hole in my eye, I couldn't see 'me'. The 'I' – myself – was invisible, just as I had always imagined it to be ever since I first became conscious on this earth. Even in the mirror I could not see *me*, only my face, my *mask* and the two black holes in my eyes out of which I was looking. "... but what will you be looking at the world through, when these eyes are some day closed?"
>
> "Through two other eyes!" I answered without a moment's hesitation. "Here I will close these eyes, and in a new body I will open two new eyes."
>
> "And what if there is a time delay between the two bodies; what if you ... have to wait a week, or perhaps months, years, even thousands of years?"
>
> "That just cannot be," answered the little girl that I was then, "for when I fall asleep, I do not know, on awakening, how long I have been asleep. In sleep there is no time, and

---

1:30. Brunton, Dr Paul: *The Wisdom of the Overself.* pp. 143-145.
[British writer on ancient philosophy; 19/20th C.] Source A-d.

> in death it will be the same. ... But my ceasing to exist just cannot be!"[31]

This intuitive child had understood reincarnation!

1:32. But the film star and writer, Shirley Maclaine, asked the question that was now gnawing at my mind: "Do you believe all this? ... Do you really believe in reincarnation?" Shirley was with a friend, looking at a library bookshelf labelled Reincarnation and Immortality, and she saw the *Egyptian Books of the Dead*, the *Bhagavad Gita* and some specialist books on the *Holy Bible* and the *Kabala.* Her friend replied:

> "Why, yeah, I do. It's the only thing that makes sense. ... You should read some of the works not only on this shelf but also of Pythagoras, Plato, Ralph Waldo Emerson, Walt Whitman, Goethe, and Voltaire."
>
> "Did those guys believe in reincarnation?"
>
> "Sure, and they wrote extensively about it. ... [Voltaire] said he didn't find it any more surprising to be born lots of times than to be born once. I feel the same way. ... Do you want me to compile a kind of reading list for you?" ...
>
> "Sure," I said ...
>
> "Great. ... For me, real intelligence is open-mindedness."[32]

"Oh! I do hope that's true!" I thought, and realised that I had been caught up on a roller coaster of ideas. "But where have all these concepts come from – in terms of history and religion? And how can they all hang together and relate so well, when they've come from such a wide variety of sources?"

Then I knew that I would have to learn something about the origins of these concepts, in order to answer my own questions, and that I should compile them for useful reference from time to time, as 'The Sources'.

1:31. Haich, Elisabeth: *Initiation.* pp. 81-82.
[Swiss writer/yoga teacher; 19/20th C.]

1:32. Maclaine, Shirley: *Out on a Limb.* pp. 48-49.
[American filmstar/writer; 20th C.]

"But I can't do that just now," I exclaimed. "All these library books are calling me, and there's so much to read! But the really important thing – *the most important thing* – is to remember that 'real intelligence is open-mindedness' – as I have the feeling that these books may explore life and death in some very strange ways."

2

The Rounds of our Returning

2:1. Shirley Maclaine had been intrigued by her friend's interest in reincarnation, and his suggestion that she should read more on the subject, so she started with an encyclopaedia and discovered that the concepts of rebirth were really very old as they had been found in some of the earliest scripts that had survived through the centuries. Many of these concepts were based on the understanding that the evolution of mankind is directed towards our return to the 'common source and origin of all life': that is to God. And reincarnation is the repeated embodiment of a soul-entity during this evolutionary progress, with the entity existing in some kind of disembodied state – or 'astral form' – between its incarnations. Maclaine then explains that the encyclopedia said –

> ... the companion subjects of karma – that is, working out one's inner burdens – and reincarnation – the physical opportunity to live through one's karma – were two of the oldest beliefs in the history of mankind and more widely accepted than almost any religious concepts on earth.

So countless generations have believed in the concepts of reincarnation and karma; the ancient Egyptians and Greeks did, and so did the early Hindus and Buddhists – in fact, the present-day Hindus and Buddhists still do. And there are references to reincarnation in the Judaic scriptures; but these beliefs seem to have disappeared in the transition from Judaism to present-day Christianity – and Maclaine wondered how this might have affected her own ideas, saying: "Hundreds of millions of people believed in the theory of reincarnation (or whatever the term might be); but I, coming from a Christian background, hadn't even known what it actually meant."[1]

Guy Playfair discusses this point in his book, *The Indefinite Boundary*, and says:

> 2:2. To many intelligent people in the Western Christian world, the idea of reincarnation is still anathema.

"But I don't really know what 'anathema' means," I said as I scanned the fine print of the dictionary. Its definition was brief but explicit, saying that 'anathema' was something 'accursed or detested' by the Christian church. Playfair, however, suggests that reincarnation should not be regarded in this way. In the first place, millions of people from non-Christian religions have believed in reincarnation for more than 2,500 years; and secondly, he stresses the point that some Jews – including some of Jesus' followers – discussed the concept quite openly. And Playfair goes even further, saying:

> The Bible is full of clear references to reincarnation as an established belief, and while it is true that this belief is never explicitly stated, it is never attacked or contradicted. Such remarks as "Ye must be born again" may perhaps be considered as symbolic but there was nothing symbolic about Jesus's disciples' reactions on being asked what people were saying about their master's origins.[2]

To my surprise, I found this to be true when I looked up the Gospel accounts in the *Holy Bible*. For example:

2:1. Maclaine, Shirley: *Out on a Limb*. pp. 51-52.
[American filmstar/writer; 20th C.]

2:2. Playfair, Guy: *The Indefinite Boundary*. pp. 158-159.
[British writer; 20th C.]

> 2:3. Jesus ... asked his disciples, saying, "Whom do men say that I, the Son of man, am?"
>
> And they said, "Some say that Thou art John the Baptist; some, Elias; and others Jeremias, or one of the prophets."[3]
>
> 2:4. And ... Jesus began to say unto the multitudes concerning John [the Baptist], ... "this is he, of whom it is written, 'Behold, I send my messenger before thy face, which shall prepare thy way before thee.' ...
>
> "For all the prophets and the law prophesied until John. And if ye will receive it, this is Elias, which was for to come.
>
> "He that hath ears to hear, let him hear."[4]
>
> 2:5. And his disciples asked him, saying, "Why ... say the scribes that Elias must first come?"
>
> And Jesus answered and said unto them, "Elias truly shall first come, and restore all things.
>
> "But I say unto you, that Elias is come already, and they knew him not, but have done unto him whatsoever they listed." ...
>
> Then the disciples understood that he spake unto them of John the Baptist – [who had been beheaded].[5]

As I studied these accounts, I found myself thinking that they might have been based on inaccurate memories of the disciples and not on factual conversations. This could be the case, as there is evidence that the Gospel of Matthew was written many, many years after Jesus had died. But the fact that these accounts are found in the New Testament implies that the writer – or Jesus or His followers – thought reincarnation could be feasible. One can therefore conclude that reincarnation was mooted in their society, and this would explain why Jesus did not condemn their discussion on reincarnation – let alone curse it. On the contrary, these accounts suggest that Jesus invited such discussions and even added to them Himself, and it seems reasonable to suspect that it was the Christians who changed their views on reincarnation at some later date.

2:3. *Holy Bible.* Matthew. Ch. 16. vs. 13-14.
[St. Matthew's Gospel in the New Testament.] Source D-b.
2:4. Ibid. Ch.11. vs. 7; 10; 13-15.
2:5. Ibid. Ch. 17. vs. 10-13.

Now the writers, Joseph Head and Sylvia Cranston, provide some important evidence that shows that the early Christian churches did not treat reincarnation as if it were a forbidden or anathematised subject. In their book, *Reincarnation*, they say that the concept was discussed quite openly by several Church Fathers until the year 553 AD, but that all this changed when a special meeting – the Fifth Ecumenical Council – was set up. There is further evidence that suggests that the decisions of this Council were biased, and that some of their documents were falsified – as explained by Head and Cranston:

> 2:6. Recently disclosed evidence advanced by Catholic scholars – who now have access to the original records – throws an entirely new light on what actually occurred at this council, as shall be seen shortly. The story surrounding the anathemas is an engrossing one, and as these curses brought in their wake serious consequences affecting for many centuries the life and thoughts of milions in the West, the whole matter seems worth exploring ... at length.

The early history of Christianity was apparently peppered with power struggles and protracted arguments on theological doctrine, and church councils were arranged from time to time in an attempt to discuss and smooth over these problems; but their repeated efforts were in vain, and the Christians were finally divided in the 6th century, with Pope Vigilius remaining as head of the Western Church, based in Rome. Emperor Justinian headed the breakaway Eastern Church, which was based in Constantinople; but he was dissatisfied as the division had not ended the conflict between the churches, and it was not long before the Pope suffered the great indignity of being kidnapped from Rome, and taken to Constantinople as Justinian's prisoner.

The Pope was incarcerated there for eight long years. Then Justinian released him, and tried to repair their damaged relationship by setting up the historic Fifth Ecumenical Council. The Council, however, was flawed from the start as Justinian arranged the agenda on his own terms, and he included an item that was designed to anathematise certain beliefs that were held by the influential and beloved Western Church Father, Origen – including his concept that souls exist *before* their incarnation. Origen was not alone in holding such beliefs, and one can only assume that Justinian was jealous or afraid of his doctrinal influence.

There were other things that were incorrect at this Council – and Head and Cranston make a dramatic statement, saying:

> The *Catholic Encyclopaedia* gives some rather astonishing information concerning this Fifth Ecumenical Council, permitting the conclusion, on at least technical grounds, that there is no barrier to belief in reincarnation for Catholic Christians. With the exception of six Western bishops from Africa, the council was attended entirely by Eastern bishops; no representative from Rome was present. Although Pope Vigilius was in Constantinople at the time, he refused to attend.

The Pope had been treated so badly that one can understand his refusing to attend; yet despite this, he tried to insist that an equal number of Western and Eastern bishops should be present at the Council. Justinian, however, would not agree to this, so the Pope decided to have no more dealings with him. And Head and Cranston add their own conclusion:

> When we learn that of the 165 bishops at the final meeting, 159 were from the Eastern Church, it can safely be concluded that the voting during all the sessions was very much in Justinian's hands.[6]

When I had read this revealing study, I turned to the relevant pages of the *Catholic Encyclopaedia* and found the following statements:

> 2:7. In the next General Council of Constantinople (680 AD) it was found that the original Acts of the Fifth Council had been tampered with, ... [and it is not] certain that in their present shape we have them in their original completeness. This has a bearing on the much disputed

---

2:6. Head, Joseph; Cranston, Sylvia: *Reincarnation*. pp. 156-157. [American writers; 20th C.] Source D-e.

question concerning the condemnation of Origenism at this council.[7]

2:8. Were Origen and Origenism anathematized? Many learned writers believe so; an equal number deny that they were condemned; most modern authorities are either undecided or reply with reservations.[8]

Head and Cranston, however, clearly believe that Origen's concepts were not anathematised properly, and they say that –

> 2:9. ... one far-reaching result ... still persists, namely, the exclusion from consideration by orthodox Christianity of the teaching of the pre-existence of the soul and, by implication, reincarnation. Probably many a good Christian would have another look at the whole subject if he were only aware of the foregoing facts. ... [And] it seems likely that these doctrines must have been widely held, else why go to the trouble of condemning them?[9]

2:10. The writer Guy Playfair now takes his turn in describing Origen as a confident and influential philosopher, whose teaching included the concept of pre-existence, and he quotes Origen as saying that the soul "puts off one body and exchanges it for a second" which is determined by "the soul's previous merits or demerits".[10]

2:11. Plato had also taught his followers that their souls would be reincarnated, and that "if you become worse, you will go to the worse souls, and if better to the better souls". He had been highly respected as a Greek philosopher in the 3rd century BC, and his influence was considerable. Some notable Christians respected his views in later years, and Saint Augustine hinted that Plotinus – who was a Roman

---

2:7. *Catholic Encyclopaedia*: Vol. 4. pp. 308-309.
[*Catholic Enclyclopaedias*; 20th C.] Source D-d.

2:8. Ibid. Vol. 11. pp. 311-312.

2:9. Head, Joseph; Cranston, Sylvia: *Reincarnation*. pp. 158-159.
[American writers; 20th C.] Source D-e.

2:10. Playfair, Guy: *The Indefinite Boundary*. p. 160.
[British writer, 20th C.]

philosopher in the 3rd century AD – was possibly a reincarnation of Plato. And Playfair adds: "Plotinus taught that the soul entered the body 'through a certain voluntary inclination' in order to acquire experience of both good and evil, and that it rose again after death to its former non-material condition."

These concepts never faded completely from the West, despite the increasing public interest in the realms of science and education, and Playfair lists some of the proponents of reincarnation in the 19th and early 20th centuries – including Schopenhauer, Kant, Hume, Shelley, Browning, Tennyson and Masefield.[11]

John Masefield – who was a relative of mine, by marriage – penned this view:

> 2:12. I held that when a person dies
> His soul returns again to earth;
> Arrayed in some new flesh-disguise
> Another mother gives him birth.
> With sturdier limbs and brighter brain
> The old soul takes the roads again.[12]

Masefield wrote this poem at a time when there was a marked revival of European interest in the concept of reincarnation. Several travellers had returned from the East, and some wanted to share their appreciation of the philosophies of Hindu and Buddhist literature. There were many allusions to rebirth in these works – as in these extracts from the *Bhagavad Gita*, the favourite Hindu classic that was written before the 5th century BC:

> 2:13. Just as the dweller in this body passes through childhood, youth and old age, so at death he merely passes into another kind of body ...[13]

2:11. Ibid. pp. 159-160.
2:12. Masefield, John: *The Collected Poems of John Masefield.* p. 69.
[British Poet Laureate; 19/20th C.]
2:13. *Bhagavad Gita: The Song of God.* p. 40.
[Krishna's teaching; pre-5th C. BC.] Source A-b.

2:14. Worn-out garments
Are shed by the body:
Worn-out bodies
Are shed by the dweller
Within the body.
New bodies are donned
By the dweller, like garments.[14]

2:15. Buddhists also hold these views – as Dr Rahula explains in his book, *What the Buddha Taught.* When a body dies, he says, its functions simply cease, but its inner energy never dies as it continues to exist in some other 'shape or form'. So reincarnation is a continuing process through which this energy evolves, –

> ... like a flame that burns through the night: it is not the same flame nor is it another. A child grows up to be a man of sixty. Certainly the man of sixty is not the same as the child of sixty years ago, nor is he another person. Similarly, a person who dies here and is reborn elsewhere is neither the same person, nor another.[15]

This changing, evolving nature of the personality between death and rebirth is also described by the American theosophist, Henry Olcott:

> 2:16. In each birth the *personality* differs from that of the previous or next succeeding birth, ... now in the personality of a sage, again as an artisan, and so on throughout the string of births. But though personalities ever shift, the one line of life along which they are strung like beads runs unbroken; it is ever *that particular line*, never any other.[16]

2:14. Ibid. p. 42.
2:15. Rahula, Dr Walpola: *What the Buddha Taught.* pp. 33-34.
[Buddha's teaching; 6th C. BC.] Source B-a.
2:16. Olcott, Henry S: *The Buddhist Catechism.* p. 65fn.
[American Founder: Theosophical Society; 19/20th C.] Source I-b.

Now the English Buddhist, John Blofeld, takes up the theme:

> 2:17. What we call 'life' is a single link in an infinitely long chain of 'lives' and 'deaths'.

And Blofeld plays with this idea, wondering whether we might be able to look back over the chains of all our lives. Perhaps we could do this if our subconscious memories were lifted, somehow, into our conscious minds. Would the chains of our lives be so long that they could reach right back to a time before we were humans on this earth? And his questions flow on, –

> ... why just this earth? Why should not many of our previous lives have been passed upon other earths contained within this stupendous universe? Perhaps the recollection would include hundreds or thousands of millions of lives lived here or elsewhere, and at this or other levels of consciousness, perhaps in states of being previously unsuspected. Only, it is hard to understand how any mind could encompass so vast an accumulation of memories.[17]

Blofeld's ideas were mind-boggling! But I came down to earth when I remembered reading about some children in the West, who had surprised their parents by mentioning specific names, details and incidents that did not relate in any way to their present lives. It is sad that such innocent remarks are so often ignored, or thought to be amusing.

2:18. In some other societies, however, people believe that memories of this kind have been carried over from earlier incarnations. Jeffrey Iverson makes this point in his book, *In Search of the Dead*, and says that many cases of reincarnation have been documented in scientific studies. For example, Dr Ian Stevenson is a professor of psychiatry at the University of Virginia, and he has done a great deal of research with around 2,500 children who have retained such memories. Stevenson's work has taken him to distant parts of the world to meet these children – and their

---

2:17. Blofeld, John: *The Wheel of Life*. pp. 28-29.
[British Buddhist; 20th C.] Source B-d.

families, neighbours and associates – and he has checked their accounts against any records that were held by police, doctors, government officials and others. In describing Stevenson's research, Iverson says:

> He has a compelling dossier of children who recall the life and death of someone else – sometimes they have the mannerisms and habits of the dead person, and some even bear physical marks that correspond with aspects of that person's life.[18]

2:19. Having read this, I turned with interest to one of Stevenson's books, *Twenty Cases Suggestive of Reincarnation,* and found an account that fitted this description exactly. It described a North American Tlingit family in which the father, William George, was a firm believer in the concepts of rebirth, and on one occasion, he said to his daughter-in-law:

> "I will come back and be your son. ... And you will recognize me because I will have birthmarks like the ones I now have. ... Keep this watch for me. I am going to be your son."

William George gave her his gold watch, and two months later – 'in August 1949' – he met his end. He had been fishing out at sea in his boat, and was thought to have drowned. His body was never found, but the strong currents along that coastline would have carried him away. His daughter-in-law, Mrs Reginald George, was soon expecting a baby, and her son was born in May 1950. He had small moles on his body – which were like those of his grandfather, and in the same positions – and his parents were so impressed that they named the baby William George Junior.

As the years passed by, the family became more and more convinced that the child was the true reincarnation of his grandfather: he had the same behaviour and mannerisms, and he liked and disliked the same

---

2:18. Iverson, Jeffrey: *In Search of the Dead.* p. 145.
[British writer; 20th C.]

things; he was good at the same activities and appeared to know all about boats; he seemed to understand how fishing nets should be used, and he knew about the local fishing conditions and the coastline when he was very young; but despite his love of boats, he was very afraid of the sea.

In addition to this, William George treated his family in the way that his grandfather had: he behaved in the same way with each one of them, mixing the generations by addressing 'his uncles and aunts' as though they were 'his sons and daughters', and he was rather concerned – as his grandfather would have been – when two of his uncles became too fond of their drink. His mother was much impressed when William George laid claim to the watch that had been given to her by his grandfather. The boy was only four when he found her sorting out the jewel-box in which she kept the treasured watch. "That's *my* watch," he said as he snatched it up, and his mother retrieved it with difficulty. And as the boy grew older he liked to examine the watch, saying that it should be returned to him. But the years were passing, and he was changing – as Stevenson explains:

> By 1961, William George, Jr. had largely lost his previous identification with his grandfather, and apart from his occasional requests for 'his watch' ... he behaved like a normal boy of his age. I talked with him in Alaska and hoped that he would have more to say about the watch which his mother brought out in my presence. He handled it fondly, but did not talk about it. I cannot say whether his reticence arose from shyness with me or from a fading of the images that originally led him to claim it as his own.[19]

Now Stevenson is only one amongst a number of psychiatrists who are interested in reincarnation, and another is Dr Guirdham, who found that he was involved with several patients who knew that they had lived in the past. In his book, *The Cathars and Reincarnation*, Guirdham describes his first case:

2:19. Stevenson, Dr I: *Twenty Cases Suggestive of Reincarnation*. pp. 232-235.
[Canadian Professor of Psychiatry; 20th C.]

> 2:20. This is not just another tale of reincarnation. The justification for writing it is that its origins and substance are unique [as my patient recalled her past] ... by direct experience through visions, dreams and intuitions, without having studied the period or subject. The major proportion of her revelations occurred twenty-six years ago, in an intensive uprush of memory in her early teens. It gave her a detailed knowledge of Catharism.

Catharism was a Gnostic tradition that was cruelly suppressed by the Inquisition in France in the 13th century – and Guirdham explains that children were not taught about the horrors of persecution when his patient was at school in England in the early 1940s. And he adds:

> Nor is it, nor has it ever been, a practice for English girls of thirteen to transcribe their thoughts, visions and feelings in mediaeval French.[20]

2:21. Yet this patient had written poetry and notes in this language when she was only thirteen and – "a few were found, with her school reports, among a few special possessions her father kept in an old dispatch box."[21]

2:22. Guirdham also explains that she had neither studied French medieval history nor Gnostic beliefs, saying, –

> ... she herself had at that time no realisation whatever that she had been a Cathar. Her ignorance of mediaeval history was such that although she recollected perfectly and in detail certain Cathar rituals, she did not know that they characterised a particular sect to which she had belonged.[22]

2:23. In addition to this, her notes revealed the fact that she was familiar with certain details that were not recognised by the historians

---

2:20. Guirdham, Dr Arthur: *The Cathars and Reincarnation.* pp. 9-10.
[British physchiatrist; 20th C.]
2:21. Ibid. p. 176.
2:22. Ibid. p. 20.

of Cathar history in the 1940s. For example, these historians were convinced that Cathar priests always wore black; but Guirdham explains that his patient knew better:

> For twenty-six years, including her six years correspondence with me, she stubbornly maintained that they wore dark blue. She was proved correct by Jean Duvernoy of Toulouse, but only in the last four years. In editing the register of the Inquisition of Jacques Fournier, Monsieur Duvernoy revealed that Cathar priests wore sometimes dark blue or dark green. [His] ... book was published in 1965. The truth was known to my patient as far back as 1944.[23]

Many more of her memories were found to be accurate, but several of them were making her present life difficult – and she wrote to Guirdham in January 1965, saying:

> 2:24. "I vowed to myself years ago, when at the age of thirteen these inexplicable occurrences started to take place, that no one should ever know. I feared, as perhaps I fear now, that I would be regarded as a crank and eventually go mad."[24]

Although she was able to unburden herself to Dr Guirdham in this way, she remained haunted and confused by her dreams and memories, and sent the following note to him when he was about to travel:

> 2:25. "If when you are in France you should meet Fabrissa, Roger, Pierre de Mazerolles or any of this mad crowd, tell them to go to hell. They'll be better off there than in my imagination."

But Guirdham comments, quite simply, that they were not imaginary people. They were people whom she had known in the past:

2:23. Ibid. pp. 10-11.
2:24. Ibid. p. 44.

"You can read about them in various depositions made to the Inquisition."[25]

2:26. And in another note, she said that she was extremely troubled by switching to and fro between past and present times: "It has always landed me in trouble, caused me great unhappiness, and I hate it."[26]

2:27. These experiences were all distressing; but her worst memory of all was of being burnt at the stake, when the Church Inquisitors had condemned her to death – and Guirdham received her tragic and yet revealing account of dying:

> "I must have committed a fearful crime to deserve such an agonising death. So must the others. ... We all walked barefoot through the streets towards a square where they had prepared a pile of sticks all ready to set alight. There were several monks around [who sided with the Inquisition] singing hymns and praying. I didn't feel grateful. I thought they had a cheek to pray for me. ... I hated those monks being there to see me die ...
>
> "The pain was maddening. You should pray to God when you're dying, if you can pray when you're in agony. In my dream I didn't pray. ... I thought of Roger and ... I knew he was dead. – I felt suddenly glad to be dying. ... [But] I hate the thought of going blind. ... In this dream I was going blind. I tried to close my eyelids but I couldn't. They must have been burnt off, and now those flames ... weren't so cruel after all. They began to feel cold. Icy cold. ... I was numb with the cold and suddenly I started to laugh. I had fooled those people who thought they could burn me."[27]

2:28. "She was dying – but not dying. She was staying alive," I thought, remembering the words of a Hottentot legend in which the

2:25. Ibid. pp. 59-60.
2:26. Ibid. p. 62.
2:27. Ibid. pp. 88-89.

moon says: "As I die and rise to life again, so shall you die and rise to life again."[28]

And the Buddhist teacher, Lama Govinda, carries this even further:

> 2:29. In fact, we all have died many deaths before we came into this incarnation. And what we call birth is merely the reverse side of death, like one of the two sides of a coin, or like a door which we call 'entrance' from outside and 'exit' from inside a room. ... Not everybody remembers his or her previous death; and, because of this lack of remembering, most persons do not believe there was a previous death. But, likewise, they do not remember their recent birth – and yet they do not doubt that they were recently born. They forget that active memory is only a small part of our normal consciousness, and that our subconscious memory registers and preserves every past impression and experience which our waking mind fails to recall.[29]

Now the Cambridge philosopher, John McTaggart, was particularly interested in the subconscious and the influence that it bears on our present lives, and he discusses this point with some deliberation, saying –

> 2:30. ... it might be said that our chief ground for hoping for a progressive improvement after death would be destroyed if memory periodically ceased. Death, it might be argued, ... would deprive us of all memory of what we had done, and therefore whatever was gained in one life would be lost at death. ... We must ask, therefore, what elements of value ... can be carried on *without* memory ...
>
> Let us consider wisdom first. Can we be wiser by reason of something which we have forgotten? Unquestionably we can. Wisdom is not merely, or chiefly, amassed facts, or even recorded judgements. It depends primarily on a mind

---

2:28. In Lorimer, David: *Survival?* p. 26.
[South African Hottentot proverb.] Source F-e.

2:29. In Evans-Wentz, Dr W.Y: *Tiebetan Book of the Dead.* p.liii.
[Lama Govinda: Buddhist teacher; 19/20th C.] Source B-b.

> qualified to deal with facts, and to form judgements. ... And so a man who dies after acquiring knowledge – and all men acquire some – might enter his new life deprived indeed of his knowledge, but not deprived of the increased strength and delicacy of mind which he had gained in acquiring the knowledge. And, if so, he will be wiser in the second life because of what has happened in the first ...
>
> With virtue the point is perhaps clearer. For the memory of moral experiences is of no value to virtue except in so far as it helps to form the moral character, and if this is done, the loss of memory would be no loss to virtue. Now we cannot doubt that a character may remain determined by an event which has been forgotten. I have forgotten the greater number of the good and evil acts which I have done in my present life. And yet each must have left a trace on my character. And so a man may carry over into his next life the dispositions and tendencies which he has gained by the moral contests of this life.[30]

"But this could explain why Blofeld was so fascinated by Buddhism, despite his being born and brought up as a Christian," I said to myself. "Buddhism would have left a 'trace on his character' in the past, and it's now come through into this life." Blofeld's book, *The Wheel of Life*, was obviously significant – so I flicked through its pages and found these relevant passages:

> 2:31. Teachers have held that this present life leads us forwards or backwards from precisely the point reached by the end of the preceding life. (Thus, the belief that a man may immediately be reborn as a pig or, conversely, as a god would seem to be a popular misunderstanding of the implications of the doctrine of reincarnation – an over-simplification of a little-understood truth.)

2:30. McTaggart, John E: *Human Immortality and Pre-Existence.* pp. 105-108. [British philosopher; 19/20th C.]

Our human characters, however, evolve 'from life to life' – Blofeld continues – yet every baby has to relearn the ordinary things of its new life. If this were not the case, 'babies would be born as wise as their grandparents'. But we return to earth-life with 'abstract propensities', these being our –

> ... talents, bents, abilities, personal likes and dislikes, and a host of others. ... It is the method of applying these propensities to the exterior world which has to be relearnt. Thus ... it follows that, if for some Karmic reason a devout Hindu or Buddhist is reborn in a Christian community, though the spiritual aspect of RELIGION may appeal strongly to him even in his childhood, the form of his religion will be Christian. He will normally remain a Christian all his life – probably a very good one – unless the thinness of the dividing curtain enables him to re-establish links with his former faith.

Blofeld is convinced that he was a Buddhist in the past, and that he had attained a degree of 'spiritual advancement' in that life, as he felt an extraordinary surge of 'subconscious recognition', reverence and traditional respect when he first saw a Buddha-statue in this life. He also believes that the great Gurus can recall their earlier incarnations as they have developed themselves, in spiritual terms, and the memories from their past lives are now accessible within their conscious minds. Then Blofeld adds:

> My years of seesawing between Buddhism and Christianity resulted from an unconscious conflict between a faith 'remembered' below the surface of normal consciousness and that other faith bequeathed to me by my parents and strengthened by the presence of its adherents all around me. Thus, my conversion to Buddhism was in fact a RECONVERSION, which took place after the veil separating me from a conscious recollection of my previous life had now and then been momentarily blown aside.[31]

2:31. Blofeld, John: *The Wheel of Life.* pp. 29-30
[British Buddhist; 20th C.] Source B-d.

The Jewish writer, Sholem Asch, suggests that we all experience fragmented memories of the past, as –

> 2:32. ... our senses are haunted by fragmentary recollections of another life. They drift like torn clouds above the hills and valleys of the mind, and weave themselves into the incidents of our current existence.[32]

2:33. And Carl Jung – the German-Swiss psychiatrist – understands this too, saying: "I might have lived in former centuries."[33]

2:34. Jung came to this conclusion because he had had some very strange experiences. Once, when he was a schoolboy, he went to stay with a friend whose family lived by a lake, and he was delighted to find that they owned a small boat. The two boys were given permission to go rowing on condition that they would be very careful, but Jung stepped onto the seat and thrust the boat from the shore with an oar. His friend's father was furious and immediately summoned them back. He was really angry, and this somehow triggered Jung's subconscious memory – as he says:

> I was thoroughly crestfallen but had to admit that ... his lecture was quite justified. At the same time I was seized with rage that this fat, ignorant boor should dare to insult ME. This ME was not only grown up, but important, an authority, a person with office and dignity, an old man, an object of respect and awe. Yet the contrast with reality was so grotesque that in the midst of my fury I suddenly stopped myself, for the question rose to my lips: "Who in the world are you, anyway? You are reacting as though you were the devil only knows how important! ... You are barely twelve years old, a schoolboy." ... This 'Other' was an old man who lived in the eighteenth century, wore buckled shoes and a white wig and went driving in a fly with high,

---

2:32. Asch, Sholem: *The Nazarene.* p. 3.
[Jewish writer; 19/20th C.]

2:33. Jung, Dr Carl G: *Memories, Dreams, Reflections.* p. 294.
[German-Swiss psychiatrist; 19/20th C.]

> concave rear wheels between which the box was suspended on springs and leather straps.

Then Jung switched to an earlier memory – a little boy's memory – of watching a vintage carriage that was driven past his home:

> It was truly an antique, looking exactly as if it had come straight out of the eighteenth century. When I saw it, I felt with great excitement: "That's it! ... That comes from *my* times." It was as though I had recognised it because it was the same type as the one I had driven in myself. ... The carriage was a relic of those times! I cannot describe what was happening in me or what it was that affected me so strongly: a longing, a nostalgia, or a recognition that kept saying "Yes, that's how it was! Yes, that's how it was!"

Jung had also been fascinated by an 18th century statuette of a doctor from Basel, saying:

> This statuette of the old doctor had buckled shoes which in a strange way I recognised as my own. I was convinced that these were shoes I had worn. The conviction drove me wild with excitement. "Why, those must be my shoes!" I could still feel those shoes on my feet, and yet I could not explain where this crazy feeling came from. I could not understand this identity I felt with the eighteenth century. Often in those days I would write the date 1786 instead of 1886, and ... I was overcome by an inescapable nostalgia.[34]

So Jung had been assailed by all these memories while being summoned from the boat, and realised that he had been behaving in quite a dangerous way; but he was a boy whose antics had been foolish, and he was duly punished.

Sholem Asch would have sympathised with Carl Jung, as he says:

2:34. Ibid. pp. 44-46.

> 2:35. Not the power to remember, but its very opposite, the power to forget, is a necessary condition of our existence. ... But it sometimes happens that the Angel of Forgetfulness himself forgets to remove from our memories the records of the former world. ... They assert themselves, clothed with reality, in the form of nightmares which visit our beds.[35]

The writer and healer, Allegra Taylor, would understand this too. She had just joined a training course and met a fellow student called Patrick – and then the unexpected happened:

> 2:36. That night in the limbo land between sleeping and waking, I suddenly 'knew' with suffocating crushing horror, with anguished certainty, that Patrick and I had both been children together in a very recent incarnation and had died a violent and horrible death, snuffed out, bewildered, in the flower of innocence in a Nazi concentration camp. It entered my mind as a vivid subliminal flash like a scene lit up by lightning on a dark night – me with ratty pigtails, taller than him; both of us thin and raggedy, holding hands by a muddy trench. Palpitating, heart-stopping fear followed by blackness ...
>
> I sat up in bed profoundly shaken and pondered this revelation: it could explain a lot of puzzling aspects to this intense relationship. He frees me to feel very young and truthful. I have only known him for such a short time and yet, more than anyone I have ever met, he really sees me as I am. ... We can lark about with the artless daftness of kids, and there is also between us a grave childlike quality of reverence and awe. ... I feel as if I've found him again, and that we can now finish our childhoods together and finally be allowed to grow up.
>
> I guess that the whole episode is probably a symbol somewhere in the deep rivers of my psyche, a metaphor in my subconscious, for the omnipresent melancholy about

---

2:35. Asch, Sholem: *The Nazarene.* p. 3.
[Jewish writer; 19/20th C.]

the holocaust that infiltrated my childhood to a degree where unbearable feelings and unendurable realities had to be suppressed in order for life to go on. The knowledge of that horror and evil was always there at the back of my mind no matter how much I refused to face it, the burden of it somehow robbing me of the lighthearted innocence of childhood.[36]

And the American writer, Emmet Fox, concludes:

2:37. Nature has drawn a veil of forgetfulness over our beginnings on this plane, and for excellent reasons she hides away the memory of previous lives until we are sufficiently developed to be ready to remember them. ... so the past is mercifully withheld from us until we can regard our own histories impersonally and objectively, and when we do reach that stage it is possible to remember.[37]

2:36. Taylor, Allegra: *I Fly Out with Bright Feathers*. pp. 159-160. [British novice healer; 20th C.]

2:37. Fox, Emmet: *Power Through Constructive Thinking*. pp. 245-246. [American writer; 19/20th C.]

3

Karma, and its Consequence

When Emmet Fox said that 'the past is mercifully withheld from us' I felt that his words were a little too bland, as I could neither forget Guirdham's young patient who had suffered the memories of her Cathar life, nor Allegra Taylor's nightmare of being killed by the Nazis. Their experiences suggest that memories from a past life can sometimes rise spontaneously from the subconscious to the conscious mind. And I was now reading about a doctor, Dr Edith Fiore, who uses hypnosis to gain access to any subconscious memories – from past lives – that might underlie her patients' current psychological or behavioural problems.

3:1. In the early years of her career, Fiore had naturally assumed that she was exploring the hidden memories of her patients' present lives; but then she had a surprise, and it opened her mind to the wider view that has helped her treat her patients more effectively. For example, she had hypnotised a man who was troubled by 'sexual problems' – but while he was in trance, he described the frustrated memories of a 17th century Catholic priest. When he regained normal consciousness, they discussed these memories, and he said that he felt he had lived in the past. Fiore had thought this strange, saying: "Since the concept of past lives had never occurred to me as anything but a rather fascinating and archaic Eastern viewpoint, I was intrigued."[1]

In fact she was so intrigued that she studied the subject in greater depth, and her work was more successful when she accepted the idea that past-life experiences might be affecting her patients' lives.

3:1. Fiore, Dr Edith: *The Unquiet Dead.* p.9.
[American psychologist; 20th C.]

3:2. Now the Canadian psychiatrist, Dr Joel Whitton, has used hypnosis over a twenty year period of research, saying to his patients: "Go to the time you were incarnate before this life. Now, *who* are you, and *where* are you?" And following this order, his patients describe – and apparently re-live – the happenings "from another time, another place." This enables Whitton to explore an extraordinary amount of stored information that can only have had its origins in his patients' earlier lives; and he writes:

> Once guided to another lifetime, the hypnotic subject assumes a different personality and acknowledges a different body while being aware of sharing with this other self the same basic identity. ...
>
> The past-life personality can be directed to any point between its birth and death and will often discuss freely the experiences of that lifetime in a voice that reflects its age, gender, culture, language, character, and placement in historical time. When the store of emotionally significant memories from that life is exhausted, Dr Whitton might decide to move his subject to an even earlier existence. The person in trance then summons up another offshoot of the core identity – another unique personality grappling with a completely different existence.[2]
>
> 3:3. Dr Whitton learned how to compile personal inventories of past lives stretching across thousands of years. ... He saw how the trials, the successes, and the failures of each life contributed to the formation of the present-day individual. Moreover, no matter how disparate the various lives in each person's reincarnational history might be, they always unfolded according to cause and effect. In other words, the actions and attitudes in one life would determine the setting and challenges of a life or lives to come.[3]

3:2. Whitton, Dr Joel and Fisher, Joe: *Life Between Life*. pp. 4-5.
[Canadians: psychiatrist and writer; 20th C.]
3:3. Ibid. p. 17.

"But why does it have to happen like this?" I asked myself. "Why should we live such a series of lives? Is one not enough?" Then the British philosopher, John McTaggart, answered my questions, saying:

> 3:4. No man can learn fully in one life the lessons of unbroken health and of bodily sickness, of riches and of poverty, of study and action, of comradeship and isolation, of defiance and of obedience, of virtue and of vice. ... (And though the way is long, it can be no more wearisome than a single life. For with death we leave behind us memory and old age, and fatigue. We may die old, but we shall be born young.)[4]

3:5. These ideas are taken even further by Professor von Stietencron, whose subject is Hindu philosophy. He explains that people are quite unlike each other from the moment of their birth. They differ in so many ways – physically and intellectually – in looks, personality, likes and dislikes, health and sickness, and in social behaviour. And he makes the point that –

> ... even where they seem to be of a similar predisposition, they are born into different conditions of life, castes, and families. They do not have the same chances or get the same education. They are rich or poor, meet good fortune or bad.

The ancient Hindus tried to accept the idea that such disparity was, for some reason, the work of God. And Stietencron describes how they went over and over the problem, trying to make sense:

> Neither the environment nor genetics offers a satisfactory explanation for the phenomenon of individual differences. Because even if one assumes that they correctly describe the causes and effects, they do not answer the question of meaning at all.

3:4. McTaggart, John Ellis: *The Nature of Existence,* Vol. II. p. 397.
[British philosopher; 19/20th C.]

> Why does it befall one man that he is blind, deaf, or crippled from birth, or that he must be shunned by his fellows and agonize in a leprous body? Why do others enjoy life in health and prosperity? What principle determines how happiness or suffering, talent or stupidity, birth into a rich or a poor family ... is allotted to individual beings? ...
>
> Hindu religions are sure that these qualitative differences in the fate of individual persons (with all the pain, the injustice, the physical, psychic, and social inequality this implies) cannot be blamed on the deity: It could not contain such wickedness. The qualitative differences must have been acquired by the creatures themselves.
>
> Yet it is also clear that they do not emerge only after birth, as a result, say, of external influences. Rather, they are already present, most of them, at the child's conception, in the form both of hereditary traits and of the social milieu into which it will be born. Thus if the individual soul exercises an influence on its own destiny, this can only have happened in a previous existence ...
>
> The Hindus speak in this connection of *karma.* Karma that has accrued from earlier lives, they say, decides both the physical and the psychic qualities of the individual creature and the environmental conditions to which it is exposed in the new birth.[5]

Now one of the Founders of the Theosophical Society, William Judge, joins the discussion to define karma:

> 3:6. Karma ... is the twin doctrine to reincarnation. So inextricably interlaced are these two laws that it is almost impossible to properly consider one apart from the other. ... Applied to man's moral life, [karma] is the law of ethical causation, justice, reward and punishment; the cause for birth and rebirth, yet equally the means for escape from

3:5. In Kung, Hans: *Christianity & the World Religions.* pp. 212-214.
[Prof von Stietencron: German professor of theology; 20th C.] Source A-e.

incarnation. Viewed from another point it is merely effect flowing from cause, action and reaction, exact result for every thought and act.[6]

This reminded me of the second verse of John Masefield's poem on reincarnation. The verse had made little sense when I first read it, as I had not known about the concept of karma; but Masefield had, as he said:

3:7. All that I rightly think or do,
Or make, or spoil, or bless, or blast,
Is curse or blessing justly due
For sloth or effort in the past.
My life's a statement of the sum
Of vice indulged, or overcome. ...
My road shall be the road I made;
All that I gave shall be repaid.[7]

Karma was well defined by Judge, but no definition can fully encompass this concept. So I searched for Madame Blavatsky's introductory work – *The Key to Theosophy* – as she had been the most influential thinker and Founder of their Society. Her description of karma was detailed, and written in her own splendid style:

3:8. Those who believe in Karma have to believe in destiny, which, from birth to death, every man is weaving thread by thread, around himself, as a spider does his cobweb. ... When the last strand is woven, and man is seemingly enwrapped in the network of his own doing, he finds himself completely under the empire of this self-made destiny. ... But verily there is not an accident in our lives, not a misshapen day, or a misfortune, that could not be traced back to our own doings in this or in another life. ... Nothing but such certainty can quiet our revolted sense of justice.

3:6. Judge, William: *The Ocean of Theosophy*. p. 89.
[American Theosophist; 19th C.] Source I-a.
3:7. Masefeld, John: *The Collected Poems of John Masefield*. p. 70.
[British Poet Laureate; 19/20th C.]

> For, when one ... observes the inequalities of birth and fortune, of intellect and capacities; when one sees honour paid [to] fools and profligates, on whom fortune has heaped her favours by mere privilege of birth, and their nearest neighbour, with all his intellect and noble virtues – far more deserving in every way – perishing of want and for lack of sympathy; when one sees all this and has to turn away, helpless to relieve the undeserved suffering, ... that blessed knowledge of Karma alone prevents [one] from cursing life and men, as well as their supposed creator. ...
>
> Karma creates nothing, nor does it design. It is man who plants and creates causes, and Karmic Law adjusts the effects; which adjustment is not an act, but universal harmony, tending ever to resume its original position, like a bough, which, bent down too forcibly, rebounds with corresponding vigour. If it happens to dislocate the arm that tried to bend it out of its natural position, shall we say it is the bough which broke our arm, or that our own folly has brought us to grief?[8]

The American writer, Emmet Fox, now takes up the theme:

> 3:9. If you touch a red-hot stove, you will burn your finger. This will hurt you, and perhaps incapacitate you for a few days, but it is not punishment, only a natural consequence. Nevertheless it is a benign and reformative thing, for after one or two such experiences in childhood, you learn to keep your fingers away from hot iron. If that stove did not hurt you, you would some day have your whole hand burned off before discovering your loss. So it is with all natural retribution – you suffer because you have a lesson to learn, [and then] the ill consequences cease, for nature is never vindictive.[9]

3:8. Blavatsky, H. P: *The Key to Theosophy.* pp. 210-212.
[Russian, Founder of the Theosophical Society; 19th C.] Source I-c.

3:9. Fox, Emmet: *Power Through Constructive Thinking.* p. 261.
[American writer; 19/20th C.]

"So this is what karma really is. It's teaching us – and developing us," I thought as I turned to read Edgar Cayce. I had heard that he was an extraordinary man who lived in the 19th and 20th centuries, and his biography was intriguing. He was not a Theosophist, however, but an intuitive healer and visionary – who said:

> 3:10. Karma ... is often wrongly and unjustly confused with retribution. It is too meticulous and dispassionate for that; its ultimate purpose too benign. But while it is acting as a painful cure for an even more painful relapse, it can be bitter gall indeed.
>
> Apparently a certain type of mortal suffering can be a salutary astringent to the torpors of the subconscious mind when all subtler warnings have failed to persuade the ego to exert itself in its own best interests.[10]

Now the analyst of such philosophy, Paul Brunton, explains this in similar terms, saying:

> 3:11. The depressions of carking illness awaken ... [the subconscious] to yearn for the Undecaying. The agony of unexpected loss arouses it to seek for the Peaceful. The touch of chill death drives it to look for the Deathless.

The unhappy ego is longing for peace in eternity; but Brunton explains that it is impossible for the ego to be released prematurely from its cycle of earth lives, and he adds: "The multitude of impressions which it has gained during its incarnation have worn certain furrows of desire and habit."

So the ego – or soul – has been marked by its past, and although it longs to escape from the problems of life it usually fails to understand the full purpose of its daily experiences. It therefore fails to work through and learn from its problems, and it continues to indulge and develop its desires and habits – its karmic inheritance. Then Brunton explains that a soul of this kind is unable to loosen its attachment, either to these experiences or to the people whom it either hated or loved too selfishly:

3:10. In Langley, Noel: *Edgar Cayce on Reincarnation.* p. 51.
[Edgar Cayce's teaching: American healer; 19/20th C.]

> All these are mental ties, and so long as they exist the 'I' necessarily continues to feel the need of the physical body in which it formed them. And thought being creative, it will be driven by its own forces, that is its own karma, sooner or later to return to earth again. ... Hence the birth of every baby is never a biological accident but always a psychological necessity. Sexual union brings two cells together, which unite into a single germ and grow, but it does not create new life. It merely creates the new conditions in which an old life can express itself.[11]

Now William Judge agrees with this, saying:

> 3:12. It is desire and passion which caused us to be born, and will bring us to birth again and again in some body on this earth or another globe. It is by passion and desire we are made to evolve through the mansions of death called lives on earth. [12]

And the Buddhist teacher, Walpola Rahula, emphasises this point:

> 3:13. Will, volition, desire, thirst to exist, to continue, to become more and more, is a tremendous force that moves whole lives, whole existences, that even moves the whole world. This is the greatest force, the greatest energy in the world.[13]

3:14. 'Thirst' is the term that Rahula uses for all the sensual longings, worldly ambitions and intellectual aspirations in our lives. Rahula says that the Buddha Gautama believed that the 'evils in the world', the disputes great and small, and the many, many problems between people, families and nations have all been caused by this 'thirst'. And he adds:

3:11. Brunton, Dr Paul: *The Wisdom of the Overself.* pp. 150-151.
[British writer on ancient philosophy; 19/20th C.] Source A-d.

3:12. Judge, William: *The Ocean of Theosophy.* p. 46.
[American Theosophist; 19th C.] Source I-a.

3:13. Rahula, Dr Walpola: *What the Buddha Taught.* p. 33.
[Buddha's teaching; 6th C. BC.] Source B-a.

> Great statesmen who try to settle international disputes and talk of war and peace only in economic and political terms touch the superficialities, and never go deep into the real root of the problem ... [which is] that all the evils in the world are produced by selfish desire.[14]

At this point, Madame Blavatsky rejoins the discussion and says:

> 3:15. The evils that you speak of are not peculiar to the individual or even to the Nation, they are more or less universal.[15]

And her reasoning is straightforward, as she explains that –

> 3:16. ... every atom is subject to the general law governing the whole body to which it belongs, and here we come upon the wider track of the Karmic law. Do you not perceive that the aggregate of individual Karma becomes that of the nation to which those individuals belong, and further, that the sum total of National Karma is that of the World?[16]

William Judge now supports and develops this view:

> 3:17. Nations cannot escape their national karma, and any nation that has acted in a wicked manner must suffer some day, be it soon or late. ... [The] misery of any nation or race is the direct result of the thoughts and acts of the Egos who make up the race or nation. In the dim past they did wickedly and now suffer. They violated the laws of harmony. The immutable rule is that harmony must be restored if violated. So these Egos suffer in making compensation and establishing the equilibrium of the occult cosmos.[17]

3:14. Ibid. p. 30.
3:15. Blavatsky, H. P: *The Key to Theosophy*. p. 202.
[Russian, Founder of the Theosophical Society; 19th C.] Source I-c.
3:16. Ibid. p. 202.
3:17. Judge, William: *The Ocean of Theosophy*. pp. 95-96.
[American Theosophist; 19th C.] Source I-a.

And Edgar Cayce gives a tragic example of this, saying –

> 3:18. ... the souls involved in the Conquistador invasions of Mexico and South America ... paid proportionately for their plunder and slaughter of the Aztecs. This annihilation of an entire civilization is sickening to read even now; but the gold-hungry adventurers ... returned en masse to Spain during the period of the Spanish Civil War in this century. There, brother and mother and father and sister turned against one another until their civilization was a shambles. Does this throw a clearer light on the reason why certain groups of apparently innocent people are subject to undeserved horror and tragedy?[18]

3:19. Many souls may need such experiences – Brunton says – to help them evolve in karmic terms, and the ensuing horror in their lives will show them that they should reform themselves in every way so that they are able to co-operate with 'the cosmic order'. In doing this, they overcome the cruel karmic ties which they themselves had created, and then – Brunton adds – the 'evil and pain would vanish' as 'evil is ephemeral':

> In the end it defeats itself. It has only a negative life. It represents the not-seeing of what *is*, the not-doing in harmony, the not-understanding of truth. Evil is, in short, a lack of proper comprehension, a too-distant wandering from true being, an inadequate grasp of life. When insight is gained and these deficiencies are corrected, it ceases its activity and vanishes.[19]

Now these ideas reflect the Buddha's teaching on the concept of karma in the 6th century BC, and he is quoted as saying:

3:18. In Langley, Noel: *Edgar Cayce on Reincarnation.* p. 254.
[Edgar Cayce's teaching: American healer; 19/20th C.]
3:19. Brunton, Dr Paul: *The Wisdom of the Overself.* p. 179.
[British writer on ancient philosophy; 19/20th C.] Source A-d.

> 3:20. Deep indeed is this causal law, and deep it appears to be. But it is by not knowing, by not understanding, by not penetrating this doctrine that the world of men has become entangled like a ball of twine, unable to pass beyond the Way of Woe and the ceaseless round of rebirth.[20]

We are, indeed, living in a world in which we are entangled in wrongdoing and evil, as seen by glancing through newspapers or turning on the news.

3:21. And Brunton chews over this problem, trying to understand why this evil, which is 'ephemeral', remains "inseparably present throughout the history of the universe". He feels that there are two reasons for this: "First, this earth provides a theatre for life's evolutionary activities, and thus ultimately for man, and that evolution is the orderly unfoldment of latent possibilities." We are on earth for our own development – he continues – as we have failed to correct enough of our faults, and we still need to evolve, in general terms, through further karmic life-experiences. Yet despite our efforts we are often far from perfect and add further wrongs to the world from time to time. Some souls, however, will reach the level at which they need not return for further experience; they have virtually overcome their problem with evil and have, to a great extent, developed their 'latent possibilities'. So they may leave the earth for good, but their places are not left empty, as they are immediately filled by manifestations of human life in the earlier stages of karmic development. And Brunton concludes this point, saying:

> There is no such thing as an unbroken ascent, a smooth and merely mechanical progress. The evil in man is strong enough to prevent it. But the ascent and progression themselves are true facts...
>
> Second, although good triumphs ultimately over evil when the ego's journey along the ... spiritual path finally terminates, we do not see this ultimate triumph of the natural processes of development because it occurs in a realm beyond our sight.

3:20. In Cerminara, Dr Gina: *The World Within.* pp. 199-200.
[Buddha's Teaching; 6th C. BC.] Source B-a.

While we are living on the earth – Brunton adds – we are too limited by our material bodies and our 'ignorant' minds to be able to visit such a spiritual 'realm', and we seem to be constantly bound by evil. [21]

3:22. But we can, in fact, make things better for ourselves. We have to be on the earth in the karmic roles that we had prepared for ourselves in earlier lives, but we are quite free to improve these roles. Indeed, that is why we are here.

And Brunton rounds this up by saying:

> Our past free will is the source of our present fate, as our present one will be the source of our future fate. ... This yields the clear implication that what happens to [us] ... happens by the secret will of ... [our] own innermost being.[22]

And Edgar Cayce agrees with this:

> 3:23. We have free will. We participate in our destiny. Our choices have inevitable, even predetermined results, but which choices we have made or will make have not been and are not now predetermined.[23]

"Well, I wonder what the spirit Seth would add to this?" I asked myself with some reservation. "If he really is a developed soul – coming from above or beyond 'physical reality' – he might be able to explain predetermination." So I hunted for my copy of *Seth Speaks*, and found that he said:

> 3:24. Predetermination is never involved, for the ... 'laws' of reincarnation are adapted by the individual personalities to suit themselves.[24]

3:21. Brunton, Dr Paul: *The Wisdom of the Overself.* pp. 179-181.
[British writer on ancient philosophy; 19/20th C.] Source A-d.

3:22. Ibid. pp. 188-190.

3:23. In Cochran, Lin: *Edgar Cayce on Secrets of the Universe.* p. 107.
[Edgar Cayce: American healer; 19/20th C.]

3:24. In Roberts, Jane: *Seth Speaks.* p. 216.
[Seth: Spirit teacher, through medium, Jane Roberts; 20th C.]

3:25. Seth explains that we can use our incarnations to grow consciously and intellectually to widen our horizons, and this enables us to free ourselves gradually from our karmic ties. And we can develop ourselves, in spiritual terms, by opening up our minds to the concepts of our existence.[25]

3:26. Seth also describes the way in which we select our incarnations before we return to the earth plane, being guided by wise counsellors who understand the meaning of all that lies behind our lives, and the various options that are open to us. Our decisions may seem difficult at the time, Seth adds: "But this is not a time of confusion, but of great illumination, and unbelievable challenge. ... The planning itself is all a part of experience and of development."[26]

3:27. Now the psychiatrist, Joel Whitton, understands the care and attention that is taken in planning each incarnation, as he has gathered many relevant memories from his hypnotised patients. For example, one of them said:

> "I am being helped to work out the next life so that I can face whatever difficulties come my way. I don't want to take the responsibility because I feel that I don't have the strength. But I know we have to be given obstacles in order to overcome those obstacles – to become stronger, more aware, more evolved, more responsible."

Dr Whitton believes that each incarnation is carefully planned in a way that is challenging, and difficult enough to enable the subject to evolve in karmic terms. He also believes that souls consult each other while making these plans – especially when they have been in a close relationship during their previous lives – and this enables them to return to the earth in selected partnerships or groups, so that they can evolve 'through constantly changing relationships in different lives.'[27]

And Seth would clearly agree with this, as he says:

3:25. Ibid. p. 202.
3:26. Ibid. pp. 182-184.
3:27. Whitton, Dr Joel and Fisher, Joe: *Life Between Life*. pp. 43-44.
[Canadians: psychiatrist and writer; 20th C.]

> 3:28. Oftentimes members of various groups – military groups, church groups, hunting groups, will in another life form family relationships in which they will work out old problems in new ways. Families must be considered as gestalts of psychic activity; they have a subjective identity, of which no particular member of the group may be aware.
>
> Families have subconscious purposes, though the individual members of the family may pursue these goals without conscious awareness. ... Those who have been closely bound through emotional ties often [form] ... tied physical relationships that continue through many lifetimes.[28]

3:29. If we understand this – Seth continues – it will help us with our day-to-day relationships. If we allow ourselves to hate certain people, for example, we are forming a karmic connection that will bind us to them until we have overcome the negative emotion, even though this may take several lifetimes. And we may 'attract' some other things that we dislike:

> If you vividly concern yourself with the injustices you feel have been done to you, then you attract more such experience, and if this goes on, then it will be mirrored in your next existence. ... You are setting the stage for your 'next' life now.[29]

3:30. Now Dr Whitton claims that he has some evidence which shows that unpleasant emotional ties can bring people together in their successive incarnations. Such ties, however, may be used beneficially – as described by a hypnotised subject who recalled the period of planning between his previous death and recent rebirth, saying:

3:28. In Roberts, Jane: *Seth Speaks.* pp. 204-205.
[Seth: Spirit teacher, through medium, Jane Roberts; 20th C.]
3:29. Ibid. p. 203.

> "There are people I didn't treat too well in my last life, and I have to go back to the Earth plane again and work off that debt. This time, if they hurt me in return, I'm going to forgive them because all I really want to do is to go back home. This is home."

And in contrast to this, Whitton explains that 'soul mates' are those who select particularly close relationships through several incarnations, while they help each other evolve in karmic terms. But the majority of souls are not so lucky, and when they are advised as to whom they should be associated in their next incarnation, they may dislike the advice: "Oh no – not *her* again!" groaned one subject, ... on being told his personal evolution would best be served by being reborn to a woman he had murdered in a previous life.[30]

This was, quite clearly, a very dramatic case!

3:31. But Shirley Maclaine surprised her own mother by discussing the idea that we might have chosen our relationships for this life. And her mother exclaimed:

> "Oh, ... be serious now." ...
>
> "I think we *choose* to be together," [Shirley went on,] "to work out our drama. We choose our parents, and I think the parents choose the children they want to have before they ever come into an incarnation."
>
> "You do?" said Mother, astonished at the thought and realizing, at the same time, the implications of what I'd said. "You mean you believe you chose to have your father and me as your parents?"
>
> "Yes," I answered, "and I believe that we all agreed to be part of this family unit before any of us were born."
>
> "Oh, my goodness," exclaimed Mother. "You believe all this was preordained?"
>
> "Yes, and not by God, but by each of us."[31]

3:30. Whitton, Dr Joel and Fisher, Joe: *Life Between Life.* pp. 44-45.
[Canadians: psychiatrist, and writer; 20th C.]

3:31. Maclaine, Shirley: *Dancing in the Light.* pp. 42-43.
[American filmstar/writer; 20th C.]

Now Helen Wambach has published some evidence that supports the idea that we can set up our family and group relationships before we return to earth-life. As a research psychologist, she hypnotises many volunteers and asks them to recall certain stages of their lives, including their pre-birth and birth memories. Some of these memories are really quite extraordinary – unless one thinks about them carefully. Are they, in fact, quite ordinary?

> 3:32. "My children told me they wanted to be my children before I was born, and I knew them not only from past lives, but from the between-life period."[32]

> 3:33. "When you asked if I knew my mother-to-be or my father-to-be, ... of course I knew them. They had been children of mine in a past life. In that life I had been quite frivolous and had deserted both of them when they were both young children. I became clearly aware that I was choosing this lifetime in order to experience a feeling of abandonment by my parents. An important part of my life lesson was to be learned here at the beginning, to be thrown onto the sympathies of strangers. I did not know my adoptive parents; ... the only people I knew from a past life were my natural parents."[33]

> 3:34. "My mother had been my sister in a past life where we fought all the time. My father had been my grandfather in another lifetime. My husband was a Sioux Indian when I was a French padre, and I didn't like him then either! ... This has been a very enlightening hypnotic experience as I have had the feeling since my earliest memories that I was here for a reason ..."[34]

> 3:35. "I was persuaded to be born with others that I knew to tie up all residual loose ends from my most immediate

---

3:32. In Wambach, Dr Helen: *Life before Life.* p. 93.
 [Pre-birth memories, recounted under hypnosis; 20th C.]
3:33. Ibid. pp. 165-166.
3:34. Ibid. p. 38.

life before. When you asked about helping to choose, I became aware of some old mentors of mine, three of them, but I recognized only one. When you asked about the prospects of living the coming lifetime, I had a feeling of tedium and homesickness for the place I left (not on earth), and I determined to do it right this time once and for all."[35]

3:36. " ... there seemed to be some counselors around me. I felt very depressed and unhappy. Tears ran down my cheeks here during the hypnosis."[36]

3:37. "... my feelings about the prospect of being in this lifetime were of anger. I felt shocked and stifled at the prospect of being in a body once more."[37]

3:38. "I was very resistant to the idea of choosing to be born, but I know I had to make the decision myself. My feelings about the prospect of living another lifetime were that it was really a drag. This surprises me because I love living so much."[38]

And now Ben Okri has the final word. He is a very sensitive writer who described his life in Nigeria, and made the following comment:

3:39. There was not one amongst us who looked forward to being born. We disliked the rigours of existence, the unfulfilled longings, the enshrined injustices of the world, the labyrinths of love, the ignorance of parents, the fact of dying, and the amazing indifference of the Living in the midst of the simple beauties of the universe. We feared the heartlessness of human beings, all of whom are born blind, few of whom ever learn to see.[39]

3:35. Ibid. pp. 48-49.
3:36. Ibid. p. 55.
3:37. Ibid. p. 55.
3:38. Ibid. p. 57.
3:39. Okri, Ben: *The Famished Road.* p. 3.
[Nigerian writer; 20th C.] Source F-d.

4

Chosen Lives in Childhood

4:1. Our birth is but a sleep and a forgetting:
The Soul that rises with us, our life's Star,
Hath had elsewhere its setting,
And cometh from afar:
Not in entire forgetfulness,
And not in utter nakedness,
But trailing clouds of glory do we come
From God, who is our home.[1]

Wordsworth writes as a truly inspired poet, and in this verse he gives a hopeful impression of our return to earth, in contrast to the despair of Ben Okri and to the selected memories from Wambach's book, *Life before Life.*

4:2. But the psychologist, Gina Cerminara, draws attention to the fact that Wordsworth's opening lines give the same message as that found in the 'ancient wisdom' – the compilation of old beliefs that underlie many concepts of life. Cerminara says that the lines, 'the soul that rises with us ... and cometh from afar' are often used by advocates of reincarnation. She is not happy, however, with the bit about 'trailing clouds of glory do we come,' and says:

4:1. *The Oxford Book of English Verse.* p. 628.
[William Wordsworth: English poet; 18/19th C.]

> In an ultimate sense it is true of course that the soul comes originally from Divinity and therefore shares – forgetfully – in its pristine purity and splendor. ... The psychological facts of the matter, however, ... [are] that we do not come trailing clouds of glory so much as we come trailing a very substantial cargo of accumulated abilities and disabilities, defects and capacities, weaknesses and strengths.[2]

Ben Okri would seem to agree, as he writes:

> 4:3. To be born is to come into the world weighed down with strange gifts of the soul, with enigmas and an inextinguishable sense of exile. So it was with me.[3]

"Now, this could be true," I said to myself thoughtfully as I turned back to the bookshelves. "And Seth – the spirit who apparently spoke through the entranced Jane Roberts – is bound to have something about the beginning of a new life on earth." So I scanned through the pages of *Seth Speaks* and found his description of the 'process' of incarnation. He explains that a returning soul will usually join the foetus in the womb:

> 4:4. The process is gradual, individual and determined by experience in other lives. It is particularly dependent upon emotional characteristics – not necessarily of the last incarnated self, but the emotional tensions present as a result of a group of past existences. ... The womb state under these conditions is a dreamlike one, with the personality still focused mainly in the between-life existence. Gradually the situation reverses, until it becomes more difficult to retain clear concentration in the between-life situation.

Alternatively, the incoming soul may join the baby-to-be at the time of its conception. This tends to happen when the personality has

---

4:2. Cerminara, Dr Gina: *Many Mansions*. pp. 213-214.
[American psychologist; 20th C.]

4:3. Okri, Ben: *The Famished Road*. p. 5.
[Nigerian writer; 20th C.] Source F-d.

formed close karmic bonds with its parents-to-be, either in a past life or between its incarnations. Or the soul, Seth continues, may be hastening back to this world when –

> ... there is an unceasing and almost obsessional desire to return to the earthly situation – either for a specific purpose, or ... as a result of seemingly less worthy motives – greed, for example, or an obsessional desire that is partially composed of unresolved problems.

Some other personalities, however, are less keen to come back and may remain free until the baby is born. And then Seth says: "The shock of birth has several consequences ... that usually draw the personality full blast, so to speak, into physical reality." Birth is certainly a 'shock' as the simple 'body consciousness' of the foetus has identified itself, both physically and telepathically, with its mother:

> This support is suddenly denied at birth. If the new personality has not entered earlier to any full extent, it *usually* does so at birth, in order to stabilize the new organism. It comforts the new organism, in other words. The new personality, therefore, will experience birth to varying degrees according to when it has entered this dimension.[4]

Seth's disclosures are supported by one of Dr Wambach's research projects, in which she hypnotised her volunteers and asked them if they had any memories of being a baby *in utero*, and of their experiences of birth. Their recorded memories were numerous – of which these are samples:

> 4:5. "I felt such sadness to leave the place where I was to come back into physical life. It seemed so hard to be confined in a little body, and to lose the lightness and the love I had known in the between-life state."[5]

4:4. In Roberts, Jane: *Seth Speaks*. pp. 229-231.
  [Seth: spirit teacher, through medium, Jane Roberts; 20th C.]

4:5. In Wambach, Dr Helen: *Life before Life*. p. 25.
  [Birth memories, recounted under hypnosis; 20th C.]

4:6. "I suddenly flashed on being very uncomfortable and cramped. I was back in prison. Negative sensations. I was aware under the hypnosis that my mother did not want the pregnancy and had much mental turmoil with physical and emotional trauma."[6]

4:7 "I seemed to be in and out of the fetus to check on development. After birth I stayed with the baby more, but I could still leave the body."[7]

4:8. "... it felt like I was floating above the delivery table until the birth. ... But I was aware that my mother was very loving and eager to receive me."[8]

4:9. "I joined just as the baby was delivered, I felt cramped at first, then wondered, 'How do I communicate with these people?'"[9]

4:10. "Immediately after birth I felt that they were pulling me unnecessarily. I felt drained and angry. I felt raw from the light, the air, everything. They were so *rough.* The atmosphere was rude. I had expected playing, but it was all commotion, and I longed to be back in space where everything was light."[10]

4:11. "I felt extreme sadness. I am crying. I am too freaked out by the strong stimuli to be very aware. ... I feel so sad that I am so alone and my life will be so hard."[11]

4:12. "After birth I felt uncomfortable, and it felt strange because I was so tiny for who I really was inside!"[12]

4:6. Ibid. p. 119.
4:7. Ibid. p. 106.
4:8. Ibid. p. 101.
4:9. Ibid. p. 126.
4:10. Ibid. pp. 140-141.
4:11. Ibid. p.125.
4:12. Ibid. p. 149.

> 4:13. "When you asked if I were aware of other people's feelings, for some reason I felt like laughing at them, I'm not sure why. I think it was because they had no idea who I really was and what birth was all about."[13]

So what is birth – or rather, *rebirth* – all about?

This question was discussed by Raynor Johnson in his book, *A Religious Outlook for Modern Man.* He was a physicist, and the Master of a College in Melbourne University at one time, and an intuitive philosopher.

4:14. He believes that every soul has its own "evolutionary history" – and that when it is reincarnated, the soul returns with its "desires and tendencies, interests and latent capacities, and a store of wisdom". These traits are the distillation of the soul's previous experience, so that every child is unique:

> Doubtless bodily differences are adequately accounted for by the genetic regroupings which take place in the fertilized ovum. What chiefly arouses comment is that children of the same parents, subject approximately to the same environment, may early manifest striking differences of temperament, sensitivity, interests, intellectual and artistic capacity, etc. Here we have evidence of the awakening soul which from birth until well into adult life is gradually infusing more of itself into the new personality ...
>
> The acorn has in its being a latent principle of oakness which can be awakened only if it falls from the tree, is buried in the soil, and subjected to the influences of this environment. So the souls of men at the beginning ... have a wealth of possibilities latent within them. They must sow themselves (perhaps again and again) in physical bodies, and be subject to the influences of this physical order if their latent possibilities are to be unfolded.[14]

4:13. Ibid. p. 146.

4:14. Johnson, Dr Raynor: *A Religious Outlook for Modern Man.* pp. 37-38. [British physicist; 20th C.]

Now Plato – the philosopher – was convinced that we return to earth with these latent possibilities. He had lived in the 4th and 5th centuries BC, and described a conversation between Socrates – who was Plato's Greek contemporary – and his pupil, Meno, on the theme of latent knowledge:

> 4:15. *Socrates*: "I have heard from men and women who understand the truths ... that the soul of man is immortal: at one time it comes to an end – that which is called death – and at another is born again, but is never finally exterminated. ...
> "Thus the soul, since it is immortal and has been born many times, ... can recall the knowledge of virtue or anything else which, as we see, it once possessed. ... When a man has recalled a single piece of knowledge – *learned* it, in ordinary language – there is no reason why he should not find out all the rest, if he keeps a stout heart and does not grow weary of the search; for seeking and learning are in fact nothing but recollection." ...
> *Meno*: "I see, Socrates. But what do you mean when you say that we don't learn anything, but that what we call learning is recollection?"

At this point Socrates decided that it would be easier to demonstrate his theory than explain it, and he suggested that Meno should summon one of his young slaves. A boy was called over, and Socrates asked if he spoke Greek. Meno said that he did, having been 'born and bred in the house' – and Socrates said: "Listen carefully then, and see whether it seems to you that he is learning from me or simply being reminded."[15]

4:16. He then turned to the boy, and questioned him on an abstruse Pythagorean theory in geometry in such a way that the boy could sift through his own memories and come up with the right answers. And Socrates continued, saying:

> "You see, Meno, that I am not teaching him anything, only asking ...[16]

4:15. Plato: *Protagoras and Meno.* pp. 129-130.
[Greek philosopher; 5/4th C. BC.] Source C-a.
4:16. Ibid. p. 132.

> 4:17. "Has he answered with any opinions that were not his own? ... These opinions were somewhere in him, were they not?" ...
>
> *Meno*: "It would appear so." ...
>
> *Socrates*: "Has anyone taught him all these? You ought to know, especially as he has been brought up in your household."
>
> *Meno*: "Yes, I know that no one ever taught him." ...
>
> *Socrates*: "Then if he did not acquire them in this life, isn't it immediately clear that he possessed and had learned them during some other period?"[17]

This argument impressed me, and it seemed to explain an article that I had read in *The Times* newspaper which described a boy, Ganesh, as some sort of genius. Here was a lad – I thought – whose ability in maths could only be attributed to some particular knowledge that he 'possessed and had learned' in an earlier life.

4:18. Ganesh was only thirteen when he graduated from an English university with a brilliant 'First', and younger than any other student who had received a degree at this level in four hundred years. In fact he was so young that he had to complete a third of the syllabus at home before the authorities would allow him to join the university, and even then he was only allowed to attend for a single day each week. Despite these severe restrictions, Ganesh graduated with first class honours and was delighted that he had achieved his goal.[18]

4:19. His father was understandably proud of his son's achievement, but he insisted that Ganesh had never been pushed through the syllabus, and that he had only helped Ganesh when the boy wanted some tuition. Maths had just fascinated the boy; maths was somehow there within him.[19]

Now the Rosicrucian, Max Heindel, takes up the theme, saying:

> 4:20. Genius is the hall-mark of the advanced soul, which by hard work in many previous lives has developed itself in

---

4:17. Ibid. pp. 137-138.

4:18. In *The Times*. London, July 14, 1992. p. 1.
[Article by John O'Leary.]

4:19. Ibid. p. 3.

> some way beyond the normal achievements. ... It cannot be accounted for by heredity, which applies only in part to the dense body and not to qualities of the soul. ... The body is simply an instrument, the work it yields being dependent upon the Ego which guides it.[20]

And Emmet Fox adds his views:

> 4:21. The born musician is a man who has studied music in a previous life, perhaps in several lives, and has therefore built that faculty into his soul. He is a talented musician today because he is reaping what he sowed yesterday ...
>
> Child prodigies are always souls who have acquired their proficiency in a previous life; and it is noticeable how often such children are born into circumstances favorable for their talent. [21]

4:22. The prodigy, Mozart, was born into a musical family in Austria in the 18th century. Ann Lingg describes him in her book, *Genius of Harmony*, and says that "Wolfgang was only ... three years old" when he kept playing on the harpsichord; so his father decided he should teach him to play it properly, and Mozart would work for hours at a time without any encouragement. His father kept a detailed diary – which is now in the Salzburg Mozarteum – and his concise entries are filled with pride. For example: "The above minuet Wolfgangerl knew by heart when he was not yet four." ... "On January 26, 1761, the day before his fifth birthday, Wolfgangerl learned this minuet and trio within half an hour, at 9.30 p.m."

On one occasion Mozart was left at home, playing the harpsichord as usual while the maid cooked the dinner. But then he decided to "write a concerto". He had often watched his father copying music, so he collected Papa's writing materials and set to work. Papa, however, had never had such trouble with the feather pen and ink! Yet despite

---

4:20. Heindel, Max: *Rosicrucian Cosmo-Conception.* pp. 155-156. [American Rosicrucian; 19/20th C.] Source H-b.

4:21. Fox, Emmet: *Power Through Constructive Thinking.* pp. 252-253. [American writer; 19/20th C.]

this problem, Mozart was working steadily when "Papa and his friend, Schachtner," returned – and Papa exclaimed:

> "What are you doing here, Wolferl? What *is* this mess?" Papa ... took the sheet away from Wolferl and laughed at the mixture of circles and lines, blots and smears. But suddenly Leopold Mozart stopped laughing and studied the sheet of paper closely.
>
> "Schachtner," he said quietly. ... "Look. ... Everything is set properly and symmetrically. Almost perfect. Only it's too difficult for anyone to play."
>
> "But that's why it's a concerto," Wolfgang interrupted. "One must practice it until it goes well. Listen, like this." ... And he ran to the harpsichord and played. He couldn't really play what he had written, but he did it well enough to make the two men understand that he knew what he wanted.
>
> For the rest of the evening, Leopold was very thoughtful: ... "This isn't talent. This is a miracle. ... There is nothing I could teach Wolferl which he wouldn't already know. ... It's just *in* him. We all like music, but with him it's different."[22]

4:23. Now the mystic, Paracelsus, has been quoted as saying: "To be taught is nothing; everything is in man, waiting to be awakened."[23]

"But this repeats the same message – in rather generous terms," I said to myself. "It's backing the stuff that I've just read – stuff which suggests that we do retain knowledge from our previous lives. And if that knowledge surfaces, it makes some kids seem brilliant: kids like Ganesh, with his maths – and Mozart, with his music. But come to think of it, their fathers did help them.

"So the real question is this: are there any children who know certain things that they could not possibly have learnt in this life?" I thought for a while, and then remembered an extraordinary case that shows that this can happen – as described in Raynor Johnson's book, *A Religious Outlook for Modern Man.*

4:22. Lingg, Ann: *Mozart, Genius of Harmony*. pp. 10-14.
[Describing Mozart: Austrian musical genius; 18th C.]

4:23. In Playfair, Guy: *The Indefinite Boundary*. p. 272.
[Paracelsus: Swiss Rosicrucian; 16th C.] Source H-a.

4:24. This case describes a little girl who had no brothers or sisters. She was often lonely, and amused herself by reciting strange words and ditties, which her parents thought were some sort of baby-talk.

Now her father's cousin had been abroad for some years, as he was working in the East as a Jesuit priest. But then he came to stay with them – and Johnson continues:

> The child, then about five, grew weary of listening to grown-up conversations, and sitting in a corner began to murmur to herself her usual recitations. The priest stopped talking and listened, and then asked, "Where did Laurence learn Persian?"
>
> "Persian!" said her father, "it's nonsense, sound without sense." The priest then asked her to speak to him in her own language – which she did, and he said to her father, "This is Persian, not Persian of today, but of the epic era."
>
> The parents were amazed: they said nobody who knew Persian had been near the child or near them. They could not account for her conduct.[24]

4:25. A further example of hidden, inner knowledge was described by the mystic, 'AE'. He said that he had been a very ordinary child, apart from having a 'vivid imagination'. He had, therefore, assumed that he had conjured up his own private saga –

> ... of gods and demi-gods, and miraculous happenings in some Valhalla, and to these characters he assigned names. ... But one day while waiting at the desk of the village library for the librarian to bring him a story book, he happened to glance at the open page of a book that was lying there, and his eye encountered the word 'Aeon'. He declared that his surprise and excitement were so great that he left the library empty-handed and walked about the streets for two hours before he could muster up sufficient calmness and courage

---

4:24. In Johnson, Dr Raynor: *A Religious Outlook for Modern Man.* p. 186.
[Private communuication to Raynor Johnson; 20th C.]

> to ask the librarian what book it was, and if he might look at it. For the name Aeon was one which he had given to the hero of one of his own stories, a name which he regarded as peculiarly his own, or of his own invention, and it was upsetting to discover that such was plainly not the case.

The volume, in fact, was a study of abstruse Gnostic belief and cosmology, and 'AE' was extremely surprised to find that his private saga of imagined characters was clearly not his own: it was based on Gnostic concepts that were centuries old.[25]

'AE' had remembered and not imagined his Gnostic inheritance, and little Laurence had spoken 'epic' Persian, so it is logical to conclude that they had acquired their abstruse knowledge in earlier incarnations. But some people have been able to foretell certain facts about their *future* incarnations.

For example, I remembered that the American Eskimo, William George Senior, had said that he would be reborn to his daughter-in-law, and he gave his gold watch to her to keep for his return. William George had also predicted that certain moles on his *future* body would be positioned like those that were on his present body. And apparently, this had all come true.

4:26. And Alexandra David-Neel said that a dying lama - a *tulku* - would often foretell where he could be found in his next incarnation. David-Neel was a French explorer, who was given the honourable Buddhist title of 'Lama' while she was in Tibet. She explained that a dying lama would provide -

> ... various particulars about his future parents, the situation of their house and so on. ... Sometimes a young boy is quickly found whose birthplace and other characteristics answer the directions given by the late lama or the astrologer. In other cases, years elapse without finding anyone, and some 'incarnations' even remain undiscovered ...
>
> When a child is discovered who nearly answers the prescribed conditions, a lama clairvoyant is again consulted,

4:25. Bragdon, Claude: *Merely Players*. p. 174.
[Describing 'AE': an Irish mystic; 19/20th C.]

> and if he pronounces in favour of the child the following final test is applied.
>
> A number of objects such as rosaries, ritualistic implements, books, tea-cups, etc., are placed together, and the child must pick out those which belonged to the late *tulku,* thus showing that he recognizes the things which were *his* in his previous life. ...
>
> Countless tales are told throughout Tibet about extraordinary proofs of memory from previous lives, ... but I prefer to confine myself to the relation of facts connected with people whom I have personally known.

David-Neel stayed for a while in Kum-Bum, next to a large estate that had been the home of Lama Agnai tsang. He had died seven years earlier, but his monks had failed to find his long-awaited incarnation. David-Neel, however, felt that the 'steward of the lama's household' was really rather comfortable in this situation: he was running the 'estate' himself and living rather well. He had to travel from time to time to do the estate's trading; but while he was resting at a farm one day, he was opening a jade snuffbox – which he had brought with him – when a small boy came up, and asked:

> "Why do you use my snuff-box?"
>
> The steward was thunderstruck. Truly, the precious snuff-box was not his, but belonged to the departed Agnai tsang, and though he had not perhaps exactly intended to steal it, yet he had taken possession of it.
>
> He remained there trembling while the boy looked at him as his face suddenly became grave and stern, with no longer anything childish about it.
>
> "Give it back to me at once, it is mine," he said again.
>
> Stung with remorse, and at the same time terrified and bewildered, the superstitious monk could only fall on his knees and prostrate himself before his reincarnated master.

Some time later, the steward and his party returned to the Kum-Bum estate in a triumphal procession, with the little boy seated 'in state' on a pony. David-Neel watched their arrival and was very interested to hear the lad ask, "Why do we turn to the left to reach the second courtyard? The gate is on our right side."

The monks were impressed by his question, as they knew that the old gate had been 'walled up' and a new gate made on the left when the last lama died. The fact that the boy had noticed this gave them proof, they were sure, that he was the reincarnation of the lama – and they hastened to take tea with him, in the lama's 'private apartment'.

The boy was seated carefully on cushions, and a special cup with a 'jewelled cover' was set before him. But he seemed dissatisfied:

> "Give me the larger china cup," he commanded. Then he described one, mentioning the very pattern that decorated it.
>
> Nobody knew about such a cup, not even the steward, and the monks respectfully endeavoured to convince their young master that there was no cup of that kind in the house. ...
>
> "Look better, you will find it."
>
> And suddenly ... he added explanations about a box painted in such a colour, which was in such a place in the store-room.
>
> The monks had briefly informed me of what was going on and I waited with interest to see how things would turn out. Less than half an hour later, the set, cup, saucer and cover, was discovered in a casket that was at the bottom of the very box described by the boy.[26]

Now Raynor Johnson introduces a new point, saying –

> 4:27. ... [the] permanent soul which stores the wisdom, goodness, artistic sensitivity, interest, and skills of the past, surely influences in some degree the new personality which it is sending forth into the world.[27]

4: 26. David-Neel, A: *Magic and Mystery in Tibet.* pp. 94-98. [French explorer and Lama; 19/20th C.] Source B-C.

4:27. Johnson, Dr Raynor: *A Religious Outlook for Modern Man.* p. 180. [British physicist; 20th C.]

This seems very logical, and it would explain why some children are so set in their ways of doing certain things, or believing certain things, that they simply follow their own way of life – even against their parents' wishes.

4:28. Saint Catherine, for example, lived in Sienna in the 14th century – and the Reverend Butler describes her as a little girl who insisted on kneeling on every stair to whisper her favourite prayer, *Hail Mary*. She spent all her time in praying or performing 'pious practices' of one sort or another, and only tolerated the company of other children if they joined her in these practices.

Her mother, quite naturally, was worried as the years passed by and Catherine failed to change; and when she turned twelve, her parents said that she should prepare herself for marriage, insisting that she should have her hair arranged properly and wear the fashion of the day. Catherine tried to please her mother by allowing herself to be made attractive in this way, but inevitably she failed as she disliked the frippery and nonsense. It was just not her style.

And the Reverend Butler takes on her saga - from *Lives of the Saints:*

> Uncompromisingly she now declared that she would never marry, and, as her parents still persisted in trying to find her a husband, she cut off her golden-brown hair – her chief beauty.
>
> The whole family, roused to indignation, ... [were] determined to overcome her resolution by a system of petty persecution. ... All these trials she bore with a sweet patience which nothing could ever ruffle. ... At last her father realized that further opposition was useless, and ... she was allowed to lead the life to which she felt herself called. In the small room now ceded for her use, ... which she kept shuttered and dimly-lighted, she gave herself up to prayer and fasting, scourged herself thrice daily with a heavy chain, and slept upon a board.[28]

4:28. Butler, Rev. Alban: *Lives of the Saints.* pp. 337-338.
[Describing St. Catherine; 14th C.]

Now Catherine was quite unlike another of the famous saints – Saint Teresa of Avila – though both were remarkably pious. Catherine's life was one of extreme self-discipline, in contrast to Teresa's loving dedication and social activity; and Catherine, as a child, was treated severely by her parents, her siblings and herself, whereas Teresa was a very natural member of a loving family. And in her autobiography, Teresa says:

> 4:29. … my brothers and sisters never stood in the way of my serving God. I had one brother almost of my own age, whom I loved best. ... We used to read the lives of the Saints together, and when I read of the martyrdoms which they suffered for the love of God, I used to think that they had bought their entry into God's presence very cheaply. Then I fervently longed to die like them. ... I used to discuss with my brother ways and means of becoming martyrs, and we agreed to go together to the land of the Moors, begging our way for the love of God, so that we might be beheaded there. I believe that our Lord had given us courage enough even at that tender age, if only we could have seen a way. But our having parents seemed to us a very great hindrance.[29]

But her parents' instinct was to keep their children safe and sound!

Parents fear that death will be the end, the passing into some form of unknowable eternity or nothingness, whereas children are generally much less afraid. And one mother wrote to Dr Kübler-Ross – a specialist who worked with the dying and their loved ones – describing her small daughter's lack of fear:

> 4:30. My daughter ... slept in my bed that night, and I was awakened by her hugging and shaking me, saying, "Mom, Mom, Jesus told me I'm going to heaven! ... and it's all beautiful … and Jesus and God are there." ... She was talking so fast that I could barely follow her. Almost euphoric. This scared me…

4:29. Teresa of Avila: *The Life of Saint Teresa by Herself.* pp. 23-24.
[Spanish Prioress and mystic; 16th C.]

The girl's strange 'excitement' frightened her mother, as the child was normally quiet and sedate:

> To find her so excited that she was stammering and tripping over her words was very unusual. In fact, I don't remember *ever* seeing her in such a state, not at Christmas, birthdays, or the circus.
>
> I told her to hush, slow down, not talk that way (mostly a superstitious fear on my part). I'd had a 'feeling' since she was born that she somehow wouldn't be with me long. ... [But] I couldn't succeed in slowing her down. She went on and on, telling me ... how happy she was going to be there, ... and how Jesus had *told* her. Very emphatic, so excited that she was difficult to follow ...
>
> I said, "Honey, wait, settle down now," and begged her back, "if you went to heaven, I'd miss you, honey. And I'm glad that you had such a happy dream, but let's slow down and relax a minute, OK?"
>
> It didn't work. She said, "It was *not* a dream, it was *real*" (in that emphatic way that four-year-olds have), ... and laid in my arms for a while and said I shouldn't worry 'cause Jesus would take care of me, climbed out of bed, and ran off to play.
>
> I got up, too, and fixed breakfast. We had a normal day, but somehow between 3:00 and 3:30 that afternoon, ... [the little girl] was murdered.[30]

Death is now described by Dr Kübler-Ross, in her gentle way:

> 4:31 And so it is with death – the culmination of life, the graduation, the good-bye before another hello, the end before another beginning. Death is the great transition.

4:30. In Kübler-Ross, Dr Elizabeth: *On Children and Death*. pp. 131-133. [A mother's letter; 20th C.]

Kübler-Ross has been with very many people while they died, and she is convinced that death teaches us about life and its 'ultimate mysteries.' She writes:

> Those who learned to KNOW death, rather than to fear and fight it, become our teachers about LIFE. There are thousands of children who know death far beyond the knowledge adults have. Adults may listen to these children and shrug it off; they may think that children do not comprehend death; they may reject their ideas. But one day they may remember their teachings ...[31]

Edou, for example, was a remarkably matter-of-fact and fearless little boy while he was facing his impending death, and said:

> 4:32. "I prayed to God, I wanted to live until I was seven. – After that day or maybe a little later, I could die as I would like to die."

Edou explained that he wanted to die because he was so ill, and he was sure that his spirit would be free of pain after death. Then he added: "When you choose your life in heaven, you can come back to earth in a healthy life or no life or in a sick life, but you can't remember what you chose."

When asked what he thought about 'life in heaven', Edou said that his body would not be there, although his spirit would be, and that dying was a bit like 'walking into your mind'. He explained that some people were afraid of dying as it might be painful, and if they were in pain already they would be afraid of having even more pain; but his own problem about dying was that he knew he would miss his mother. If she also chose to die – he continued – they would be together in spirit; but even if she did not die, he would be able to return in his own spirit to see her from time to time. Asked whether he thought he would be able to visit other people, Edou said:

4:31. Ibid. p. xvii.
[Dr Elisabeth Kübler-Ross: American specialist for the dying; 20th C.]

"Yes, I do. ... One time in the middle of the night I heard something going through the house – the spirit of my grandfather. I think Mom heard it too." ...

"Do you think he will be waiting for you?"

"Yes, I do."[32]

There are other children who have said that they saw the spirit of a person who has died, and one of these children clearly chose to die to be with his little brother – as his mother explains in the following account:

4:33. In 1883 I was the mother of two strong, healthy boys. The eldest was a bright boy of two years and seven months. The other a darling baby boy of eight months. August 6th, 1883, my baby died. Ray, my little son, was then in perfect health. Every day after baby's death (and I may safely say every hour in the day) he would say to me, "Mamma, baby calls Ray." He would often leave his play and come running to me, saying, "Mamma, baby calls Ray all the time." Every night he would waken me out of my sleep and say, "Mamma, baby calls Ray all the time. He wants Ray to come where he is; you must not cry when Ray goes, Mamma; you must not cry, for baby wants Ray."

One day I was sweeping the sitting-room floor, and he came running as fast as he could run. ... I never saw him so excited, and he grabbed my dress and pulled me to the dinning-room door, jerked it open, saying, "Oh, Mamma, Mamma, come quick; baby is sitting in his high chair." As soon as he opened the door and looked at the chair, he said, "Oh, Mamma, why didn't you hurry; now he's gone. ... Ray is going with baby, but you must not cry, Mamma." Ray soon became very sick. Nursing and medicine were of no avail. He died Oct. 13th, 1883, two months and seven days after baby's death.[33]

4:32. Ibid. pp. 221-223.
[Edou's understanding of impending death; 20th C.]

4:33. In Barrett, Sir William: *Death-Bed Visions*. pp. 38-39.
[A mother's account; 19/20th C.] Source J-f.

Now the American Rosicrucian, Max Heindel, explains that –

> 4:34. ... children can 'see' the higher Worlds and they often prattle about what they see until the ridicule of their elders or punishment for 'telling stories' teaches them to desist.
>
> It is deplorable that the little ones are forced to lie – or at least to deny the truth – because of the incredulity of their 'wise' elders. Even the investigations of the Society for Psychical Research have proven that children often have invisible playmates who frequently visit them until they are several years old.[34]

4:35. Some children describe their 'invisible playmates' quite readily – as in this article, from *The Times*:

> Scott helps with maths problems; Mr Green tells jokes and his daughter shares midnight feasts; Jessica can be as small as a mouse or as big as a giant and flies around the room, and Gemma, who lives in the mirror in the bathroom, just talks. ...
>
> "She's very pretty" ... [child A] confides about Jessica. [Child B] ... says that Gemma ... "is nicer than me. She tells me the right things to do." [Child C] ... describes Scott ... as an older brother, "the perfect person, always happy, never ill, just the sort of person I'd like to be."
>
> Some of the children admit to loneliness or bullying, but in times of uncertainty or misery, these friends have been there to see them through. "He's like a guardian angel," says ... [child D].[35]

Now, despite the fact that I was reading about children who had these spirit friends, I was very surprised when my small granddaughter suddenly greeted the empty air at her side while she sat swinging on the

4:34. Heindel, Max: *The Rosicrucian Cosmo-Conception.* p. 140.
[American Rosicrucian; 19/20th C.] Source J-f.

4:35. In *The Times.* London, April 4, 1992. p. 3.
[Article by Belle Grey.] Source J-f.

lowest branch of a tree. She was acting as though she was with a solid and responsive friend! Then a smile, and a 'bye, and more swinging on her own. The incident was matter-of-fact, somehow, rather than imaginative, and I found it a little blood-chilling at the time! But I was not alone in reacting like this – as the writer Elisabeth Haich describes how she became frightened when she first heard about spirits and ghosts, saying:

> 4:36. I could learn all sorts of exciting things about superstition from our washwoman. As fast as I possibly could I sought out opportunities for clandestine conversation with her. Thus I came to hear some of the most horrible stories about ghosts, superstitions and witchcraft until I got into such a state of fear that I no longer dared to enter a dark room alone. Then Uncle Stefi asked me once why I was afraid.
>
> "Because I might see a ghost," I said.
>
> "Oh, so that's it! Want to know an easy way to defend yourself? ... Just whistle real loud, and all the ghosts will scamper away instantly," he answered.
>
> From then on I was constantly whistling, while at the same time delving further into ghost stories. Thus, on the one hand, I extended my knowledge about the lowest levels of mysticism, and on the other, developed an above-average ability for whistling.[36]

4:36. Haich Elisabeth: *Initiation.* p. 49.
[Swiss writer/yoga teacher; 19/20th C.]

5

Spirits and Inspiration

Elisabeth Haich kept her ghosts at bay by whistling 'real loud', but now I would have to deal with them as they had slipped into my spheres of interest. My doubts about their existence were lessening a little, but I felt that I should read more about them to see where they would take me. So I armed myself with the useful phrase that 'real intelligence is open-mindedness' - and picked out a book by the sensitive South African author, Laurens Van der Post, and soon found this spooky passage:

> 5:1. I soon came to believe ... that the country was haunted. Late at night on lonely journeys when I climbed out of cart or wagon to open a gate in a pass, I would suddenly tremble with fear for the nearness and certainty of unacknowledged being. It was not just a normal fear of darkness. Often I would find the horses sharing my feeling and shivering deeply under my hand as I laid it on their necks as much to comfort myself as to calm them. ... Another time, out with a Hottentot groom on the veld many miles from any habitation in a night as black as an Old Testament Bible, our horses reared, stopped dead and stood, legs wide apart, heads up, snorting with terror and trembling all over. The Hottentot groom, who believed as do all his kind that horses have second sight, cried hysterically: "Please, little

> master, let's turn back! Please don't go on!" But he would never say what he thought he had seen.[1]

This was, indeed, quite chilling; but I found a letter that was far more chilling – a letter that was published by the Harvard Professor, William James, that said:

> 5:2. I have several times within the past few years felt the so-called 'consciousness of a presence'. ... It was about September, 1884, when I had the first experience. On the previous night I had had, after getting into bed at my rooms in College, a vivid tactile hallucination of being grasped by the arm, which made me get up and search the room for an intruder; but the sense of presence properly so called came on the next night. After I had got into bed and blown out the candle, I lay awake awhile thinking on the previous night's experience, when suddenly I *felt* something come into the room and stay close to my bed. It remained only a minute or two. I did not recognize it by any ordinary sense, and yet there was a horribly unpleasant 'sensation' connected with it. It stirred something more at the roots of my being than any ordinary perception; ... something was present with me, and I knew its presence far more surely than I have ever known the presence of any fleshly living creature. I was conscious of its departure as of its coming: an almost instantaneously swift going through the door, and the 'horrible sensation' disappeared.[2]

"But this is *really* horrible!" I thought. "And what on earth should I make of it?" As if in answer, an Arab princess from Zanzibar described – in her memoirs – how her people viewed such happenings:

> 5:3. In our parts people are fond of everything supernatural; the more mysterious and incomprehensible it

---

5:1. Van der Post, Laurens: *The Lost World of the Kalahari.* p. 59. [South African writer; 20th C.] Source F-e.

5:2. In James, Prof William: *The Varieties of Religious Experience.* pp. 59-60 [Testimony from a friend; 19/20th C.]

appears the more faith it receives. Everybody believes in spirits, good and evil, ... and as it is a general belief that the soul of the departed has a longing to return to and especially prefers to stay in its former abode, no person cares to enter the same in the daytime, and flies from it at night.[3]

This princess had married the German Consul to Zanzibar in the late 19th century, and had taken the name, Emily Said-Reute. They had then moved to Europe, and many years passed by before she was able to return to Zanzibar with her children, to show them her old home. She now describes their extraordinary visit, saying:

5:4. Had I expected what was awaiting me in the old house of my birth, I should have paid it a preliminary visit by myself. The figures of former residents seemed to me to be hovering around and gliding from under the dangerously-leaning roofs, the half-hanging doors and falling beams. More and more vividly did their faces and shapes grow upon me. I was moving in their midst, and could hear their own familiar voices. How long this ... lasted I know not, but I was suddenly roused into the actual present again by ... my children coming to draw me away from the scenes that affected me so deeply.[4]

Now Jane Roberts – the medium, through whom Seth the spirit speaks – writes in her own intuitive way:

5:5. And so there may be others now ... without images, but knowing – others who have been what we are and more – others who remember what we have forgotten. They may have discovered through some acceleration of consciousness other forms of being, or dimensions of reality of which we are also part. ... Yet they are all about us, in the wind and trees, formed and unformed, more alive in many ways perhaps than we are – the speakers.

5:3. Said-Ruete, Emily: *Memoirs of an Arabian Princess*. p. 102.
[Omani Arab princess; 19th C.] Source F-b.

5:4. Ibid. p. 296.

> Through these voices, these intuitions, these flashes of insights and messages, the universe speaks to us, to each of us personally ... saying, "while you are conscious bodies, remember what it was like and will be like to be bodiless. ... We are yourselves, turned inside out."[5]

The French medium, Allan Kardec, adds a more prosaic view:

> 5:6. The souls, then, that people space, are ... the souls of men stripped of their envelope of gross terrestrial matter; ... if we admit that souls exist, we must also admit that spirits are nothing else but souls.[6]
>
> 5:7. ... it follows that the souls of men are spirits in flesh, and that we, on dying, become spirits.[7]

5:8. Carl Jung recalls a strange episode which helped him understand that a dying man becomes a spirit. Jung had been to a funeral, and was mulling over the sad occasion in the late evening when he became aware that his supposedly dead neighbour was standing at the end of his bed. Despite his initial surprise, Jung assumed that he was imagining his friend, and he asked himself:

> "Do I have any proof that this is a fantasy? Suppose it is not a fantasy, suppose my friend is really here and I decided he was only a fantasy – would that not be abominable of me? ... I might just as well give him the benefit of the doubt and for experiment's sake credit him with reality."

As soon as Jung had made this decision, he felt that the presence was beckoning him and moving towards the door. He had not expected this, and hesitated before allowing himself – in thought, as it were – to follow. Jung followed his friend out into the road and down to his house, and was

---

5:5. Roberts, Jane: *Seth Speaks.* pp. xxi-xxii.
[American medium/writer; 20th C.]

5:6. Kardec, Allan: *Experimental Spiritism: The Mediums' Book* p. 4.
[French Spiritist medium; 19th C.] Source J-b.

5:7. Ibid. p. 46.

then led up to the study. The apparition mounted a small stool, and drew Jung's attention to a row of five red books on the second top shelf. He pointed to the second of these books, and then disappeared. Jung had never been in his neighbour's study, and he could not read the book's title; but he was so impressed by the whole episode that he called on his neighbour's widow the next day, and asked if he could consult one of her late husband's books. She led him up to the study, he says, and –

> … there was a stool standing under the bookcase. … I could see the five books with red bindings. I stepped up on the stool so as to be able to read. ... The title of the second volume read: *The Legacy of the Dead.* The contents seemed to me of no interest. Only the title was extremely significant in connection with this experience.[8]

Jung's neighbour had simply appeared before him as a realistic and interactive spirit. And the British Society for Psychical Research has published many accounts from others who were convinced that they have seen visions of the dead. One description from the 19th century explains this, in particularly vivid terms:

> 5:9. I had not been thinking of my late sister, or in any manner reflecting on the past, ... [when] I suddenly became conscious that some one was sitting on my left, with one arm resting on the table. Quick as a flash I turned and distinctly saw the form of my dead sister, and for a brief second or so looked her squarely in the face; and so sure was I that it was she, that I sprang forward in delight, calling her by name, and, as I did so, that apparition instantly vanished. Naturally I was startled and dumbfounded, almost doubting my senses; but ... I satisfied myself I had not been dreaming and was wide awake. I was near enough to touch her, had it been a physical possibility, and noted her features, expression, and details of dress, etc. She appeared as if alive. Her eyes looked kindly and perfectly naturally

---

5:8. Jung, Dr Carl G: *Memories, Dreams, Reflections.* pp. 289-290.
[German-Swiss psychiatrist; 19/20th C.]

into mine. Her skin was so life-like that I could see the glow of moisture on its surface, and, on the whole, there was no change in her appearance, otherwise than when alive ...

This visitation, or whatever you may call it, so impressed me that I took the next train home, and in the presence of my parents and others I related what had occurred. My father, a man of rare good sense and very practical, was inclined to ridicule me; ... but he, too, was amazed when later on I told them of a bright red line or *scratch* on the right-hand side of my sister's face, which I distinctly had seen. When I mentioned this, my mother rose trembling to her feet and nearly fainted away, and as soon as she sufficiently recovered her self-possession, with tears streaming down her face, she exclaimed that I had indeed seen my sister, as no living mortal but herself was aware of that scratch, which she had accidentally made while doing some little act of kindness after my sister's death. She said she well remembered how pained she was to think she should have, unintentionally, marred the features of her dead daughter, and that unknown to all, how she had carefully obliterated all traces of the slight scratch with the aid of powder, etc., and that she had never mentioned it to a human being, from that day to this. In proof, neither my father nor any of the family had detected it, and positively were unaware of the incident, *yet I saw the scratch as bright as if just made.* So strangely impressed was my mother that even after she had retired to rest, she got up and dressed, came to me and told me *she knew* at least that I had seen my sister. A few weeks later my mother died, happy in her belief she would rejoin her favourite daughter in a better world.[9]

5:10. Many people have been comforted by seeing the apparition of a loved one who has died. To give an example, Dr Kübler-Ross described a woman whose daughter had been raped and then drowned.

5:9. *In Proceedings of the Society Psychical Research*: Vol. 6. p.13.
[F. G.'s testimony; 19th C.] Source K-c.

For the next few days the despairing mother wandered about in abject misery, till at last she lay down. And then "... she noticed a bright light coming through the window and in it appeared her little first-grader, healthy, radiant, and smiling – with outstretched arms: 'Look, Mom!' Her daughter disappeared after a few moments but the sight filled her with such peace and love that she was in a much better mental condition after this incident than the rest of the still frightened community!"[10]

5:11. Kübler-Ross now describes the emptiness of a home that has suffered the loss of a teenager. There's no lively music, no friends crowding in, chattering and laughing. The house feels frigid 'like a morgue' – one Mom said – and she found it terrible to bear her loss as she paced the empty rooms:

> It is on days like this, weeks and months after the funeral, that the arrival of an old school pal can be the greatest gift. One boy [called Rick] came to the door of Mrs L. and asked for permission to continue to play ball on their front yard, "like we used to do." God, was she happy to give that permission. Before long, other classmates came, and she saw herself busy in the kitchen, fixing cold drinks and snacks and laughingly bringing back old memories. "One day I have to tell Rick that he saved my life by doing that. I don't know how he knew ..."
>
> I advised Mrs L. to tell Rick *today* and not postpone it for tomorrow. ... When she did, Rick told her in the most matter-of-fact way that it was her son who had told him that it was time to resume the old games on his front yard. ... [Rick had] only "followed orders" given by his old pal who "visited him occasionally in his dreams."[11]

"But can a dream *really* let us have some contact with the dead?" I asked myself doubtfully. And I turned again to the books and found that a young man, James Chaffin, had had no such doubts. In fact James had

---

5:10. Kübler-Ross, Dr Elisabeth: *On Children and Death*. p. 177.
[American specialist for the dying; 20th C.]

5:11. Ibid. pp. 147-148.

won an extraordinary court case after giving some evidence that was provided by his deceased father, James L. Chaffin; and the British Society for Psychical Research published young James's account, in which he said:

> 5:12. I began to have very vivid dreams that my father appeared to me at my bedside but made no verbal communication. Some time later, I think it was the latter part of June, 1925, he appeared at my bedside again, ... wearing a black overcoat which I knew to be his own coat. This time my father's spirit spoke to me; he took hold of his overcoat this way and pulled it back and said, "You will find my will in my overcoat pocket," and then disappeared. The next morning I arose fully convinced that my father's spirit had visited me for the purpose of explaining some mistake.

James then decided that he should try to find his father's coat. It was not in his mother's house, however, as she had passed it on to his brother, John; so James went to John's house and, to his relief, the coat was there. James gave further details about this in court, saying:

> On examination of the inside pocket I found that the lining had been sewed together. I immediately cut the stitches and found a little roll of paper tied with a string which was in my father's handwriting and contained only the following words: "Read the 27th chapter of Genesis in my Daddie's old Bible."

With this paper in his hands, James felt that he should find a witness to help him check the Bible in his mother's house. A neighbour agreed to do so, and when they found the Bible he leafed through Genesis, and found that the pages which contained Chapter 27 had been folded together to hold the father's second will.[12]

5:13. This second will proved to be a really important document as it would enable the family to sort out the problems that had been

---

5:12. In *Proceedings, Soc. Psychical Research*: Vol. 36. pp. 519-520.
[J. P. Chaffin's testimony; 20th C.} Source K-c.

caused by old James L. Chaffin's first will – which had been very unfair. And the published account continues:

> On the 16th November, 1905, the Testator [James L. Chaffin] made a will, duly attested by two witnesses, whereby he gave his farm to his third son, Marshall, whom he appointed sole executor. The widow and the other three sons were left unprovided for. Some years later he appears to have been dissatisfied with this disposition of his property, and ... made a new will as follows:
>
> After reading the 27th chapter of Genesis, I, James L. Chaffin, do make my last will and testament, and here it is. I want, after giving my body a decent burial, my little property to be equally divided between my four children. ... And if she is living, you all must take care of your mammy. Now this is my last will and testament. Witness my hand and seal.
>
> James L. Chaffin. This January 16, 1919.
>
> This second will, though unattested, would according to the law of North Carolina be valid as being written throughout by the Testator's own hand. ... The Testator, having written out this will, placed it ... [in] the 27th Chapter of Genesis, which tells how the younger brother Jacob supplanted the elder brother Esau, and won his birthright and his father's blessing. The sole beneficiary under the first will was, it will be remembered, a younger brother.

Old James L. Chaffin, however, had obviously failed to tell the family that he had made a second will after reading the chapter in Genesis, which made him regret his first will. (Perhaps he had planned a deathbed scenario – I surmised – in which he would call for his Bible and reveal the hidden will, to the shame of his younger son, Marshall, and the joy of the rest of the family.) But the old man had died suddenly when he had a bad fall, and his first will, of course, was put into effect.[13]

5:13. Ibid. pp. 517-518.

5:14. The family had been treated unfairly; but this was put right when their case was finally taken to court, in December 1925:

> A jury was sworn ... and the court then adjourned for lunch. When the hearing was continued one of the lawyers announced that during the interval an amicable adjustment of the issues had been arrived at, and that the new will would be admitted to probate without opposition.[14]

Now the young James Chaffin ends his account with the following statement:

> 5:15. During the month of December, 1925, my father again appeared to me, ... [though many] of my friends do not believe it is possible for the living to hold communication with the dead. But I am convinced that my father actually appeared to me on these several occasions and I shall believe it to the day of my death.[15]

Young James would clearly have welcomed the understanding and support of Emanuel Swedenborg – who was the remarkable Swedish scientist and mystic in the 17th and 18th centuries, who wrote:

> 5:16. I am well aware of the fact that many people will say that nobody can possibly speak with spirits or angels as long as he is living in the body, and that many will call it delusion. ... But none of this deters me; for I have seen, I have heard, I have felt.[16]

5:17. His biographer, Cyriel Sigstedt, describes Swedenborg as being an extraordinary but very able man. His fame was spreading, and the former Prime Minister of Sweden, Carl Gustaf Tessin, was very keen to meet him. This was somewhat surprising, as Tessin had made some unfavourable comments in a scribbled note in his journal when he first

---

5:14. Ibid. p. 521.
5:15. Ibid. p. 520.
5:16. Swedenborg, Emanuel: *Arcana Caelestia*: Vol. 1. para. 68.
[Swedish scientist/mystic; 17/18th C.] Source J-a.

heard of Swedenborg, saying: "Councillor Swedenborg is a living instance among us of the height to which vapors may rise in a man's head and imagination. He ... believes that he sees and can speak with all the dead, both known and unknown."

Despite this belittling judgement, Tessin did call on Swedenborg and was obviously impressed by him:

> "Merely out of curiosity, to make the acquaintance of a singular man I went to see Assessor Swedenborg on the afternoon of March 5, 1760. He ... was cheerful, friendly, and talkative. It seemed that I was welcome. ... I never concern myself with other people's affairs, ... but I nevertheless intend to do everything I can to become informed of Assessor Swedenborg's life and mode of living, in order that our biographies may contain everything relating to a man who will come to occupy the foremost place among visionaries."[17]

5:18. Tessin was clearly fascinated, as were others – particularly in Stockholm, where the news of Swedenborg's visionary powers spread quickly amongst the elite. These powers, for example, were demonstrated after the death of the Dutch Ambassador, when his widow – Madame de Marteville – received a bill for an expensive set of silver that he had given to her before he died. Madame was very distressed when she saw the price on the invoice, but knowing that her husband had always paid punctually, she searched and searched for the receipt. She could not find it, and discussed the problem with her closest friends, and one of them said that she should ask Swedenborg to help her. Madame liked the idea, and invited these friends to join her in visiting the 'strange and wonderful man'. He greeted them kindly, and listened to Mme de Marteville as she explained her problem, and then said that he would help her. So she 'made her request':

> If, as people said, Swedenborg possessed the extraordinary gift of conversing with the souls of the departed, would he have the kindness to ask her husband about the matter of the silver service?

5:17. Sigstedt, Cyriel Odhner. *The Swedenborg Epic*. pp. 272-274.
[Describing Emanuel Swedenborg; 17/18th C.] Source J-a.

> Swedenborg had no objection to complying with her request, ... [and] he promised her that if he should meet de Marteville he would mention the matter to him. This he did when, a few days later, he encountered the ambassador in the spirit world. M. de Marteville assured Swedenborg that he would "go home that same evening and look after it." "But I did not receive any other answer for his widow," Swedenborg added.
>
> According to Mme de Marteville, eight days after her visit to Swedenborg her late husband appeared to her in a dream and pointed out the place where the receipt lay. ... "My child, you are worried about the receipt. Just pull out the drawer of my desk all the way. In pulling it out, the receipt was probably pushed back and is lying behind it."

When Madame de Marteville awoke she followed his advice, and was delighted to find the receipt in the little space that was behind the drawer; so she went back to bed and slept late. And Swedenborg's biographer continues:

> About eleven o'clock Swedenborg came and begged to be announced. Before he had heard a word from Mme de Marteville, he told her that, during the night, he had seen various spirits, among them Monsieur de Marteville. Swedenborg had desired to converse with the ambassador but he refused because, as he said, he had to go to his wife and tell her something of importance.[18]

"I guess de Marteville forgot the first message, till he was reminded by seeing Swedenborg," I said to myself, thinking that Monsieur was still 'very human' despite the fact that he was a spirit. And this train of thought made me realise that I was becoming less sceptical: "That's just as well. It'll make it easier for me to read through this stuff about spirits." I had opened a heavy tome that was written by the French medium, Allan Kardec, and seen that his prose was ponderous. But it soon proved to be fascinating:

5:18. Ibid. pp. 277-278.

> 5:19. The faculty of perceiving the presence of spirits is developed by habit, and may become so subtle as to enable one who is endowed with it to recognise, by impression, not only the good or evil nature of the spirit at his side, but even his individuality; just as a blind man, by an undefinable faculty of perception, recognises the approach of such and such a person, so a medium ... recognises the presence of certain spirits. A good spirit always produces an agreeable impression; an evil spirit, on the contrary, produces an impression that is painful and disagreeable and causes a feeling of anxiety; it seems to bring with it, so to say, an odour of impurity.[19]

"So evil spirits might really be real!" I said to myself, recalling those 'disagreeable' sensations of ghostly presence that had been described by Van der Post and William James.

But Allan Kardec continues, saying:

> 5:20. To suppose that all spirits have the same mental outlook is to suppose them all to be on the same level of advancement; to attribute to all of them the same clear vision of the truth of things, is to assume that all of them have already attained to perfection; but, spirits being nothing more than human beings stripped of their fleshly envelope, this is not, and cannot be, the case ...[20]
>
> 5:21. And here let us remark that inspiration comes to us all, from spirits who influence us, for good or for evil, in every circumstance of our lives, and in every resolution we make, and it may therefore be truly said that ... there is no one who has not about him his familiar spirits, who do their utmost to suggest salutary or pernicious counsels to those with whom they are connected.[21]

5:19. Kardec, Allan: *Experimental Spiritism: The Mediums' Book.* p. 178. [French Spiritist medium; 19th C.] Source J-b.

5:20. Ibid. p. 374.

5:21. Ibid. p. 192.

Kardec's views are a little unsettling when they suggest that we live with these 'familiar spirits' around us! So I turned again to William James' book, *The Varieties of Religious Experience*, which he wrote when he was a Harvard professor. I felt that I would be on safe ground if a man of his calibre was interested in this subject, and was reassured to find that he had published an extraordinary account - from a reformed alcoholic – which described the opposing pull of 'salutary and pernicious counsels':

> 5:22. I had not eaten for days, and for four nights preceding I had suffered with delirium tremens, or the horrors, from midnight till morning. I had often said, "I will never be a tramp. I will never be cornered, for when that time comes ... I will find a home in the bottom of the river." But the Lord so ordered it that when that time did come I was not able to walk one quarter of the way to the river. As I sat there thinking, I seemed to feel some great and mighty presence. I did not know then what it was, ... [but, strengthened by this presence], I said I would never take another drink, if I died on the street, and I really felt as though that would happen before morning. Something said, "If you want to keep this promise, go and have yourself locked up." I went to the nearest station-house and had myself locked up.
>
> I was placed in a narrow cell, and it seemed as though all the demons that could find room came in that place with me. This was not all the company I had, either. No, praise the Lord; that dear Spirit that came to me in the saloon was present, and said, "Pray." I did pray, and though I did not feel any great help, I kept on praying ...
>
> I was finally released, and found my way to my brother's house, where every care was given me. While lying in bed the admonishing Spirit never left me, and when I arose the following Sabbath morning I felt that day would decide my fate, and toward evening it came into my head to go to Jerry M'Auley's Mission. I went [there], ... and I found myself saying, "I wonder if God can save *me*?" I listened to the testimony of twenty-five or thirty persons, every one of

> whom had been saved from rum, and I made up my mind that I would be saved or die right there. When the invitation [to dedicate myself] was given, I knelt down with a crowd of drunkards. ... Then Mrs M'Auley prayed fervently for us. Oh, what a conflict was going on for my poor soul! A blessed whisper said, "Come"; the devil said, "Be careful!" ... [So] I promised God that night that if he would take away the appetite for strong drink, I would work for him all my life. He has done his part, and I have been trying to do mine.[22]

Now Swedenborg discusses these good and bad influences in a way that helped me understand that they might operate in karmic ways:

> 5:23. With every individual there are good spirits and evil spirits. Through the good spirits, man has conjunction with heaven, and through the evil spirits with hell. ... The reason that spirits who communicate with hell are adjoined to man is that man is born into evils *["if his karma from an earlier life makes this necessary for his development," I thought.]* ... He is therefore held in his own life by means of evil spirits and withheld from it by means of good spirits, and by the two kept in equilibrium. Being in equilibrium, he is in his freedom, and can be drawn away from evils and turned towards good ...
>
> Again, it has been shown that so far as a man's life is from what he inherits, and thus from self *["which is certainly karma"]* ... he cannot be forced to good, and what is forced does not abide; further that the good that man receives in freedom is implanted in his will and becomes, as it were, his own. These are the reasons that man has communication with hell and communication with heaven.[23]

5:22. In James, Prof William: *The Varieties of Religious Experience.* pp. 201-203. [Testimony from a friend; 19/20th C.]

5:23. Swedenborg, Emanuel: *Heaven and Hell.* paras. 292-293. [Swedish scientist/mystic; 17/18th C.] Source J-a.

> 5:24. The spirits adjoined to man are such as he himself is, in respect to affection or love, but ... are changed in accordance with the changes of his affections. ... [When men] are lovers of self or lovers of gain, or lovers of revenge, or lovers of adultery, similar spirits are present, and dwell, as it were, in their evil affections, and man is incited by these, except so far as he can be kept from evil by good spirits.[24]

These ideas seemed to be more and more plausible, and they are taken even further by the medium, W. T. Stead, in his study of spirit communications:

> 5:25. We have all our [spirit] guides. These angels, unknown and unseen by us, prompt us to all good actions and dissuade us from evil. They are with us in thought, and we often receive their warnings as if they were the promptings of our own spirit ...
>
> This is perhaps a little difficult to understand, but it is true. There are, as well as good, evil angels, who are with us not less constantly, ... [and we] are always swaying hither and thither towards our good and evil guides. We call them ... impulses, wayward longings, aspirations, coming we know not where or whence. ... [For the] soul in the body hears but dimly, and sees not at all the innumerable influences with which it is surrounded. The first and most startling thing we have to learn is that our senses, material senses, are not so much to help us to see and hear as to bar us off from seeing and hearing. We are on earth, as it were, with blinkers on. We must not see or hear or know much that surrounds us. The physical consciousness which is part of us, needs for its development the temporary seclusion of life from the realities of the world of spirit into which it is ushered at death. ... We then can see what were the sources of these vague impressions, intuitions, and aspirations. [25]

5:24. Ibid. para. 295.

5:25. Stead, W. T: *Letters from Julia.* pp. 45-47.
[Stead's analysis of Julia's spirit communications; 19th C.]

5:26. These 'vague impressions, intuitions, and aspirations' affect us all; but inspiration is much more dramatic – and Dr Rosamond Harding has done some careful research on this subject, saying that inspiration is best explained by those who are truly inspired:

> The letters of Tchaikovsky are particularly suitable for this purpose. ... Tchaikovsky writes: "generally speaking, the germ of a future composition comes suddenly and unexpectedly." Now the suddeness with which an idea of value makes its appearance is a characteristic not only of musical thought but also of every type of creative mind. For example, ... George Eliot, in a letter ... of February 1861, says: "I am writing a story which came across my other plans by a sudden inspiration."[26]

The same theme is taken up by Kardec, who says:

> 5:27. From the foregoing consideration it is evident that [some people], ... without any modification of their normal state, have flashes of intellectual lucidity which give them, for the moment, an unusual facility of conception and of expression. ... In what are rightly spoken of as 'moments of inspiration,' the flow of ideas is abundant and continuous, our thoughts succeeding one another in an orderly enchaining, through the action of an involuntary, spontaneous, and almost feverish impulsion; it appears to us, at such times, as though some superior intelligence has come to our aid.[27]

And Dr Harding now continues:

> 5:28. Blake, referring to his poem *Milton*, ... says, "I have written this poem from immediate dictation, twelve or sometimes twenty or thirty lines at a time, without

---

5:26. Harding, Dr Rosamond E. M: *An Anatomy of Inspiration*. p. 7.
[British researcher; 20th C.]

5:27. Kardec, Allan: *Experimental Spiritism: The Mediums' Book*. pp. 192-193.
[French Spiritist medium; 19th C.] Source J-b.

> premeditation, and even against my will." Goethe looked upon his genius as a mysterious power; his poems came to him of themselves and at times even against his will. "The songs made me," he said, "not I them; the songs had me in their power." The description of Apollo in the third book of Hyperion seemed to Keats to have come "by chance or magic – to be as it were something given to him." He said also that he had often "not been aware of the beauty of some thought or expression until after he had composed and written it down. It has struck him with astonishment and seemed rather the production of another person than his own." ... George Eliot told [a friend] ... "that, in all that she considered her best writing, there was a 'not herself' which took possession of her, and that she felt her own personality to be merely the instrument through which this spirit, as it were, was acting."

Harding gives more examples of this, saying, –

> Dickens declared that when he sat down to his book "some beneficent power" showed it all to him. Thackeray says in *The Round-about Papers* "I have been surprised at the observations made by some of my characters. It seems as if an occult Power was moving the pen." ... Tchaikovsky tells us how he sketched the whole of the *Tempest* overture as if he were possessed by some supernatural force. Parry refers to "exaltation so great that the vitality becomes almost supernatural." Elgar looked upon himself as the "all but unconscious medium – by which his works had come into being." ... Alfred Russel Wallace [who, with Darwin, described the theory of evolution], was led to say "I have long since come to see that no one deserves either praise or blame for the *ideas* that come to him, but only for the actions resulting therefrom. Ideas and beliefs are certainly not voluntary acts. They come to us – we hardly know *how* or *whence* ..."[28]

5:28. Harding, Dr Rosamond E. M: *An Anatomy of Inspiration*. pp. 14-15. [British researcher; 20th C.]

5:29. Jung, too, was aware of the fact that ideas just came to him. They simply appeared and followed their own course within his mind. Jung suspected that a particular 'force' or personality, whom he called Philemon, was responsible for these thoughts. He would often converse with Philemon, who replied with his own views, revealing his considerable intellect. Jung was a little mystified, but also quite intrigued:

> At times he seemed to me quite real, as if he were a living personality. I went walking up and down the garden with him, and to me he was what the Indians call a guru ...
>
> More than fifteen years later a highly cultivated elderly Indian visited me, a friend of Ghandi's, and we talked about ... the relationship between guru and chela. I hesitantly asked him whether he could tell me anything about the person and character of his own guru, whereupon he replied in a matter-of-fact tone, "Oh, yes, he was Shankaracharya."
>
> "You dont mean the commentator on the Vedas who died centuries ago?" I asked.
>
> "Yes, I mean him," he said to my amazement.
>
> "Then you are referring to a spirit?" I asked.
>
> "Of course it was his spirit," he agreed.
>
> At that moment I thought of Philemon.
>
> "There are ghostly gurus too," he added. "Most people have living gurus. But there are always some who have a spirit for teacher."
>
> This information was both illuminating and reassuring to me. Evidently, then, I had not plummeted right out of the human world, but had only experienced the sort of thing that could happen to others who made similar efforts.[29]

5:30. Shirley Maclaine was also intrigued when she learned – like Jung – that she had received spirit guidance. She had asked a friend if he thought that people could have spirit guides. "Why sure," he replied, and explained that there are souls in the afterlife who help those of us

---

5:29. Jung, Dr Carl G: *Memories, Dreams, Reflections*. pp. 176-177.
[German-Swiss psychiatrist; 19/20th C.]

who are on the earth. He also suggested that Shirley should look back over her life to see if she had felt some kind of 'force' guiding her from time to time. Shirley tried doing this, and realised that there had been occasions when this might have been happening, although she had assumed it was just 'intuition'. She had, for example, been prompted to visit a group of lamas who were practising some strange meditations, and this had encouraged her to study meditation, and to pursue her deepening interest in spiritual matters.[30]

And at another level, Kardec had known that we all have spirit guides – as he explained in his 19th century style, saying –

> 5:31. ... all have a spirit-guide who, if they listen to him, directs them in the right way. ... Call it as you will – your familiar spirit, inspiration, reason, intelligence – it is always a voice that answers the inner voice of your soul, and addresses to you wise counsel, though you do not always profit thereby. All men are not yet able to follow the suggestions of reason ... which raises a man above himself. ... [It is] the sacred flame which inspires the artist and the poet, the divine thought which elevates the mind of the philosopher, the vital impulsion which carries forward not only individuals but peoples, the reason ... which lifts man ever nearer and nearer to God, the reason which leads him on from the known to the unknown, and enables him to achieve the sublimest results. Listen to the monitions which come to you incessantly, and your perceptions will gradually be opened to the voice of your guardian-angel, who holds out to you a helping hand from the celestial heights. The inner voice which speaks to the heart of every man is the voice of the good spirits around him ...[31]

So we should listen to our spirit guides, though it is difficult to do so in this age of hectic rush and mental stimulation. But certain people

---

5:30. Maclaine, Shirley: *Out on a Limb*. p. 184.
[American filmstar/writer; 20th C.]

5:31. Kardec, Allan: *Experimental Spiritism: The Mediums' Book*. pp. 423-424.
[Spirit quidance through medium, Allan Kardec; 19th C.] Source J-b.

can help us – and they are the mediums who are naturally psychic, and have developed their gifts as sensitive channels.

5:32. A few of these mediums work at the College of Psychic Studies in London – where Paul Beard was the president for a number of years. He feels that the people who consult mediums have often left their 'readings' with the false impression that they have a spirit guide who is constantly with them. Many Spiritualists believe this too; but Beard suggests that the special link between a guide and person is, in fact, some form of 'contact of a telepathic kind'. And he continues now, explaining:

> The pupil, consciously or unconsciously, can perhaps call for help from the guide; the guide may have means of discovering when his help is needed, ... [but he] can only be expected to be concerned with the moments of Spiritual significance.[32]
>
> 5:33. Whether or not a guide is a being of wisdom, what is certain is that his knowledge of his pupil is not at all like the facts in a Scotland Yard dossier. It almost seems as if he sees him, not as we see our friends, from without to within, but from within to without. ... When the sitter – [the pupil] – attempts to put a gloss upon his own character and actions, it produces an uneasy feeling that he is certainly not deceiving the guide but only himself. The sitter soon realises, if he has any powers of self-criticism, that he is quite unable to project his own image of himself upon the guide. He has to take or leave himself as the guide sees him...
>
> The sitter in turn gradually gains a view of the guide's own character. ... He is likely to find him even-tempered, wise, benevolent, far-sighted, tolerant, humorous, patient, and probably extremely subtle. A strong sense of dignity may convey itself, and ... an impression of great humanity combined with an apparent freedom from the smaller human failings ...

5:32. Beard, Paul: *Survival of Death*. p. 115.
[British, President of the College of Psychic Studies; 20th C.] Source K-b.

> Unlike some who are regarded on earth – or regard themselves – as paragons of virtue, guides are altogether delightful companions. Their company is not spoiled but enhanced by the knowledge they show of the sitter's deeper character, and the marked ability they demonstrate to read his unspoken thoughts. ... An outstanding characteristic of any responsible guide is his scrupulous respect for the free-will of his listener; in particular he never tries to impose beliefs upon him, still less to make him dependent upon him. On the contrary, the guide's teaching is frequently directed towards enabling his charge to work without the intervention of a medium, not by developing mediumistic gifts of his own, but by what can better be described as the reaching of an interior awareness of how to deal correctly with his own problems. The guide cannot do the pupil's work; the pupil can only do it for himself.[33]

This description of a guide and his 'pupil' woke something within me, and I found myself yearning for my guide. I longed for his reassurance that I was working well as I tried to unravel these concepts of life, and I needed his encouragement as I struggled to explain them. And I felt so alone.

Then my daughter phoned me, unexpectedly, to say that she had seen a remarkable medium and felt that I would like to see him too. To my surprise, I felt dubious about her suggestion; but she was very persuasive – saying that she wanted to give me the 'reading' as a present, and would arrange a 'sitting' for me in the following week. She then put down the phone.

"But if I go to see him, will he really get it right?" I asked myself with some concern. "I mean, can this medium act as a true channel for me – and *really* get me something from my guide? I need some real, *real* guidance about my work now. But I'm not sure that it can come this way." And through that long week of waiting I begged my guide to help me – till the day came at last.

5.33: Ibid. pp. 118-119.

The medium greeted me, and checked I was 'Jenny', and I sat and waited hopefully to hear from my guide. But the medium just studied me for a while, and then gave me a 'reading' of my inner, spiritual self – explaining its development, its strengths and weaknesses, and its areas of influence. He could 'read' me better than I had thought was possible, and he explained me to myself in an extraordinary and enlightening way. It all rang true, and was very sensitive and helpful – but he had failed to make the contact that I longed for from my guide. My disappointment grew when I thought he had finished. But then he said slowly – so very, very slowly – "that's all – I think – that I should say. – No – Wait. – "

And then he just sat quietly – and I could see him change – and I realised that he was going into some sort of trance. And when at last he spoke again, his voice had changed – his style had changed – and he spoke in a way that I somehow recognised – yes – in the way that I recognised as that of my seemingly unknown and yet familiar guide:

> 5:34. "... what you are working on must come through, and can come through, into society – into the ideas and knowledge of your people around you.
>
> "You are working to assimilate these ideas, these philosophies, these concepts, and to put them together in a very practical way, in a way that can tie in to the understanding of those others about you in the world as they are coming to these ideas. You are working in an intellectual, rational way to spread the philosophy in a form which can attract the more rational, the scientific and mathematical minds. ... Science is reaching the stage at which people are nearly ready to accept and support these philosophical ideas. The two are being brought together – the scientific and mathematical outlooks – and philosophy is the connection.
>
> "In spiritual and cosmic terms, your work is to cut across the barriers of cultures, beliefs and time. It's your ability to understand that is needed here, and ... your understanding is real, valid and has force.
>
> "You will not always find people around you prepared to understand your work, but you must not allow yourself to

be emotionally upset by this. You will leave your work in a visible form, and the energy will bring it all through so that people will come to witness the philosophy in your creation.

"Don't be emotional over opposition. It will eventually all come through to the understanding of those who are becoming prepared to receive it. But don't be too hasty with what you are creating. This is important. Understand that although you had no knowledge of what you are now creating, you do understand it – so you can be level and open about it. It will become conscious knowledge."[34]

5.34. Through a medium at the College of Psychic Studies.
[My guide's message; 20th C.] Source K-d.

6

Mediums and their Messages

My visit to the medium had astounded me. The fact that he had been able to read and interpret the spiritual side of my character was extraordinary enough; but I had been changing secretly within myself, through all my reading and thinking, and unbelievably the medium could see this too. He had understood my spiritual development in a way that no one else could. But the most crucial and awe-inspiring moment of the whole reading was when I recognised my guiding spirit as he spoke to me through the medium. This recognition of my guide caught alight inside me, and I knew that the marvellous message came straight from him to me. My guide had clearly heard my silent calls for help because he spoke to me with such strengthening and yet such gentle words, and although I did not understand how mediums worked at this stage of my development, I knew now that their gift was true.

Through our centuries of time, people – and even nations – have listened to their mediums. And Allan Kardec says that the –

> 6:1. ... prophets were mediums; the mysteries of Eleusis were founded on medianimity; the Chaldeans, Assyrians, Egyptians, and all the people of antiquity, had their mediums.[1]

His rolling phrases sent me in search of the most ancient book on my bookshelf, the Holy Bible, and there I found descriptions of mediums – as in the book of Samuel:

6:1. Kardec, Allan: *Experimental Spiritism: The Mediums' Book.* p. 424.
[French Spiritist medium; 19th C.] Source J-b.

6:2. And it came to pass in those days, that the Philistines gathered their armies together for warfare, to fight with Israel ...

And when Saul saw the host of the Philistines, he was afraid, and his heart greatly trembled.

And when Saul inquired of the Lord, the Lord answered him not, neither by dreams, nor by ... prophets.

Then said Saul unto his servants, "Seek me a woman - [a medium] - that hath a familiar spirit, that I may go to her, and inquire of her." And his servants said to him, "Behold, there is a woman that hath a familiar spirit at Endor."

And Saul disguised himself, ... and they came to the woman by night: and he said, "I pray thee, divine unto me by the familiar spirit, and bring me him up, whom I shall name unto thee." ...

Then said the woman, "Whom shall I bring up unto thee?" And he said, "Bring me up Samuel" [who had recently died].

And when the woman saw Samuel ... she said, "An old man cometh up; and he is covered with a mantle." And Saul perceived that it was Samuel, and he stooped with his face to the ground, and bowed himself.

And Samuel said to Saul, "Why hast thou disquieted me, to bring me up?" And Saul answered, "I am sore distressed; for the Philistines make war against me, and God is departed from me, and answereth me no more, neither by prophets, nor by dreams: therefore I have called thee, that thou mayest make known unto me what I shall do."

Then said Samuel, "Wherefore then dost thou ask of me, seeing the Lord is departed from thee, and is become thine enemy? ... For the Lord hath rent the kingdom out of thine hand ...

"Moreover the Lord will also deliver Israel with thee into the hand of the Philistines: and tomorrow shalt thou and thy sons be with me: the Lord also shall deliver the host of Israel into the hand of the Philistines."

> Then Saul fell straightway all along on the earth, and was sore afraid, because of the words of Samuel.[2]
>
> 6:3. Now the Philistines fought against Israel: and the men of Israel fled from before the Philistines, and fell down slain in Mount Gilboa.
>
> And the Philistines followed hard upon Saul and upon his sons; and the Philistines slew ... Saul's sons.
>
> And the battle went sore against Saul, and the archers hit him; and he was sore wounded of the archers.
>
> Then said Saul unto his armour-bearer, "Draw thy sword, and thrust me through therewith: lest these uncircumcised come and thrust me through, and abuse me." But his armour-bearer would not; for he was sore afraid. Therefore Saul took a sword, and fell upon it.
>
> And when his armour-bearer saw that Saul was dead, he fell likewise upon his sword, and died with him
>
> So Saul died, and his three sons, and his armour-bearer, and all his men, that same day together.
>
> And when the men of Israel ... [saw] that Saul and his sons were dead, they forsook the cities, and fled; and the Philistines came and dwelt in them.[3]

6:4. So the skills of mediumship are old; but they are also modern, and used all around the world. John Blofeld, for example, was travelling in the East in the 20th century when he had an encounter with a huge Mongol lama, who proved to be an interesting fellow. They struck up a conversation, which moved through a series of subjects until – Blofeld says – he finally "reached the subject of what is in the West generally referred to as Shamanism, which I take to mean divination by means of a spirit deliberately invited by a medium to take possession of his body."

The Mongol then announced that he was, in fact, a 'shaman' – and said that he would be happy to demonstrate his skills at the temple, if Blofeld would call on him there. Blofeld was naturally curious; so he

---

6:2. *Holy Bible.* 1 Samuel. Ch. 28. vs. 1; 5-8; 11-12; 14-17; 19-20.
[1 Samuel: Ancient Judaic scripture in the Holy Bible.] Source D-a.
6:3. Ibid. Ch. 31. vs. 1-7.

took a rickshaw to the temple the next day, and was led down to the lama's cell. It was a little dark at first – despite the dancing flames of the butter-lamps – but Blofeld could see that the Mongol was sitting, Buddha-like, by a low lacquered table. An old man and a small boy were present, and soon set up a rhythmic beat on drum and cymbals:

> The Mongol had closed his eyes and begun to gabble mystic formulas in a deep bass voice. ... After five or ten minutes, the gabbling ceased and the Mongol's lips were still, but the music of drum and cymbals seemed to be working up to a crescendo. By the time they reached the tremendous crash which ushered in dead silence, the Mongol had fallen into a deep trance. ... The altar lamps were quite bright, but as they were behind him his face was entirely in shadow; so it may have been only my imagination which made me feel he had undergone a remarkable facial change ... to create the impression that a younger, stronger and more vigorous, *leaner* man had taken his place. ...
>
> Suddenly the whole body trembled with horrid violence and the face tightened into an angry grimace. ... A great voice filled the room, barking out a terse sentence ...
>
> "*Yau wen shenmo?*" (What will you ask?)

Blofeld was quite dumbfounded. The dreadful voice from the entranced Mongol made him realise that this was clearly no trick; but he also realised that the Mongol expected him to enquire about his future and his health problems – as others would have done when the spirit had been invited to possess the medium. But Blofeld had come to the Mongol's cell intending to observe and not to participate; so he waited silently, embarrassed by his foolishness and remarkably afraid. At last, after a long and ghastly delay, the drummer –

> ... picked up his drumstick and began to rub the instrument with it softly. Almost at once, the Mongol stirred. ... He swayed gently backwards and forwards from the waist up and then, with a gasp, slid back against some cushions, ... and lay back on them with his feet still crossed. At that moment fear vanished from the room ...

> "Well?" said the Mongol at last. "Did you learn anything of interest to you, Mr P'u?"

Blofeld felt he could say no more than confess his own stupidity. The Mongol seemed very dissatisfied, but he hid his annoyance and called for some tea. After a cup or two, Blofeld ventured:

> "The spirit which possessed you just now, was it a particular spirit, well-known to you and summoned specially by name?" ...
>
> "Most certainly I specially summoned that spirit. To lay myself open to possession by any wandering ghost might have awful consequences for myself and the others present. I should never dare to do such a thing."
>
> "And this spirit?" I urged.
>
> "It was the spirit I always summon when I wish to help people discover what is hidden in the future or hidden from them during the present. We know that this spirit was once incarnated as an important Lama. ... [He] has spoken through my lips a hundred times, but I know nothing of him except what others have told me; for, during possession, I am either unconscious or dreaming dreams having nothing to do with the spirit or the words he utters. ... His answers, they say, are never wrong. Only there are times when he so frightens those who have asked me to invoke him that they scream or run away in terror."[4]

This was an extraordinary encounter! But it seemed wise to balance it with some accounts from the West, so I looked along the library shelves and found a 19th century tome on the history of Spiritualism in the USA.

6:5. The author, Emma Hardinge, had apparently travelled a great deal in pursuit of her research, and on one occasion she stayed near a community of Shakers as she was interested in their way of life and in their beliefs. The Shakers told her that they had always trained themselves to be aware of any 'spiritual presence' that was near to them,

---

6:4. Blofeld, John: *The Wheel of Life.* pp. 97-102.
[British Buddhist; 20th C.] Source B-d.

and as a result they had often heard and seen spirits, even in the earliest days of their movement. But they wanted to tell her, in particular, about a 'multitude of spiritual beings' who had visited them in 1830. These 'spiritual beings' had told the Shakers that certain manifestations would be heard and seen by others in the future – to enable them to understand that spirits are real beings – and that these manifestations would begin in 1848 with the 'Rochester knockings', which would be heard in a particular house in Rochester that 'peculiarly suited their purpose', as did the Fox family who would be living there at the time.[5]

6:6. Hardinge described the Fox parents as being 'exemplary members' of their local Methodist church, and they were also well known for their 'unimpeachable truth and veracity'. She had found them to be pleasant and straightforward when she went to Rochester to investigate the 'knockings' and other events that did, indeed, take place there – as had been predicted by the 'spiritual beings' – and she wrote the following account of the whole strange saga:

> From the family themselves the author learns that they heard knocking very frequently. ... The family had moved into the house in December 1847, and in the February of the following year noises had become so distinct and continuous that their rest was broken night after night. ...
>
> [On March 31st] the children kept exclaiming, and sitting up in bed to listen to the sounds. Mr and Mrs Fox tried the windows and doors, but all in vain; the raps were evidently answering the noise occasioned by the father's shaking the window-sashes, as if in mockery. At length the youngest child, Kate, ... snapped her fingers and called out, "Here, Mr Split-foot, do as I do!" The effect was instantaneous; the invisible rapper responded by imitating the number of her movements ...
>
> Addressing the viewless rapper, Mrs Fox then said, "Count ten." The raps obeyed. "How old is my daughter Margaret?" then "Kate?" Both answers were distinctly and correctly rapped out. ... To the next question, "Are you a

---

6:5. Hardinge, Emma: *Modern American Spiritualism*. pp. 27-29.
[American Spiritualist; 19th C.]

man that knocks?" there was no response; but "*Are you a spirit?*" elicited firm and distinct responsive knocks. To the question whether "it would knock" if she called in her neighbors, an answer was given, whereupon she sent her husband ... to summon others.[6]

6:7. Mr Fox and his neighbors, to the number of seventy or eighty persons, ... [questioned] as best they could their mysterious visitor by the knocks. Through these, obtaining affirmative answers or silence to their suggestions, they learned that the rapper purported to be the spirit of a peddler who had been ... murdered in that house between four and five years ago. On naming over the various inhabitants of the house who might have destroyed him, the knocks emphatically and repeatedly pointed to one who had lived there at the time indicated by the spirit. It was in this way ascertained ... [that] the body was dragged through the parlor, into the buttery, and thence down the cellar stairs and buried ...

On the Monday following Mr David Fox and others commenced digging in the cellar ... [and] found a plank, a vacant place or hole, ... charcoal, quicklime, some human hair, bones ... and a portion of a human skull. ... The presence of human remains in the cellar proves that *someone* was buried there, and the accompanying quicklime and charcoal testify to the fact that all traces of that mysterious inhumation were purposely destroyed.

The Fox family did not immediately quit the scene of this mysterious haunting, but remained to witness still more astonishing phenomena.[7]

6:8. The writer, Colin Wilson, was also interested in this case; and he says that part of a wall in the cellar collapsed fifty-six years after the Fox's investigation, and that renewed digging in the affected area unearthed further remains of a skeleton, and a peddler's tin box.[8]

6:6. Ibid. pp. 31-33.

6:7. Ibid. pp. 36-37

6:8. Wilson, Colin: *Afterlife*. p. 86.
[British writer; 20th C.]

Now Emma Hardinge carries on with her account, saying:

> 6:9. [The Fox family] succeeded in communicating by raps with the invisible power through the alphabet. ... In addition to communications purporting thus to explain the object and something of the *modus operandi* of the communion, numerous spirit friends of the family, and those who joined in their investigations, gladdened the hearts of their astonished relatives by direct and unlooked-for tests of their presence. They came spelling out their names, ages, and various tokens of identity correctly, and proclaiming the joyful tidings that they all 'still lived,' 'still loved.' ...
>
> The spirits recommended the assembling of the friends of the family together in harmonious meetings, which have since obtained the name of 'spirit circles'. ... But redolent of joy and consolation as is the intercourse with beloved spirit friends at this time, when orderly communion has succeeded to doubtful experiment, it must not be supposed that any such harmonious results characterized the initiatory proceedings of this spiritual movement in Rochester ...
>
> Several persons possessed of clairvoyant and clairaudient powers had been developed as mediums, ... [yet] fanatical religionists of different sects had forced themselves into the family gatherings, and the wildest scenes of rant, cant, and absurdity often ensued. Opinions of the most astounding nature were hazarded concerning the object of this movement. ... [Despite all this], several other families of wealth and influence, both in Rochester and the surrounding towns, also began to experience similar phenomena in their own households, while the news came from all quarters ... that the mysterious rappings and other phases of what is now called 'medium power' were rapidly spreading from town to town and State to State, in fulfillment of an assurance made in the very first of the communion to the Misses Fox, namely, "that these manifestations were not to be confined to them, but would go all over the world."[9]

6:9. Hardinge, Emma: *Modern American Spiritualism.* pp. 39-40.
[American Spiritualist; 19th C.]

6:10. Guy Playfair describes how the news of the Rochester knockings and subsequent spirit communications caught people's interest right across America. Many marvelled at these strange happenings, but others went to great lengths to condemn them. Some members of the US Congress became so concerned about the level of public interest in spirit 'phenomena', and the associated mediumship, that they called for 'an investigation' in 1854 – six years after the famous 'rappings'. But their suggestion was only ridiculed, and it all came to nothing.

In New York, however, a highly placed and much respected member of the establishment announced that he had become 'a firm believer in the reality of spiritual intercourse'. He was none other than Judge J.W. Edmonds, the Chief Justice of the New York Supreme Court. He had attended an extraordinary number of spiritualist sessions, which were held by various mediums, and he went on to give numerous lectures – as a convinced supporter of the Spiritualists – to fascinated audiences throughout the country. His judgement on spirits and spirit phenomena was undoubtedly logical, as was the judgement of a highly trained scientist, Professor Hare.

And Playfair continues:

> The first American scientist to tackle the psi world was Professor Robert Hare, MD, a graduate of both Harvard and Yale, and Chemistry Professor at Pennsylvania University. In 1853, he set out to bring whatever influence he possessed "to attempt to stem the tide of popular madness, ... *the gross delusion* called Spiritualism."
>
> Unlike most sceptics then or now, Hare decided to give the gross delusion a fair trial and to examine it with all the resources at his disposal. ... [And in] 1855, Hare published his findings: ... instead of debunking this 'popular madness' and 'gross delusion,' [he] warmly embraced it.[10]

6:11. The Spiritualists were considered, thereafter, to be a little more respectable as their chief proponents, Judge Edmonds and Professor

---

6:10. Playfair, Guy: *The Indefinite Boundary*. pp. 80-82.
[British writer; 20th C.]

Hare, were of the highest calibre. And other Americans – who were enthusiastic travellers – brought the news of their Spiritualist movement to Europe, and introduced the fashion of holding séances in both London and Paris.[11]

When I turned to the subject of séances, however, I realised that I had been concentrating on the human side of mediumship. "But how do the spirits see it from their own side?" I asked myself, looking through my book of spirit teaching from Silver Birch – who had spoken through the medium Barbanell for almost sixty years. My curiosity was soon satisfied, as Silver Birch explained how the spirits had the same problems as people did when they first tried to cross the communication barriers, and more importantly, how the spirits overcame these barriers:

> 6:12. When our work was started, men despised us. ... 'Table-rappers' they sneered and jeered. But it was all part of a Plan, a mighty Purpose. Slowly our influence grew and spread. We brought within the radius of our influence those who in your world commanded respect for distinguished service in their walks of life. We chose them because we knew that their testimony would be respected. ... Gradually we brought together men of science, of medicine, of philosophy, of religion - from every activity in the world of matter, so that all could pay their tribute to facts ... which pointed the way to a new and higher conception of life.[12]

Silver Birch expressed himself in such an elegant style – whereas Kardec's discussion on spirit communication was more down to earth:

> 6:13. The means of communicating with spirits are numerous. ... The first intelligent manifestations were obtained by raps and tiltings [of tables], or typtology [from the Greek word, to strike]. This primitive method, indicative of the infancy of the art of communication, was of very narrow application, and those who employed it were

---

6:11. Ibid. p. 85.

6:12. In Ortzen, Tony (Ed.): *Silver Birch Companion*. p. 57.
[Silver Birch: Spirit teacher, through medium, Barbanell; 20th C.]

> restricted, in their communications, to mono-syllabical replies, to a mere 'yes' or 'no', signified by the number of raps previously agreed upon, as the representation of those words. ... Answers were obtained in two ways: ... by the movement of a table, and by raps which seem to be produced in the substance of the wood, in the walls, or in the air.[13]

"Oh, my goodness!" I said to myself. "Raps? Are they what I've been hearing?"

I had been looking through some books on the subject of spirit communication, over the last few days, and kept hearing a sudden, loud click. At first I had wondered if it was coming from the light fitting above me. Was the metal overheating, or something like that? But the sharp, single clicks were repeated every day – even when I had not switched on the light. And now, as I re-read Kardec's words, it struck me that he had provided a possible answer. "What if the clicks are a sort of communication?" I whispered incredulously. And then – feeling very foolish and even more doubtful – I demanded, loudly: "Are you a spirit? If so, please make two clicks – TOGETHER."

Immediately two clear, sharply defined clicks snapped out. Then – total silence.

I confess that I was overcome by a severe attack of shivering! But despite this, I wanted to hear the proof again – and asked for another distinctive double click. But the lasting silence was even more meaningful: I had been given the remarkable evidence in response to my demand, and that was quite enough.

When I had recovered myself, I turned back to Kardec's work and found that he had more to say on the early development of spirit communication:

> 6:14. Typtology was speedily improved by the adoption of a more extended method of communication, ... in designating the letters of the alphabet by tilts: words, sentences, and even long communications are thus obtained ...

6: 13. Kardec, Allan: *Experimental Spiritism: The Mediums' Book.* pp. 156-157. [French Spiritist medium; 19th C.] Source J-b.

> All mediums are not equally successful in obtaining both kinds of typtology, for some can only obtain tilts, while others can only obtain raps. ... [And] the raps also can be imitated by untruthful mediums, for the best things may be counterfeited; a fact which proves nothing against their reality.[14]

Guy Playfair was also concerned about untruthful mediums, saying:

> 6:15. This seems to be the right moment to deal with the subject of fraud, which has been connected with psi phenomena throughout recorded history and remains very much so today.

The Greeks – Playfair continues – had problems with 'fake mediums'. They had many good mediums, who were frequently consulted in ancient Greece, but some became greedy and fabricated further messages 'from the dead' to get extra money from the grieving relatives. And then he adds:

> These individuals were known as necromancers, and they were strongly disapproved of by the Greeks and actively persecuted by the Romans. Plato recommended solitary confinement for life for those who "fool many of the living by pretending to raise the dead."[15]

6:16. Sir Edward Marshall Hall – who was a very senior lawyer – wrote with disapproval on the subject of fraud at the time of the 1914-18 war, saying:

> ... charlatanism and trickery are rife; unscrupulous swindlers disguised as mediums are imposing on the credulity of tens of thousands of persons who are only too willing to believe anything, and pay any price for the

---

6:14. Ibid. pp. 159-160.

6:15. Playfair, Guy: *The Indefinite Boundary*. p. 41
[British writer; 20th C.]

> information, if only it can assuage the terrible grief in which they find themselves by the loss of some loved one. ... The mischief that is wrought by persons of this class is incalculable; ... but just as there are in every profession great men and women who love their work, and are content to live for it, so are there many whose only object is to live by it, and stop at nothing in their determination to make the practice as remunerative as possible, no matter what means are employed to attain their end. Why, then, should those who really believe in communication with those who are no longer with us in the flesh be condemned as impostors and charlatans, and sometimes even be charitably described as lunatics, merely because unscrupulous adventurers have made use of the existence of such real communication to arrogate to themselves powers which they do not possess, and by this fraudulent use of trickery ... extort money from the all too credulous natures on whom they impose?
>
> Are there no dishonest lawyers, no medical quacks, no charlatan priests? And yet who would dare to deny that the professions of law, medicine and surgery, and the church have produced, and hold today, some of the finest men and women the world has ever known ...[16]

Marshall Hall's sentiments had echoed those of Allan Kardec, who wrote earlier in the 19th century, saying:

> 6:17. There are quacks who vend their worthless nostrums in the streets and squares, and even physicians who ... impose upon the confidence of their patients; but does it follow, from the fact of these abuses, that all physicians are charlatans, and that the whole medical body is unworthy of respect? Because some dealers sell dye-stuffs for wine, does it follow that all wine-merchants are adulterators, and that pure wine is not to be found? All things, even the best, are imitated, and to such a point that

---

6:16. In Wingfield, K: *Guidance from Beyond*. pp. 11-13.
[Sir Edward Marshall Hall: British King's Counsel Lawyer; 19/20th C.]

> fraud may even be said to assume in some cases the stamp of genius. But fraud has always a personal object, a material interest, of some kind or other, to compass; where nothing is to be gained, there is no temptation to deceive; *and ... the best of all guarantees of the genuineness of the phenomena is the absolute disinterestedness of the mediums through whom they occur.*[17]
>
> 6:18. What alone removes all doubt is the *expression of thought*, ... [and some spirit] communications are so far beyond the knowledge, or the intellectual grasp, of the medium that it would be impossible to attribute them to him. We admit that charlatanism is very skillful, and that it possesses a great variety of resources; but we do not admit that it can give knowledge to the ignorant, intellect to the stupid, or familiarity with names, dates, places, and circumstances unknown to the medium.[18]

So Kardec had stressed the fact that the actual content of some spirit communication was far above the level of intellect or the range of knowledge of the receiving mediums; and this was later demonstrated by F.W.H. Myers – as I will explain.

Myers was an interesting character. He was a brilliant scholar – a classicist – who gave up a promising university career in teaching so that he could concentrate his efforts on researching psychic matters. He became one of the founders of the Society for Psychical Research in London in 1882, and spent the rest of his life working for the Society; but the most surprising thing about Myers' commitment was that he carried on with his own research *in the years that followed his death.* Paul Beard was one of a number of authors who wrote about this research, and he described Myers' posthumous projects in considerable detail. Since Beard was the President of the College of Psychic Studies, I read his account with interest.

6:17. Kardec, Allan: *Experimental Spiritism: The Mediums' Book.* pp. 392-393. [French Spiritist medium; 19th C.] Source J-b.

6:18. Ibid. pp. 396-397.

6:19. Beard explained that some of Myers' psychic colleagues found that they could still make telepathic contact with him, even *after* he had died. So they decided to see if he could prove – 'through the little-educated medium, Mrs Piper' – that he could remember abstruse details from the Latin and Greek classics that he had known so well. Mrs Piper had never been taught any Latin or Greek, and she knew nothing of their ancient literature.

And Beard continues:

> Asked some simple questions about the Aeneid, Myers ... [revealed his] considerable knowledge of the book, and some familiarity with its language, and he made points, and insisted upon them, which were correct but contrary to his questioner's own memory. At another time a translation of the Invocation to Zeus was read, and the posthumous Myers recognised that it came from the Agamemnon, and eventually correctly stated it was by Aeschylus and formed part of a trilogy. Again, he was questioned about Lethe, and gave replies which showed more classical knowledge than his questioner possessed.

This remarkable evidence of Myers' knowledge satisfied his examiners. But it became apparent that the 'posthumous' Myers was determined to prove his continuing existence by setting up a more complicated project, in which certain communications – known as the 'cross-correspondences' – would be sent through a number of mediums by Myers himself. Paul Beard explains this in simple terms:

> By cross-correspondence is meant an apparent attempt to give a fragment of a message ... to one medium, another fragment of the same message through a second, and perhaps another part again through a third, of such a kind that the whole will only be fully understood when the fragments are pieced together.
>
> If one [medium] writes 'death', a second 'mors', and a third 'thanatos', it suggests that one mind is at work through all three; in a true cross-correspondence something more is produced than simple repetition of the same idea in

> different forms: the common factor which solves the puzzle is only introduced at the end, and shows the intended but hitherto unguessed connection between earlier writings ...

Some of the mediums received more than a few words from Myers:

> In one type of case, quotations from English and Classical poetry, and fragmentary references which would be understood by educated minds, appear over and over [again] in the writings of several mediums in such a way as to be clearly associated with one another. ... [They build up, as it were, a] symbolic portrait of a particular dead person, in which the name and some of the events of the life are indicated, thus pointing to a common meaning and purpose concealed from the mediums until at a late stage.

These cross-correspondences were very complex: their meaning was unintelligible to the mediums who were transcribing them, and it was difficult – but not impossible – for those who were analysing the communications to understand their final messages. Myers, however, was not satisfied that he had done enough – as Beard says that "twenty-five years after his death, Myers appears again, and this time produces, with the help of an automatic writer, Geraldine Cummins, a script giving an account of the worlds beyond death."[19]

'Automatic' writing is described in detail by the Reverend Stainton Moses, who explains that it is –

> 6:20. ... a well-known method of communication with the invisible world. ... [Some] messages began to be written through my hand just ten years since March 30, 1873. ... At first the writing was very small and irregular, and it was necessary for me to write slowly and cautiously. ... The earliest communications were ... uniform in style and in the signature, ... and there was, in short, a sustained individuality throughout his messages. He is to me an

---

6:19. Beard, Paul: *Survival of Death*. pp. 57-62.
[British, President of the College of Psychic Studies; 20th C.] Source K-b.

entity, a personality, a being with his own idiosyncrasies and characteristics, quite as clearly defined as the human beings with whom I come in contact, if, indeed, I do not do him injustice by the broad comparison.

After a time, communications came from other sources, and these were distinguished, each by its own handwriting, and by its own peculiarities of style and expression. These, once assumed, were equally invariable. I could tell at once who was writing by the mere characteristics of the calligraphy.

By degrees I found that many Spirits, who were unable to influence my hand themselves, sought the aid of a Spirit, 'Rector', who was apparently able to write more freely, and with less strain on me, – for writing by a Spirit unaccustomed to the work was often incoherent, and always resulted in a serious drain upon my vital powers. ... So it came to pass that, as a matter of ordinary course, Rector wrote: but, when a Spirit came for the first time, or when it was desired to emphasise a communication, the Spirit responsible for the message wrote for himself ...

It is an interesting subject for speculation whether my own thoughts entered into the subject-matter of the communications. I took extraordinary pains to prevent any such admixture. At first the writing was slow, and it was necessary for me to follow it with my eye; but even then the thoughts were not my thoughts. Very soon the messages assumed a character of which I had no doubt whatever that the thought was opposed to my own. But I cultivated the power of occupying my mind with other things during the time that the writing was going on, and was able to read an abstruse book, and follow out a line of close reasoning, while the message was written with unbroken regularity. Messages so written extended over many pages, and in their course there is no correction, no fault in composition, and often a sustained vigour and beauty of style. [20]

6:20. Stainton Moses, Rev William: *Spirit Teachings*. pp. 1-5.
[Founder of the London Spiritualist Alliance; 19th C.] Source J-c.

Now Sir Edward Marshall Hall – who was a King's Counsel lawyer – adds his own views on this subject:

> 6:21. My real object in writing these lines is to try to show that automatic writing, as it is called, is a real thing, and that by its means messages are conveyed through an unconscious hand from some place outside the physical world to those who are still inhabitants of it.[21]
>
> 6:22. In the hope that what I am about to write may convince others, as it did me, of the truth of this belief, I state [that] ... I first made the acquaintance of Miss K. Wingfield more than thirty years ago.

And who was Miss K. Wingfield? – Marshall Hall explains that he had called on his sister in Hampton, on a Sunday in the late 1890s, and discovered that another visitor had arrived before him. His sister introduced her guest as *the* Miss K. Wingfield – the remarkable medium who had recently demonstrated her skills as an 'automatic writer' at a big exhibition. Marshall Hall's sister then took him aside, and begged him to ask Miss Wingfield a question that would test her skills, as she was convinced that Miss Wingfield would be able to give him a satisfactory answer from the spirit world as proof of the reality of their communications. But Marshall Hall, at that time, was too sceptical about her suggestion, and refused. Then he adds:

> I shall never forget the look of pain that came over my sister's face as she replied: "What would I give to convince you." So, not believing, and yet wishing to please her, I said: "Very well, I will ask her a question."

Marshall Hall took a letter from his pocket, and folded the envelope so that neither its place of origin nor the contents could be seen, and gave it to his sister, saying, "Ask her where is the writer of the letter." They had to wait a while before Miss Wingfield wrote, "The writer of that letter is dead."

6:21. In Wingfield, K: *Guidance from Beyond*. p. 11.
[Sir Edward Marshall Hall: British King's Counsel Lawyer; 19/20th C.]

Marshall Hall was surprised by her blunt reply – but having assumed that any 'message' from Miss Wingfield would have been invented, he decided to expose the pretence by asking, "When and where did the writer die?"

"He died yesterday in South Africa."

Now Marshall Hall was really surprised. He had neither disclosed the sex of the writer nor said where the letter was from – although it was, in fact, from his brother, who had posted it three weeks earlier in South Africa. It was a rather 'unpleasant' letter, and Marshall Hall had decided to keep it from his sister. But he felt dissatisfied with Wingfield's answer.

A week later – and again in the following week – Marshall Hall heard from Archdeacon Gaul, who also lived in South Africa. He was a friend of the family, and his news about the brother was nothing out of the ordinary. But then – when the third week had passed – Marshall Hall received the sad news:

> The third succeeding Saturday I received another letter (dated the Saturday immediately preceding the Sunday on which I had asked the question at Hampton) from the Archdeacon, in which he writes: "I little thought when I wrote you last mail that I should have to tell you that your brother was found dead in his bed this morning."

And Marshall Hall adds his own conclusion:

> I need hardly say that I was staggered at the communication, and, making any and every allowance that my imagination can conceive, I came to the conclusion then, and I still believe, that the message can only have been communicated through Miss Wingfield by some agency outside this sphere.[22]

Allan Kardec, in contrast to the newly converted and enthusiastic Marshall Hall, was much more down to earth in explaining the methods of communication:

6:22. Ibid. pp. 14-18.

> 6:23. A spirit, when he wishes to communicate, makes use of the most flexible organ that he finds in the medium; from one, he borrows the hand; from another, the voice; from a third, the hearing. The speaking medium generally speaks without knowing what he says, and often gives utterance to instructions far above the reach of his own ideas, knowledge, and intelligence; ... in short, his voice is only an instrument employed by a spirit, and by means of which a third party can converse with a spirit ...[23]

And Silver Birch gives the spirit's point of view, explaining that -

> 6:24. ... mediumship is conscious co-operation between our world and yours. ... But of course [the medium's] body does not belong to us; it belongs to the tenant who inhabits it. If he cares to surrender the lease to us for a little while, that is well and good, but to rob him of his tenancy without his permission is contrary to the Law. It is a natural surrender, with a respect on both sides for the forces which will inhabit the body.[24]

This made me remember that the British Buddhist, John Blofeld, had actually seen this happening – when the Mongol lama had given him a demonstration of mediumship, terrifying Blofeld in the process. (See 6:4.) But the student healer, Allegra Taylor, was fascinated when her teacher, Rosalyn, gave the class a gentler demonstration:

> 6:25. Rosalyn said she could feel that Chi'ang, her guide, was around so she would leave and let him come in. She began to recite the Lord's Prayer, which is the method she uses to help her leave her body, and before she had finished, I witnessed an astonishing sight. Her body fleetingly took on the appearance of a person who has

---

6:23. Kardec, Allan: *Experimental Spiritism: The Medium's Book.* p. 179.
[French Spiritist medium; 19th C.] Source J-b.

6:24. In Ortzen, Tony. (ed.) *Silver Birch Companion.* p. 48.
[Silver Birch: spirit teacher, through medium, Barbanell; 20th C.]

recently died – at that moment when you just know they've gone. ... She slumped a bit and as she sat up straight again her face took on a slightly thinner, masculine, oriental appearance. Her hand gestures and body movements became more Eastern. ... Perhaps the strangest part and the most convincing was the very oriental style of the discourse, in the true tradition of sages and gurus who teach in riddles, set conundrums and leave you to figure out the meaning.

Everything she/he said was profound, mischievous, intelligent, and very different from Rosalyn's usual brash twentieth-century Californian personality. Chi'ang is rather fastidious, calm, wry and serene, although he doesn't suffer fools gladly. He admonished us for being such a humourless lot and finished his twenty-minute discourse with a few words of advice. "Laughter and joy help the masters to come in," he said. "Do not take life too seriously, rather take it sincerely." ... He left us with a Bonpo Tibetan prayer and Rosalyn opened her eyes. [25]

Now Jane Roberts explains how she became a medium, saying:

6:26. Seth, who speaks of himself as an 'energy personality essence' no longer focused in physical form ... has been speaking through me for over seven years now, in twice weekly trance sessions.

My psychic initiation really began one evening in September, 1963, however, as I sat writing poetry. Suddenly my consciousness left my body, and my mind was barraged by ideas that were astonishing and new to me at the time. On return to my body, I discovered that my hands had produced an automatic script, explaining many of the concepts that I'd been given. The notes were even titled - *The Physical Universe as Idea Construction.*

6:25. Taylor, Allegra: *I Fly Out with Bright Feathers*. pp. 154-155.
[British novice healer; 20th C.]

Jane was very surprised by this experience; but in trying to work out what had happened, she decided that she should explore some psychic activities with the help of her husband. So they started with an Ouija board – on which a pointer was supposed to move from letter to letter, spelling out messages from the spirits.

Their results were rather poor at first, but they persisted with their experiment until they began to receive messages from a personality who called himself 'Seth'. Jane suspected that the messages were coming somehow from her subconscious mind, and her suspicions increased when she realised that she knew what the next message would be *before* it was spelt out on the board; but then her sensitivity strengthened until – she says – "I felt impelled to say the words aloud, and within a month I was speaking for Seth while in trance state."

She knew, by now, that Seth's intriguing material could not have come from her own mind, and that he was the real author of *The Physical Universe as Idea Construction.* He was quite obviously an inspiring communicator, who went on to dictate several fascinating books through Jane – who adds:

> We call it the Seth Material, and it deals with such topics as the nature of physical matter, time, and reality, the god concept, probable universes ... and reincarnation. From the beginning, the obvious quality of the material intrigued us, and it was for this reason that we continued.[26]

Seth's work is certainly informative, as he explains much of what lies beyond the range of our sense perceptions and understanding. He says that he has used some of his incarnations on earth to concentrate on learning, and has, thereby, evolved as an experienced spirit teacher. His style is somehow factual, and quite startling as compared to the heavy teaching of some of the 19th and early 20th century spirits. And Kardec – as an example of the 19th century mediums – makes very heavy reading; but his definitions are precise, and the following example is apt in the context of Jane's work with Seth:

6:26. Roberts, Jane: *Seth Speaks.* pp. ix-x.
[American medium/writer; 20th C.]

6:27. Mediumship is a mission, and should always be exercised as such. Mediums are the interpreters between spirits and men.[27]

Now Silver Birch gives us his own view of his work as a spirit:

6:28. I, with others, was told that ... the world of matter required the help of beings like myself who could return, and perhaps impart some of the knowledge of spiritual laws ... so that a perplexed and weary mankind might ... find guidance and inspiration ...

We were told that power would be given to us, power to quicken men's souls. But we were also told that it would be a hard task, that we would encounter many who would not look upon our mission with favour; ... and, if I may add this, in order to accomplish it, we would have to forego all the joys, all the beauties, all that we had earned. ... Yet not one refused out of all who were approached. And so, in company with some others, I come back to your world, not to live in it, but to work within its orbit. I had to find an instrument [a medium] – always the hardest task. I had to learn your language and familiarise myself with your customs. I had to have an understanding of your civilisation.

Then I had to learn how to use this instrument [the medium] so that I could say through him those few simple truths, so simple that they would revolutionise your world if all accepted them and lived their implications. At the same time I had to learn that, whilst working close to earth, I had to maintain touch with those who sent me, so that always I could be the mouthpiece for greater wisdom, for greater knowledge, for greater learning. It was very hard at first. It is not so easy now. Gradually I was able to reach those who were amenable. Not all welcomed the news that I brought – there were many who preferred to sleep. There

6: 27. In Kardec, Allan: *Experimental Spiritism: The Mediums' Book.* p. 232. [Spirit guidance through medium, Allan Kardec; 19th C.] Source J-b.

> were others who liked their little prison that they had constructed for themselves. They were safe in their cell. They were afraid of what liberty might bring them. But here and there I made friends. I had nothing to offer them except truth, reason, common sense, simplicity and the love of a fairly old soul ...[28]

It is obvious that some spirit communications are of the highest quality; and these are a gift to us, and increase our understanding. But spirits can vary in the way that people vary, from the great and sincere intellectuals to the most foolish babblers. No one, however, would suggest that the Reverend Stainton Moses had invited babblers to add to his work – despite the fact that the quality of communications varied considerably from spirit to spirit. But one of these communicators was especially wise – as described by Stainton Moses:

> 6:29. The particular communications which I received from the Spirit known to me as Imperator, mark a distinct epoch in my life. ... It was a period of education in which I underwent a spiritual development that was, in its outcome, a very regeneration. I cannot hope, I do not try to convey to others what I then experienced. But it may possibly be borne in upon the minds of some, who are not ignorant of the dispensation of the Spirit in their own inner selves, that for me the question of the beneficent action of external Spirit on my own self was then finally settled. I have never since, even in the vagaries of an extremely sceptical mind, and amid much cause for questioning, ever seriously entertained a doubt.[29]

The lawyer, Sir Edward Marshall Hall, now adds his own conclusion:

6:28. In Ortzen, Tony (ed.): *Silver Birch Companion*. pp. 118-119.
[Silver Birch: Spirit teacher, through medium, Barbanell; 20th C.]

6:29. Stainton, Moses, Rev. William: *Spirit Teachings*. p. 7.
[Founder of the London Spiritualist Alliance; 19th C.] Source J-c.

6:30. I maintain that, so far from the real belief in these communications having a degrading or anti-religious effect, the teachings that come down to us through these means are in accord with the finest doctrines and principles of true religion. I am not referring to any particular sect or form of belief, but to that universal religion which is the basic strength of all creeds, and which, when stripped of the priest-created dogmas and anathemas, stands out in all its grand simplicity.[30]

6:31. Terrible wrongs have been perpetrated under the name of religion, or, rather, under the persecution of so-called creeds. ... [But if] one examines all the great creeds of civilized history the basic principles are found to be the same ...

It is these principles that, illustrated and amplified, form the foundation of the teaching which is conveyed in the true messages ... from outside this sphere.[31]

6:30. In Wingfield, K: *Guidance from Beyond*. pp. 11-12.
[Sir Edward Marshall Hall: British King's Counsel Lawyer; 19/20th C.]
6:31. Ibid. p. 14.

7

Possession: Depossession

"Well," I said to myself, "it's time to move on; though there's more good stuff that I could have used on the subject of spirits and mediums. – But, come to think of it, the stuff that I did use wasn't all 'good', was it? There were the nasty things too: – the fear of ghosts and haunted places, the bad spirits tormenting that poor old tramp with his drink problem, Swedenborg saying that there are good spirits – and evil spirits – with every individual. And Kardec said that too. –

"And there was the spirit called Julia, who came through the medium, Stead. I remember skimming through her book some time ago - looking for the good stuff - when I saw that she gave some kind of warning. Oh, I did mean to go back to it, to see what she was saying."

7:1. The small volume of *Letters from Julia* was still in the pile of books on my table – so I hunted down a particular passage in which Julia said: "I want to say one word now about the danger of the communications about which you hear so much."

"Yes, this is it," I thought, scanning her words of caution:

> I have not much to say. That there is love on this side is true. [Yet there] ... are evil ones, false ones, frivolous ones on this side, as there are on yours. ... But the whole question is one of balance. And what I want to ask is this, Do you or anyone else in your world ever cut off your communications with your children when they have gone into the larger life of a city, because they may bring you into the vortex of a city's temptations and the risk of evil and danger? You laugh

at the suggestion. Why not laugh equally when those whom you wish to contact have passed on [to this side of life], not to New York, or Chicago, or London? ...

You can, if you like, either on this side or on that, enter into companionship with the good or the bad. And I daresay that it is as true, on this side as on yours, that there is a possibility of making acquaintances who may be difficult to shake off. But so it is in London. You do not shrink from coming up to London from the country because in London there are many thousands of thieves, drunkards, swindlers, and men of evil and vicious life.

You say you come to London to do your work, and that it was therefore necessary to run the risk. Yes, and so it is necessary to run the risks of communicating with the wider field of spiritual existence. You say why? Oh my friend, why? Is it necessary to ask that question? If so, then you have never loved, or known the craving and passion to help the loved ones [who have passed on]. For these reasons it is necessary to risk the danger of evil spirits for the sake of keeping in conscious touch with loved ones ...[1]

So spirits, like people, can range in character from good to evil – as Emma Hardinge discovered when she was collecting material for her book on American Spiritualism. She explained that –

7:2. ... the spirit country is peopled from earth, and ... spirit-life commences from the point where mortal existence ends. Unconscious of this solemn truth, the early communicants with the unseen world were unprepared for the visitation of the *dark spirits* whom the sad experiences of the earth had manufactured into criminals. Unaware that life, whether here or hereafter, is *progress,* not violent and unnatural change, investigators were appalled at the representations, produced through mediums, of the same vicious tendencies in spirits which they had ... [while they

---

7:1. In Stead, W. T: *Letters from Julia.* pp. 32-34.
[Julia: afterlife communication; 19th C.]

were] inhabitants of earth; in a word, they did not realize the fact that spirits were still human, and that the soul in many respects remained unchanged by the mere act of physical dissolution.[2]

Canon Michael Perry now takes up the subject, saying –

> 7:3. ... the dead are as mixed a bunch as the living. We need, therefore, to ask *what* departed we are communicating with, and what spiritual influences they are under, and what influence they can have on us – malign or benign. As we are warned by *1 John 4: v.1*, we must 'not trust any and every spirit', but 'test the spirits, to see whether they are of God'. The communications we receive – like the people we meet on this present earth – *can* be good, holy, orthodox, helpful, god-fearing. Alternatively, they *can* be malevolent, blasphemous, sly, or intent on our destruction. They can be (and they often are!) just plain silly. Death does not transform Aunt Ada into Saint Augustine. She may be just as infuriatingly cretinous in the spirit world as she was in the flesh. In that case, her communications will be as vapid as her earthly conversation was.
>
> Test the spirits. Don't think that because they are departed spirits, they are ... necessarily demonic, necessarily heavenly, or necessarily profound.[3]

This suggestion seemed reasonable till I read more on the subject, and found that Allan Kardec and others were advising us to be very careful about communicating with spirits in a casual or random fashion. Kardec was quite happy, however, with the suggestion that people should deliberately evoke – or call – a particular spirit, or respond to a known spirit, as he says:

7:2. Hardinge, Emma: *Modern American Spiritualism.* p. 58.
[American Spiritualist; 19th C.]

7:3. Perry, Archdeacon Michael: *Psychic Studies: A Christian's View.* pp. 76-77.
[English theologian; 20th C.]

> 7:4. Spirits communicate spontaneously, or come at our call, that is to say, as a result of evocation. Some persons think that we should abstain from evoking any given spirit, and should wait for some one to present himself. ... In our opinion this view of the subject is a mistaken one; first, because there are always spirits around us, and most frequently of low degree, who ask nothing better than to communicate; and secondly, because such being the case, by abstaining from the evocation of a given spirit we open the door to any and every spirit who desires to enter.[4]
>
> 7:5. That there are some who are evil, astute, and profoundly hypocritical is an incontestable fact, and against these it is necessary to be on our guard.[5]

Paul Brunton reiterates this warning, and explains that:

> 7:6. Nature has very sensibly put a curtain between us and the afterworld and whoever meddles imprudently with it does so at his peril. That lying and malignant spirits lurk behind this curtain is a fact admitted even by spiritualists themselves. Most attempts, therefore, to look behind it are attempts to look for trouble.

Despite all this, Brunton believes that we have in fact benefited from the Spiritualists whose work has shown that we will survive death, and the messages that they have received from the dead have comforted those who still live in this world. Brunton, however, insists that we should not attempt to contact the spirits ourselves, but should leave this to the trained and experienced mediums and psychic researchers who "work competently and safely in such a deceptive and dangerous field". The Spiritualists are generally sincere and gifted workers – he adds – but "their number is swamped by the multitude who have ... ignorantly opened doors for lying spirits to come out of their lurking places".[6]

7:4. Kardec, Allan: *Experimental Spiritism: The Mediums' Book.* p. 319.
[French Spiritist medium; 19th C.] Source J-b.

7:5. Ibid. p. 43.

7:6. Brunton, Dr Paul: *The Wisdom of the Overself.* p. 137.
[British writer on ancient philosophy; 19/20th C.] Source A-d.

7:7. Now Dr Fiore warns us that "a practice that deliberately opens the door is 'sitting' in a séance" – and a séance is formed when the participants sit together in a circle and invite the spirits to join them. Some people who have tried to contact spirits in this way have had no idea of what they are really doing or what kind of spirit might respond to their call. And Fiore adds:

> I've heard of teenagers who – playing around half seriously – were terribly frightened when something did happen. Again, ... [when using] the Ouija board and automatic writing, the call goes out to spirits.[7]
>
> 7:8. ... the Ouija board has remained popular for decades. The game comprises a board printed with the alphabet, numbers, a 'yes' and a 'no'; and a planchette, a small triangular object with short legs and a pointer. Several people sit around the board, placing their fingers lightly on the planchette, posing questions for spirits to answer by *taking over* their hands. This causes the planchette to move around the board, spelling out responses. It can be interesting, exciting, fun – and devastating!
>
> Automatic writing is another way that people extend invitations to spirits to temporarily incorporate them. The usual practice is that they hold pens or pencils on paper, waiting for entities to use their arms and hands to write messages. This can be dangerous, because it may attract spirits who do not respect other people's properties – their bodies![8]

7:9. An example of this phenomenon was published by the science reporter Gordon Taylor, who said that a psychiatrist, Winifred Richmond, was working in Boston when she found that one of her patients – an English teacher called Violet – was in the habit of covering page after page with automatic writing. Now the strange thing about these scripts is that they changed quite considerably during a

---

7:7. Fiore, Dr Edith: *The Unquiet Dead.* p. 118.
[American psychologist; 20th C.] Source J-g.
7:8. Ibid. p. 116.

three-month observation period: they were written in seven 'styles and handwritings' and were interspersed with other scribblings. Each 'writer' would give its own name and 'spoke of itself in the first person, answered questions, gave advice and a clear account of itself'. Violet was fully aware of what was happening during this process, but she was never in control. – And Gordon Taylor continues:

> The first personality ... burst on the scene when Violet wrote in letters three inches high: "Hello, I am ANNIE McGINNIS." Violet's hand then proceeded to draw a portrait of a rather tough-looking girl. Annie's story, told in a series of installments, was that she had been seduced, become a prostitute and died while giving birth to a child. She hated men and wrote long diatribes against them, but also told crude jokes and engaged in blarney.

Annie McGinnis was then replaced by a shy and gentle character who said she was Mary Patterson, although she was very like Violet. Then a 'Mary Minott' usurped her place by calling her a 'puritanical pig'. Mary was rather worldly, and drew fashionable 'dresses' in 'numerous beautiful designs of great talent'. But the next personality to come through Violet was apparently that of a living person, called Alton.

"This is really peculiar," I said to myself with increasing discomfort. "But what's the special phrase I use? – 'Real intelligence is open–mindedness?' – Well? Okay." So I turned back to Gordon Taylor, and read his description of the next personality:

> Alton, a real person, appeared; in life he was a friend of Violet's fiancé and attempted to woo Violet, who repulsed him. ... There was a brief visit from Violet's father followed by 'The Spirit of War and Desolation', who urged her to give up automatic writing and become a medium; and finally 'Man', who developed a hatred of Alton and finally drove him from the scene.
>
> When Man was there, Violet felt a need to get up and dance. Man covered the paper with rhythmic lines and the injunction, "Let's dance, Violet." Finally Violet got up and began to dance, swaying more and more violently. Finally

> she cried out, her face depicting tremendous emotion, – ecstasy and terror. Laid on a couch, she remained stiff and moaning. Afterwards she explained that she felt another personality was attempting to take her over completely. "I wanted to give myself up to it and yet I didn't want it."[9]

Violet was not alone in suffering such invasions, as Fiore said that some of her patients were troubled in this way, being taken over by –

> 7:10. ... other personalities while in the hypnotic trance. I assumed these were multiple personalities and dealt with them as though they were. ... None of these patients seemed to benefit from the investigation of these 'personalities', except to feel more comfortable with the various aspects of their personalities that were, at times, making a mess of their lives. ... They came to grips a little better with some of their strange behavior. But there was very little change in that behavior!

As she mulled over the dilemma of these patients, Fiore remembered that she had been very surprised when she found that some of her hypnotised patients were able to recall subconscious memories from earlier incarnations. She had not understood this at the time, so she turned to the books about death and reincarnation, and found several writers who explained that dying is a wonderful process in which the soul leaves the material body and passes on into 'Light'. But there were other accounts, Fiore says, in which -

> ... spirits – or discarnates – stayed earthbound and often 'joined' living people who were unaware of their presence. They then continued to exist on the physical plane by living through these people – often bringing great misery and, at times, even death!
>
> As I read these cases I reflected back to my earlier work with patients who I assumed had multiple personalities,

---

7:9. Taylor, Gordon Rattray: *The Natural History of the Mind.* pp. 120-121. [British science reporter; 20th C.]

> and wondered whether I had been dealing with spirits. ... I began listening carefully when my patients described their problems and behaviors, to detect whether someone else could be causing their suffering.[10]

Having opened her mind to this possibility, Fiore found that she could understand more of her patients' problems and what might lie behind them. She describes – as an example – the case of Linda, saying:

> 7:11. This process was clearly illustrated in the regression of a young female patient, Linda, who was being treated for a depression so severe that she was imminently suicidal. During the hypnotic work she found herself as one of these 'displaced' spirits, a depressed male.

Fiore asked this spirit what had happened to him, and it turned out that he had killed himself in a state of despair and fury. He was convinced that he had made every effort to be a good husband, but his wife had taken a lover and his marriage was in ruins. He went down to the river in this wretched state and saw that there was only a winding stream on the dry bed, but he clambered up onto the rails of the bridge and flung himself down.

At first he thought he had not really killed himself. His body was sprawled on the sand, but he was still alive! He felt terrified and furious, and loathed the glaring light around him; so he fled away across the sand – away from his body and from his pain – and sought shelter and darkness in the bushes. But everything had gone wrong. He was lonely, unhappy, angry, and confused – especially when he heard some young people enjoying themselves on the sand – and he described all these feelings to Dr Fiore:

> They are on the beach, playing. I go up to them, but they ignore me. Why can't they help me? Why won't they help me? I'm so miserable and they are so happy. It makes me angry!

7:10. Fiore, Dr Edith: *The Unquiet Dead.* pp. 10-11.
[American psychologist; 20th C.] Source J-g.

> There's a beautiful young girl who is happy and lovely – but she won't even stop and look at me – she won't even notice me. ... [So] I tried to hit her; I don't understand ...
> It's like I'm with her now; I'm part of her, somehow. It's much better now. I'm much warmer now. She's very happy and I still feel very sad, but I can feel what she feels. I like it when she feels good. But she's the one having all the fun - and that makes me angry too. ... Now she dosen't have as much fun as she used to.[11]

Emanuel Swedenborg, in fact, had described the same phenomenon in the 17th or 18th century, and he gave a very clear explanation of this form of invasion:

> 7:12. When these [invading spirits] come to a man they do not conjoin themselves with his thought, as other spirits do, but enter into his body, and occupy all his senses, and speak through his mouth, and act through his members, believing at the time that all things of the man are theirs. These are the spirits who possess man.[12]

"But this is relevant to something I read in Stevenson's book," I said in some excitement as I hunted for the copy of *Twenty Cases Suggestive of Reincarnation* on my desk. Then I thumbed through its pages and found the intriguing case of Jasbir, son of Sri Girdhari Lal Jat, in India.

7:13. Jasbir was only three and a half when he succumbed to smallpox, and died in 1945. His father sat grieving for some hours beside the lifeless body – and then surprisingly it moved; but the boy recovered slowly, and it was a matter of days before he could talk at all, and not in his usual way. And then – some weeks later – the family was shocked to find that he really had changed! He insisted that he was 'the son of Shankar' and lived in the village Vehedi, and he wanted to go home. He had been riding in a cart – he explained – and had been given some special sweets that must have been 'poisoned' as they made him so dizzy

---

7:11. Ibid. pp. 27-28.

7:12. Swedenborg, Emanuel: *Heaven and Hell.* para. 257.
[Swedish scientist/mystic; 17/18th C.] Source J-a.

that he fell from the cart, hitting his head in the fall. Then he died. He said that the person who gave him the sweets had previously borrowed a sum of money from him, but he had never repaid the loan.

Jasbir's father was distressed and embarrassed by this strange account, and he tried to keep the story from his neighbours; but that had proved to be impossible as the gossip spread to a woman whose husband had originally come from Vehedi:

> She reported the incident to her husband's family and to members of the Tyagi family in Vehedi. The details of 'his' death and other items narrated by Jasbir corresponded closely with details of the life and death of a young man of twenty-two, Sobha Ram, son of Sri Shankar Lal Tyagi of Vehedi. Sobha Ram had died in May, 1954 in a chariot accident as related by Jasbir and in the manner described, although the Tyagi family knew nothing of any alleged poisoning or any debt of money owed Sobha Ram before they heard of Jasbir's statements. Afterwards they entertained suspicions of poisoning ...

Some weeks later a villager took Jasbir from his village, Rasulpur, to Sobha Ram's village, Vehedi. Jasbir was dropped off by the railway station and told to go to the Tyagi family's place. This proved to be no problem for the little boy, as he clearly knew his way through the village although he had never been there in his short life. But he stayed on in Vehedi for some time, and -

> ... demonstrated to the Tyagi family and other villagers a detailed knowledge of the Tyagi family and its affairs. He enjoyed himself greatly in Vehedi and returned to Rasulpur with great reluctance. Afterwards Jasbir continued to visit Vehedi from time to time, usually for several weeks or more in the summer. He still wanted to live in Vehedi and felt isolated and lonely in Rasulpur.[13]

7:13. Stevenson, Dr Ian: *Twenty Cases Suggestive of Reincarnation.* pp. 34-36. [Canadian Professor of Psychiatry; 20th C.]

Dr Stevenson heard of this case, and travelled out to India in 1961 to meet the families and villagers of Rasulpur and Vehedi. He was very impressed by the amount of detailed evidence in the case, and adds:

> 7:14. Readers may wish to know, as I did, what account Jasbir gave of events between the death of Sobha Ram and the revival of Jasbir with memories of Sobha Ram. To this question, Jasbir replied ... that after death he (as Sobha Ram) met a Sadhu (a holy man or saint) who advised him to 'take cover' in the body of Jasbir.[14]

This 'holy man or saint' was clearly from a category of spirits who would not 'loiter' mindlessly when they had died – as described by F.W.H. Myers in the following communication:

> 7:15. ... numbers of ignorant, trivially minded human beings loiter at the gates of death. They have no specially vicious tendencies and may be said to be individuals who are without any perception of the psychic evolutionary processes. During their lifetime they were incapable of any real spirituality and lived only in the material sense.
>
> Such travellers on the road to immortality have no conception of the continuous character of the journey in eternity. Craving only for sensual experiences, for the dense world of Matter, they ... have a certain cunning and regularise their position in the alien body which they seek to possess.[15]

Now this description is supported by a very unpleasant communication which was received by the Reverend Stainton Moses:

> 7:16. Round the gin shops of your cities ... hover the spirits who in the flesh were lovers of drunkenness and debauchery. They lived the drunkard's life in the body,

---

7:14. Ibid. p. 47.

7:15. In Cummins, Geraldine: *Beyond Human Personality*. p. 210.
[F. W. H. Myers: afterlife communication; 19/20th C.] Source J-d.

> they live it over again now. ... Could you but see how, in spots where the vicious congregate, the dark spirits throng, you would know something of the mystery of evil.[16]

These unpleasant gatherings could well be fact and not fiction!

When George Ritchie was a young man, for example, he was thought to have died of typhoid in an army hospital; but he had some strange experiences before he revived. One of these experiences took place in a crowded bar, and was quite unforgettable:

> 7:17. A crowd of people, many of them sailors, lined the bar three deep, while others jammed wooden booths along the wall. Though a few were drinking beer, most of them seemed to be belting whiskies as fast as the two perspiring bartenders could pour them. ... And it was obvious that these living people, ... the ones actually drinking, talking, jostling each other, could neither see the desperately thirsty disembodied beings among them, nor feel their frantic pushing to get at those glasses. (Though it was also clear to me, watching, that the non-solid people could both see and hear each other. Furious quarrels were constantly breaking out among them over glasses that none could actually get to his lips.)

Ritchie was shocked by the amount of drink that these men were pouring down their throats. It was far worse than at any party that he had ever attended – as he says:

> I watched one young sailor rise unsteadily from a stool, take two or three steps, and sag heavily to the floor. Two of his buddies stooped down and started dragging him away from the crush. ... Instantly, quicker than I'd ever seen anyone move, one of the insubstantial beings who had been standing near him at the bar was on top of him. He had been hovering like a thirsty shadow at the sailor's side,

---

7:16. In Stainton Moses, Rev. William: *Spirit Teachings*. p. 27.
[Spirit communication, via the Rev. Stainton Moses; 19th C.] Source J-c.

> greedily following every swallow the young man made. Now he seemed to spring at him like a beast of prey.
>
> In the next instant, to my utter mystification, the springing figure had vanished. It all happened even before the two men had dragged their unconscious load from under the feet of those at the bar. One minute I'd distinctly seen two individuals; by the time they propped the sailor against the wall, there was only one.
>
> Twice more, as I stared, stupefied, the identical scene was repeated. A man passed out ... [and] one of the non-solid people vanished as he hurled himself at [the man], ... almost as if he had scrambled inside the other man.[17]

And Fiore poses some questions on the subject of possession:

> 7:18. On the surface, it looks like we're puppets, manipulated against our wills by spirits or fate. Did we agree to have this experience when we planned our lives...?[18]
>
> 7:19. Are the two, the possessor and the possessee, invariably in a karmic relationship?[19]

And Allan Kardec gives his reply:

> 7:20. The motives of obsession [or partial possession] vary according to the character of the obsessing spirit. It is sometimes a vengeance exercised on some one by whom he may have been wronged during his last earthly life, or in some previous existence; but it is frequently prompted by the mere desire of doing harm. Some spirits, having suffered, like to make others suffer ...[20]

7:17. Ritchie, Dr George: *Return from Tomorrow*. pp. 59-61.
[An experience while clinically dead; 20th C.]

7:18. Fiore, Dr Edith: *The Unquiet Dead*. p. 160.
[American psychologist; 20th C.] Source J-g.

7:19. Ibid. p. 160.

7:20. Kardec, Allan: *Experimental Spiritism: The Mediums' Book*. p. 286.
[French Spiritist medium; 19th C.] Source J-b.

7:21. The method of combatting obsession varies according to the character it assumes. There is no real danger for any medium who is fully aware that he has to do with a deceptive spirit, as is the case in simple obsession; it is merely a very disagreeable thing for him. But it is precisely because *it is* disagreeable to him that the obsessor is obstinately bent on maintaining his hold upon him ...

It is well to suspend the exercise of mediality when we perceive that we are being acted upon by an evil or unreasonable spirit, and thus to show him that he is not to have the pleasure of absorbing our attention uselessly. The writing medium is able to break off connexion with a troublesome spirit by merely abstaining from writing; but the auditive medium is not so fortunate, for, in his case, the obsessing spirit sometimes pursues him incessantly, and even assails him with vile and disgusting utterances against which the unhappy victim of this species of obsession has no means of stopping his ears. ...

Corporeal subjugation [or full possession] often deprives its victim of the energy necessary for getting the better of his obsession; in such a case, therefore, the intervention of a third person is absolutely necessary, and may be exercised by mesmerism or by the mere force of will. When the co-operation of the person obsessed cannot be had, the magnetiser must endeavor to obtain an ascendancy over the obsessing spirit; but, as this ascendancy can only be a moral one, it can only be gained by a person who is morally *superior* to the obsessor, his power over whom will be in proportion to the degree of his superiority. It was the moral elevation of Jesus that gave Him boundless power over what, in His day, were called 'devils', that is to say, evil and obsessing spirits.[21]

The classic example of Jesus' power over these devils comes from Luke's Gospel in the Bible:

7:21. Ibid. pp. 286-288.

7:22. And when [Jesus] went forth ... there met him out of the city a certain man, which had devils [for a] long time, and wore no clothes, neither abode in any house, but in the tombs.

When he saw Jesus, he cried out, and fell down before him, and with a loud voice said, "What have I to do with thee, Jesus, thou Son of God most high? I beseech thee, torment me not."

(For [Jesus] had commanded the unclean spirit to come out of the man. For oftentimes it had caught him: and he was kept bound with chains and in fetters; and he brake the bands, and was driven of the devil into the wilderness.)

And Jesus asked him, saying, "What is thy name?" And he said, "Legion": because many devils were entered into him.

And they besought [Jesus] that he would not command them to go out into the deep.

And there was there an herd of many swine feeding on the mountain: and they besought him that he would suffer them to enter into them. And he suffered them.

Then went the devils out of the man, and entered into the swine: and the herd ran violently down a steep place into the lake, and were choked.

When they that fed them saw what was done, they fled, and went and told it in the city and in the country.

Then they went out to see what was done; and came to Jesus, and found the man, out of whom the devils were departed, sitting at the feet of Jesus, clothed, and in his right mind.[22]

7:23. And when [Jesus] had called unto him his twelve disciples, he gave them power against unclean spirits, to cast them out.[23]

7:22. *Holy Bible. Luke.* Ch.8 vs. 27-35.
[St. Luke's Gospel in the New Testament.] Source D-b.

7:23. Ibid. *Matthew.* Ch. 10. v. 1.
[St. Matthew's Gospel in the New Testament.] Source D-b.

Now Bishop Frank – the Bishop of Zanzibar – said that the 'Master and Teacher' of all things spiritual, both pleasant and unpleasant, was Jesus:

> 7:24. His insight into spiritual causes was superior to ours. He believed in demoniac possession and cast the demons out. He sent forth His Apostles with a commission to do likewise; and the Bishop could conclude: "I have exorcised men with success."
> *And the Bishop's biographer comments:* – I believe that there were many occasions on which he exercised this power.

Bishop Frank was working in Zanzibar in the late 19th and early 20th centuries. The missionaries were introducing Christianity into East Africa at that time, and in terms of everyday work they were all very busy, but they also had to contend with witchcraft and sorcery. The Bishop made certain rules that would guide his missionaries through these problems, and the first rule was that they should never allow the Zanzibari people to think that the missionaries themselves had the power to cast out spirits, as this power came solely from the 'faith and prayer' of the Church.[24]

7:25. There was one Zanzibari woman – known as Mama Juma – who was sometimes possessed by spirits, and apparently she said: "The Bishop told me not to be frightened, and I am *not* frightened – but oh! I am *afraid*". She had been a member of a tribal group who used to bedeck themselves as 'devils' and dance in worship of 'the spirits', but she gave this up when she 'married' a Christian convert. The missionaries, however, did not consider this to be a true marriage. And when her young husband attended classes at the Bishop's Mission he was told that he should "try to win her to desire religion", –

> … and at last by prayers and exhortations he succeeded and she began to attend the classes. They had then been married eight years and they were really fond of one another.

7:24. Maynard Smith, Canon H: *Frank, Bishop of Zanzibar.* pp. 116-117.
[British, Bishop of Zanzibar; 19/20th C.] Source F-c.

> Mama Juma then began to be troubled by a sort of trance, which came on every night between 8.30 and 9. A voice would be heard saying, "I am coming, I am coming, I am coming," and then, "I am sent to kill this woman because she follows the religion of the Europeans. I am sent by So-and-So of such a place (a well-known wizard and dealer in charms about four miles from the Mission), and I shall go on coming until I kill her; but if she will give up the religion of the Europeans, then I shall leave her in peace."
>
> The husband came to beg for help, and was taught an Act of Faith, and of defiance of the evil spirit, and told to say them and his own prayers whenever the spirit came.

This failed to ease the problem, however, and Mama Juma's condition worsened. When the missionaries heard this, they told the husband to bring Mama Juma to the Mission so that they could try to exorcise the spirit. He did so, and Mama Juma soon had another 'attack'. They took her down to the church, –

> ... and there she flung herself on the ground, writhing and trying to tear her clothes off. Finally she was exorcised, and after many prayers, penitential psalms, etc., she became quiet and lay down as if asleep. When she opened her eyes she recognized everyone, and after a short thanksgiving she went to the house provided for her.
>
> That night all was quiet, but the next night, just as Compline was over in church, we were called to Mama Juma. During the attack on the day she came in she had been very sneering and horrible, saying: "Come round me all of you. I know what you want to do; just come and see if you can do it; you never will." This night [the] attack was much the same, but she looked even more horrible, really satanic. I myself heard her (or it?) name the man who had sent the spirit, and that it had come to kill her on account of her religion. When shown the crucifix, she gnashed her teeth and tried to seize it, and made the common African

sign of contempt (a sort of sucking in of the cheeks). We prayed for about one and a half to two hours, but at last the voice said, "Oh, very well, if you want me to go, I will go." ...

On the following night she went to the house of a Christian close by, saying she felt very *odd* and would like to stay there, and by 8.45 or so she was again 'possessed'. Again we all went down to the house, and found her sitting up, looking very queer, but much less fierce than on the other occasions. This time, when shown the crucifix, she turned her head away ... and said, "What has that to do with me? Where do I come from? Don't I come from heathendom? Well, then, that has nothing to do with me."

Then suddenly, while we were praying, "You know I'm another one? I have put out that Pemba one and I am quite another one. I am a Manyema." (This was from the woman's own tribe.) ... "This woman was committed to me before she was born. But you need not mind me, I shall not hurt her, I am not like that Pemba one; she is in my charge."

We answered, "But she has chosen Another and wants no more of you, and you are afraid of Him. You are afraid even of His image. ... That is the One Whom this woman has chosen as her Lord, so you must leave her alone and go your ways."

"Can a mother forsake her child? *No*, and no more can I forsake this woman, who is *my* child, placed in my keeping before she was born."

"You will not be leaving *her*, for she has already left you, but you must cease from troubling her, for she has done with you."

This sort of argument went on for some time. ... At last it said, "Well, what *do* you really want me to do?" in a *weary* voice, as if tired out.

"We want you to leave this woman altogether and never trouble her again."

"Oh, very well then; I will go on my ways *altogether*" – (a very strong word for this).

> Then she lay down for quite a long time, seven or eight minutes, after which she sat up and said in a *very* gentle voice, "Fetch me a little water, my friends, that I may drink." And when it was brought in a coconut shell, fixed on to a long stick, she received it in her right hand, but at once transferred it to her left (which would *never* be used [in her old religion] for eating or drinking) in order to make with the right a large sign of the Cross before she drank the water.
>
> This was in December, 1920, and she has never been troubled again.[25]

The Zanzibari princess, Emily Said-Ruete, could have explained the role of the protective spirit who described Mama Juma as '*my* child, placed in my keeping' – as Said-Ruete says in her *Memoirs* –

> 7:26. ... it must be understood that the sick are not plagued by evil spirits alone – there are also good spirits, that may have taken a special fancy to a person, wishing to protect her in life. Sometimes it occurs that two spirits, a good and a bad one, contest for the same person, and during this exorcism they are sure to manifest themselves. It is said that frightful scenes sometimes ensue on such occasions, which none but the very bravest can face out.
>
> Frequently an expert woman will drive out an evil spirit; with a good one a kind of agreement is made, allowing it to pay visits to its victim at times.[26]

7:27. Protective spirits are recognised by Dr Fiore too, and she described a case in which a kind surgeon was killed in a car crash just as a woman was preparing to give birth to a premature baby. The surgeon – in spirit – went back to his hospital, and became aware of this

7:25. Ibid. *Frank, Bishop of Zanzibar.* pp. 124-126.
[An appendix by Miss Voules; 19/20th C.] Source F-c.

7:26. Said-Ruete, *Emily: Memoirs of an Arabian Princess.* p. 216.
[Omani Arab princess; 19th C.] Source F-b.

tiny fragile baby who was nearing her birth. He felt compelled to strengthen and protect her, so he somehow joined her, and stayed with her for several years. But there were increasing problems for the girl as she grew up, and she finally sought Fiore's help. When Fiore had hypnotised her, Fiore discovered that the surgeon's spirit was still with the girl – and *he* explained clearly what had happened, saying:

> "This little soul was to be born so early. ... She was too weak to survive by herself. ... I could give her the strength she needed until she could go on by herself. She was tiny, *so tiny*! She needed me – and I needed her. I still needed to experience things; with her I could experience what I hadn't and wanted to."

And Fiore adds two further comments:

> After he departed – more than twenty years later – the patient said, "He was kind, but it seems that he had taken over so much that it didn't give me a chance to grow."[27]
>
> 7:28. My therapeutic goal is to help the possessing spirits, ... even if it means that my patients must be burdened a little longer while we work on the willingness of the possessors to leave. If I were able to 'kick them out,' I would be creating a monstrous problem, because they would be, again, displaced persons and perhaps latch onto other unsuspecting people.[28]

Fiore has developed a special technique by which she persuades the possessors to move on to the higher levels. She speaks directly to them – discussing their own problems with them – while her patients are in hypnotic trance; and when these spirits seem ready but reluctant to move on, Fiore asks for help from the possessors' spirit friends and relatives, who come when thus invited, to encourage the

---

7:27. Fiore, Dr Edith: *The Unquiet Dead.* p. 34.
[American psychologist; 20th C.] Source J-g.
7:28. Ibid. p. 14.

possessing spirits to leave with them. Fiore has depossessed many patients in this way, 'freeing the lost souls' – and adds:

> 7:29. Sometimes tears streamed down my patients' faces as they resonated to emotions of the possessing spirits. They could feel overwhelming fear as spirits thought they were being cast out, and joy and relief when they saw their spirit relatives. ... Many told of feeling "something leave" – lifting up out of them. Some remarked, "It's less crowded now;" "I feel a bit empty;" "A big weight's been released;" "Now it's possible to be me. I didn't know I was me all these years – that there was a me that could be free."[29]

7:29. Ibid. p.12.

8

Withdrawal from the Body

The idea that a possessing spirit can invade a human body, and then leave it, is one thing – but the suggestion that one's own spirit can come and go from the body is quite another. Yet this is exactly what the 19th century novelist, George Eliot, suggests when she says –

> 8:1. … there might be such a thing as a man's soul being loose from his body, and going out and in, like a bird out of its nest and back.[1]

8:2. Allan Kardec would clearly support this view, as he says that when we sleep and the body 'reposes',

> … the spirit disengages itself from its material bonds; it is then more free, and can more easily see other spirits, with whom it enters into communication. A dream is only a reminiscence of this state; when we remember nothing we say we have had no dream, but the soul has none the less had its eyes open, and enjoyed its liberty.[2]

8:3. A dream – in which one dreamer saw and communicated with another – was published by the Institute of Psychophysical Research in

---

8:1. Eliot, George: *Silas Marner.* p. 9.
 [English woman novelist; 19th C.]
8:2. Kardec, Allan: *Experimental Spiritism: The Mediums' Book.* p. 106.
 [French Spiritist medium; 19th C.] Source J-b.

Oxford. The dreamer, Oliver Fox, explained that he and a couple of friends had been discussing dreams one evening, and as they parted they decided that they would try to make dream-contact with each other on Southampton Common. Later on in the night, Fox somehow met his friend Elkington on the Common – just as they had planned – and he knew that they were meeting in their dreams and that Slade had failed to join them.

When Fox met Elkington the next day he decided that he should say nothing about his own dream, but asked Elkington if he had dreamt anything. Elkington said that he had, adding: "I met you on the Common all right, ... but old Slade didn't turn up. We had just time to greet each other and comment on his absence, then the dream ended."

When they found Slade, at last, he said that he had slept soundly through the night, and they decided that this was the reason why he had failed to get to their meeting.[3]

"This is very strange stuff," I said to myself, "and where do I go from here? Perhaps I should search for some more explanations – from those on the other side." So I looked again through the books of spirit communication and found that Marshall Hall's medium, Miss Wingfield, had received some unusual details on the subject of dreams. She asks –

> 8:4. ... do you know what most dreams are? I will tell you. They are the effect of the subconscious self trying to convey to the conscious self actions and things that have taken place.[4]
>
> 8:5. That is to say, when the body here is resting, the spirit is active above, gaining knowledge and working in many ways. This in a shadowy way is again enacted through the spirit working out here below what it gained above.
>
> The soul never sleeps. Consider what is sleep? It is merely a state of inaction designed to rest the material [body] and prevent too great a wear and tear. To attain it you withdraw the active part which makes the body move and think. The

---

8:3. In Green, Celia: *Lucid Dreams*. pp. 110-11.

[Oliver Fox: British researcher in psychic experience; 19/20th C.]

8:4. Wingfield, K: *More Guidance from Beyond*. p. 26.

[Spirit guidance through medium, K. Wingfield; 19/20th C.]

soul, when it is outside the body, is always learning or working, or in some way rising to a higher level – if the human body it belongs to is doing his best to do the same in his waking hours.

"The soul is very active", the spirit continues – saying that our inability to remember what was happening while our bodies slept does not mean that the activities of our freed souls are not real.[5]

And the spirit explains this further, saying:

> 8:6. You are not permitted to bring back to earth the memory of the spheres above, because you have to live your life on earth, and were you to be wearying for that other place it might cause discontent.[6]

"But it would be wonderful if we could retain our memories of those other spheres!" I thought. The dream-memories of Fox and Elkington – who had met each other on the Common – seemed so ordinary now, and of the lower levels. In contrast to this, I longed to learn more about our visits to the higher spheres; so I turned to one of my favourite books to see if the spirit, Silver Birch, would support such a concept – and found the following passage:

> 8:7. When the activities of the day are hushed, and in the silence of the night, your souls come into their own and you leave behind the discordant vibrations of the material world and enter – for a short time, it is true – your real homes.[7]

And searching further on the library shelves I found the text of an ancient Hindu Upanishad, which says –

> 8:8. … man has only two abodes, this and the next world. The dream state, which is the third, is at the junction of the

8:5. Ibid. pp. 25-26.
8.6. Ibid. p. 30.
8.7. In Ortzen, Tony (Ed.): *Silver Birch Companion*. p. 17.
[Silver Birch: Spirit teacher, through medium, Barbanell; 20th.C.]

> two. Staying at that junction he surveys the two abodes. ... When he dreams, he ... puts the body aside and himself creates a dream body in its place ... and dreams.[8]
>
> 8:9. As a great fish swims alternately to both banks of a river, ... so does this infinite being move to both these states, the dream and waking states ...
>
> As a hawk or falcon flying in the sky becomes tired, and stretching its wings, is bound for its nest, so does this infinite being.[9]
>
> 8:10. He comes back ... to his former condition, the waking state.[10]

Then in contrast to the Hindu text, I found a modern and matter-of-fact description of 'coming back':

> 8:11. *I was half-way down the hall when I woke up.* ... "Of all things!" I said to myself, "*I have been walking in my sleep*! I surely will catch more cold. I'll have to get back to bed right away!" ...
>
> I turned around and went back, and as I passed into my bedroom through the open door, I was shaken with amazement; – there I was still lying in bed! ... Naturally, I had supposed until this moment that I had been walking in my natural physical body while in sleep. ... I can never tell you the wonderment which came over me on viewing myself there in bed.[11]

Now the Director of the Scientific and Medical Network, David Lorimer, accepts the view that the 'conscious self' can exist outside the physical body - and he introduces the subject by mentioning an 'everyday assumption':

8:8. *The Brihadaranyaka Upanishad.* para. 4.3.9.
[Ancient Hindu text: several C's. BC.] Source A-a.

8:9. Ibid. paras. 4.3.18-19.

8:10. Ibid. para. 4.3.34.

8:11. In Muldoon, S; Carrington, H: *The Phenomena of Astral Projection.* p. 88.
[An out-of-body experience; 20th C.]

8:12. Life might become altogether too bizarre and unpredictable if we could no longer assume that our centre of consciousness and identity was 'located' inside our heads. ... Despite this everyday assumption, however, people do evidently have experiences where the conscious self seems to be located outside the body and to be perceiving the world from another angle.[12]

8:13. We normally assume that the conscious self's perception and sense of identity depends on or even originates in the physical body: that without the eyes and ears, there can be no sense of sight or hearing. But ... the senses of sight and hearing seem able to function at a distance from the physical body, and on occasion even when the body is ostensibly unconscious; in many cases these senses are experienced as more acute than usual. This suggests that our normal notions need to be reversed: ... *perception is essentially extra-sensory, despite the fact that it is normally associated closely with the physical body.* Thus the physical body is an instrument of perception, but not an indispensable instrument.[13]

The experience of extra-sensory perception is described now by Emanuel Swedenborg, who explains how one's consciousness can be 'withdrawn' from the body:

8:14. I wish to relate from experience what happens when man is withdrawn from the body, and what it is to be carried away ... to another place.

As regards the first, namely, withdrawal from the body, it happens thus. Man is brought into a certain state that is midway between sleeping and waking, and when in that state he seems to himself to be wide awake; all the senses are as perfectly awake as in the completest bodily wakefulness, not only the sight and the hearing, but what is wonderful, the sense of touch also, which is then more

8:12. Lorimer, David: *Survival?* p. 226.
[British, Director of the Scientific and Medical Network; 20th C.]
8:13. Ibid. p. 231.

exquisite than is ever possible when the body is awake. ... This is the state that is called *being withdrawn from the body, and not knowing whether one is in the body or out of it.* I have been admitted into this state ... that I might know what it is, and might know that spirits and angels enjoy every sense, and that man does also in respect of his spirit when he is withdrawn from the body.

As regards the second, being carried away by the spirit to another place, I have been shown by living experience what it is. ... I wish to relate a single instance. Walking through the streets of a city and through fields, talking at the same time with spirits, I did not know otherwise than that I was fully awake, and in possession of my usual sight. Thus I walked on without going astray, and all the while with clear vision. ... But after walking thus ... I perceived that I had been in the same state as those who were said *to have been led away by the spirit into another place.* For in this state there is no reflection upon the distance, ... nor any reflection upon the time, ... neither is there any feeling of fatigue; and one is led unerringly through ways of which he himself is ignorant, even to the destined place.[14]

And Swedenborg adds the following statement:

8:15. In this way also I have been led by the Lord into the heavens and likewise to the earths in the universe. This happened as to my spirit, my body remaining in the same place.[15]

This may seem rather far-fetched – but it cannot be ignored, as Saint Paul the Apostle mentions the same experience:

8:16. I will come to visions and revelations of the Lord. I knew a man, ... (whether in the body, I cannot tell; or

---

8:14. Swedenborg, Emanuel: *Heaven and Hell.* paras. 439-441. [Swedish scientist/mystic; 17/18th C.] Source J-a.

8:15. Ibid. para. 192.

> whether out of the body, I cannot tell: God knoweth;) such an one [was] caught up to the third heaven. ...
> [He] was caught up into paradise.[16]

And the Roman philosopher, Plotinus, describes his own experiences:

> 8:17. Many times it has happened: lifted out of the body into myself; becoming external to all other things and self-encentred; beholding a marvellous beauty; then, more than ever, assured of community with the loftiest order; enacting the noblest life, acquiring identity with the divine; stationing within It by having attained that activity; ... yet, there comes a moment of descent from intellection to reasoning, and after that sojourn in the divine, I ask myself how it happens that I can now be descending, and how did the Soul ever enter into my body, the Soul which, even within the body, is the high thing it has shown itself to be.[17]

Having read this marvellous description I found it quite hard to come down from its heights. But the medium, Kardec, is more down to earth as he is intrigued by the practicalities of this phenomenon – saying:

> 8:18. Before going farther, we must reply to a question that will certainly be asked, *viz.* "How can the body live while the spirit is absent?" We reply that it is possible for the body to live with only the organic life, which is independent of the spirit's presence. But we must add that, during earth-life, the spirit is never completely detached from the body. Spirits, as well as certain seeing mediums, perceive that the spirit of one in the flesh, when away from

---

8:16. *Holy Bible.* 2 Corinthians. Ch. 12. vs. 1-2; 4.
[St. Paul: leading Christian Apostle; 1st C.] Source D-c.

8:17. Plotinus: *The Enneads.* IV. p. 357.
[Roman philosopher; 3rd C.] Source C-b.

> the body, is united to it by a luminous trail which reaches to the body; a phenomenon which never occurs when the body is dead, for then the separation is complete.[18]
>
> 8:19. This fluidic link has often been seen by clairvoyant mediums. It is a sort of phosphorescent trail between the body and the spirit; when the latter is away from the body, this trail seems to disappear in space.[19]
>
> 8:20. It is by this channel of communication that the spirit is instantaneously informed, however far away he may be, of the need which the body may have of its presence; and he then returns to the body with the swiftness of lightning. It follows, therefore, that the body can never die during the spirit's absence, and that the spirit, on his return, can never find the door of his fleshly habitation closed against him, as some romancers have pretended in their imaginary tales.[20]

The 'luminous' or 'fluidic' link between the human body and its spirit is described by the writer, Emmet Fox, – who uses the term 'etheric' for 'spirit':

> 8:21. In all these cases when the etheric leaves the physical body, it remains attached to it by an etheric ligament very like a boy's kite floating at the end of the string which he holds in his hand. This etheric connection is called in the Bible the Silver Cord. It is bluish gray in color and is so elastic that the etheric body can go very long distances away and still remain attached to the physical corpus. In sleep, by far the greater part of the etheric slips out. In very materialistic and otherwise undeveloped people the etheric remains only a yard or two from the body, usually floating overhead; but with people of some

8:18. Kardec, Allan: *Experimental Spiritism: The Mediums' Book.* pp. 129-130. [French Spiritist medium; 19th C.} Source J-b.

8:19. Ibid. p. 344.

8:20. Ibid. p. 130.

> degree of mental training, and especially with those who have some spiritual development, it passes right over into the next plane, and sometimes beyond that. The difference between normal sleep and anesthesia, and the different kinds of trance, is a question of how much of the etheric goes out at that particular time, – that is all.[21]

8:22. 'Anaesthesia' had clearly caused some out of body happenings that were observed by a natural psychic, Dr R.B. Hout. He had gone to watch some operations, and when the first anaesthetised patient was brought into the theatre, Hout saw something above the trolley – which he described as 'a vague, misty outline, having the general development and contour of the human body'. While the operation proceeded under deepening anaesthesia, Hout saw that the 'spirit form' was freed increasingly from the body, and as it intensified he could make out 'the features' of 'an elderly lady', presumably those of the patient. Hout also noted that the spirit came closer to the body as the operation was completed, though it 'had not yet re-entered its vehicle' when 'the patient was wheeled from the operating theatre.' He stayed on to watch some more operations, and describes how he –

> ... was able to see, at least part of the time, the astral cord that united these spirit bodies with their physical counterparts. This was represented to me as a silvery shaft of light. ... When the magnetic force would draw the spirit close to the physical body, this cord was more apparent, as though more concentrated. At other times the force was indistinguishable to me.[22]

From the patient's point of view, the experience of venturing from its anaesthetised body may be even more extraordinary – as described in the following accounts, which were recorded by Dr Raymond Moody:

8:21. Fox, Emmet: *Power Through Constructive Thinking*. p. 204.
[American writer; 19th/20th C.}

8:22. In Muldoon, S; H. Carrington. *Phenomena of Astral Projection*. pp. 70-71.
[Dr R. B. Hout: American doctor/psychic; 19/20th C.]

> 8:23. "I remember being wheeled into the operating room and the next few hours were the critical period. During that time, I kept getting in and out of my physical body, and I could see it from directly above. But, while I did, I was still in a body – not a physical body, but something I can best describe as an energy pattern. If I had to put it into words, I would say that it was transparent, a spiritual as opposed to a material being. Yet, it definitely had different parts."[23]
>
> 8:24. "I was out of my body looking at it from about ten yards away, but I was still thinking, just like in physical life. ... I wasn't in a body, as such. I could feel something, some kind of a – like a capsule, or something, like a clear form. I couldn't really see it; it was like it was transparent, but not really. It was like I was just there ..."[24]

8:25. In one of his afterlife communications, Sir Donald Tovey touches on the subject of etheric bodies – saying: "In actual fact, those new bodies already existed although merged with the physical bodies."[25]

And the spirit of Frederick Myers gives us more information:

> 8:26. ... there is a body vibrating at a slightly higher rate of intensity which accompanies the human being from birth till death – a body invisible to the eye, which receives the soul or conscious intelligence during sleep – a body which, at all times, acts as an intermediary between the intellect, imagination and the physical shape ...
>
> Further, this double is in the likeness of the visible manifestation of the man. So similar are they in appearance, they might be described as twins if they could be visualized together. The double, indeed, reflects the impressions of its companion, receives the memories registered by the senses

8:23. In Moody, Dr Raymond: *Life After Life.* p. 49.
[Near Death Experiences; 20th C.]

8:24. Ibid. p. 50.

8:25. In Brown, Rosemary: *Immortals at my Elbow.* p. 104.
[Sir Donald Tovey: afterlife communication; 20th C.] Source J-e.

> and imprints those impressions [upon itself]. ... This body does not imitate its companion and gradually decay as the years pass ... [as] it contains and shelters the nascent manifestation which is to be eventually the body of the soul in the world after death.[26]

8:27. Seth says that this body is the body in which one can travel when out of the physical body. It has extraordinary qualities, and performs in the way that we do in our dreams: "... it flies, goes through solid objects, and is moved directly by your will, taking you, say, from one location to another as you may think of these locations".

But Seth reminds us that this body is usually within the physical body – although we are not aware of it as being a part of ourselves – and when the time comes for us to die, this body is the vehicle that we shall use "for some time".[27]

Now the Rosicrucian, Max Heindel, introduces a further point – saying:

> 8:28. The man who is capable of extracting his own vital body by an act of will, becomes a citizen of two worlds, independent and free.[28]

8:29. And Joseph Weed – who is also a Rosicrucian – describes a technique that enables you to free yourself from your physical body. You have to relax completely on a bed or a comfortable couch, and then shut your eyes and concentrate on bringing every feeling that you have in your body right up through your body and into your head. Hold everything carefully there in your head, and then move this focus of concentration to a point "at or above the crown of your head". As you reach this level, you need to hum vibrating 'OM' sounds to produce a 'resonance'.

And Joseph Weed goes even further: "Concentrating all of your attention on the core of this resonance, let it lift slowly upward toward the ceiling. Remember, it is the resonance that ascends, not your body.

8:26. In Cummins, Geraldine: *Beyond Human Personality*. pp. 65-6.
[F. W. H. Myers: afterlife communication; 19/20th C.] Source J-d.

8:27. In Roberts, Jane: *Seth Speaks*. pp. 154-155.
[Seth: Spirit teacher, through medium, Jane Roberts; 20th C.]

8:28. Heindel, Max: *The Rosicrucian Mysteries*. p. 137.
[American Rosicrucian; 19/20th C.] Source H-b.

Then open your eyes and allow your awareness of things about you to return. Do not be alarmed when you realize that you are no longer on the bed but above it near the ceiling. Above all, do not feel shock and fear when you observe your body, seemingly lifeless on the bed below."[29]

Now this is a really strange exercise! But it is supported by the following account – which was published by Robert Crookall:

> 8:30. Gradually the consciousness, which normally suffuses the whole body, became condensed in the head. I became all head, and only head. Then it seemed that 'I' had become condensed into one tiny speck of consciousness, situated somewhere near the centre of my head. ... Then I became aware that I was beginning to travel further upwards. There came a momentary blackout, ... and then 'I' was free; I had left my body. I had projected in space somewhere above the bed on which still lay my inert body.[30]

Weed's special technique may work well for some people, but it is not the sole method by which you can leave your body – and the British science reporter, Gordon Taylor, describes an easier way – saying:

> 8:31. I once had a similar experience, lying, rather tired, on a bed ... trying to imagine how I would look to myself; I constructed, so to say, an image of myself in the air above me, when, suddenly, I was up near the ceiling, in the image, looking down at myself.[31]

8:32. The psychologist, Helen Wambach, has developed a method by which she frees people from their bodies. She invites them to relax – and says, "You are lying on your bed. ... You hear my voice, and it is easy

---

8:29. Weed, Joseph J: *Wisdom of the Mystic Masters.* pp. 196-197. [American Rosicrucian; 20th C.]

8:30. In Crookall, Dr Robert: *The Study and Practice of Astral Projection.* p. 3. [An Out of Body Experience; 20th C.]

8:31. Taylor, Gordon Rattray: *The Natural History of the Mind.* p. 222. [British science reporter; 20th C.]

for you to follow my instructions." She then tells them that they will feel a 'rising energy':

> "For some of you it may be a spinning sensation, and you're going faster and faster, though you're not dizzy. For others of you it's a feeling of expansion, as though you were growing larger and larger. There is a vibration of energy increasing all around you. The energy comes to a climax, and now you are floating out of your body. You are out of your body now. ... You are free! Remember now, your childhood dreams of flying."[32]

One Rosicrucian wondered what he should do when he found that he had freed himself from his body for the very first time, – and in his account of the experience, he says:

> 8:33. Since I knew nothing of the techniques used by birds, I hesitated to commit myself to the air. However, I knew how to swim, so telling myself that this etheric atmosphere is not too different from water, I threw myself into a horizontal position and went through the motions of swimming. To my amazement it worked. I found myself moving along about four feet above the ground at about the pace of a rapid walk. ... Soon I assumed the position of diving, with my hands clasped and extended in front of me and my feet stretched out behind. In this horizontal position I found I could propel myself by merely wishing to move forward and that I could also regulate this speed from quite slow to exceedingly fast. Once, when moving at a great rate of speed, I decided on a whim to go straight up. In a second or two I found myself far above the earth, which looked small beneath me. Around me was the immense void of space.[33]

8:32. Wambach, Dr Helen: *Reliving Past Lives*. pp. 102-103.
[American psychology researcher; 20th C.]

8:33. In Weed, Joseph J: *Wisdom of the Mystic Masters*. pp. 201-202.
[A Rosicrucian's out-of-body experiment; 20th C.]

8:34. This strange experience of rushing into space was described by Carl Jung too – *but he had not chosen to leave his body*. He was extremely ill at the time, and did not know if he was dreaming or experiencing some kind of delusion or 'ecstasy':

> At any rate, extremely strange things began to happen to me. It seemed to me that I was high up in space. Far below I saw the globe of the earth, bathed in a gloriously blue light. I saw the deep blue sea and the continents. Far below my feet lay Ceylon, and in the distance ahead of me the subcontinent of India. My field of vision did not include the whole earth, but its global shape was plainly distinguishable and its outlines shone with a silvery gleam through that wonderful blue light. In many places the globe seemed coloured, or spotted dark green like oxidized silver, ... [and] I knew that I was on the point of departing from the earth.[34]

Jung, however, recovered from his illness – and from his wonderful, and yet extraordinary experience; but I felt that the healer, Allegra Taylor, would suggest that his experience was not so extraordinary – as she says:

> 8:35. All over the world the same magical power of flight is credited to sorcerers and medicine men: changing into birds, riding on broomsticks, levitating, astral travelling. 'Among all things that fly, the mind is the swiftest,' says an American Indian proverb. 'Those who know have wings.'[35]

8:36. Now the phrase, "the mind is the swiftest", is echoed by the following passage from *The Tibetan Book of the Dead*: " ... thou canst instantaneously arrive in whatever place thou wishest; thou hast the

---

8:34. Jung, Dr Carl G: *Memories, Dreams, Reflections*. p. 270.
[German-Swiss psychiatrist; 19/20th C.]
8:35. Taylor, Allegra: *I Fly Out with Bright Feathers*. p. 84.
[British novice healer; 20th C.]

power of reaching there within the time which a man taketh to bend, or to stretch forth his hand."[36]

8:37. The spirit, Seth, takes this even further – as he says that when you feel an especially deep 'desire' to be in some other place, your 'pseudophysical form' may be seen there:

> The desire will carry the imprint of your personality and image. ... Though this thought-image *usually* is not seen by others, it is quite possible that ... such an image may be perceived by those who have developed [the] use of the inner senses.[37]

Seth's explanation is supported by a detailed account that was published by the Society of Psychical Research in the 19th century. In this account, Mr S.R. Wilmot describes how he had been sailing from Europe to New York in appalling weather. One night – when it was particularly rough – he dreamed:

> 8:38. I dreamed that I saw my wife, whom I had left in the United States, come to the door of my stateroom clad in her night-dress. At the door she seemed to discover that I was not the only occupant of the room, hesitated a little, then advanced to my side, stooped down and kissed me, and after gently caressing me for a few moments, quietly withdrew.
>
> Upon waking I was surprised to see my fellow-passenger, whose berth was above mine – but not directly over it, owing to the fact that our room was at the stern of the vessel – leaning upon his elbow, and looking fixedly at me. "You're a pretty fellow," said he at length, "to have a lady come and visit you in this way." I pressed him for an explanation, which he at first declined to give, but at length related what he had seen while wide awake, lying in his berth. It exactly corresponded with my dream ...

8:36. In Evans-Wentz, Dr W. Y: *The Tibetan Book of the Dead.* p. 159.
[Tibetan Buddhist/Bon Teaching; pre-8th C.] Source B-b.

8:37. In Roberts, Jane: *Seth Speaks.* p. 102.
[Seth: spirit teacher, through medium, Jane Roberts; 20th C.]

> The day after landing I went by rail to Watertown ... where my children and my wife had been for some time, visiting her parents. Almost her first question when we were alone together was, "Did you receive a visit from me a week ago Tuesday?" "A visit from you?" said I, "we were more than a thousand miles at sea." "I know it," she replied, "but it seemed to me that I visited you ..."
>
> My wife then told me that on account of the severity of the weather [in the Atlantic], ... she had lain awake for a long time thinking of me, and about four o'clock in the morning it seemed to her that she went out to seek me. Crossing the wide and stormy sea, she came at length to a low black steamship, whose side she went up, and then descending into the cabin, passed through it to the stern until she came to my stateroom. "Tell me," said she, "do they ever have staterooms like the one I saw, where the upper berth extends further back than the under one? A man was in the upper berth, looking right at me, and for a moment I was afraid to go in, but soon I went up to the side of your berth, bent down and kissed you, and embraced you, and then went away."[38]

The Swedish writer, Johan Strindberg, gives a similar but shorter account:

> 8:39. I pause here for a moment in order to expound the ... phenomenon known as a man's 'double'. ... Suppose that an absent person thinks of me, by evoking my personality in his remembrance; he only succeeds in creating a virtual image of me by a free and conscious effort of his own. But suppose again that an old aunt of mine in a foreign country sits at the piano without thinking of me, and sees me then standing in person behind the instrument; she has *seen* a virtual image of me.

8:38. In *Proceedings, Society for Psychical Research*: Vol. 7. pp. 42-43.
[S. R. Wilmot's testimony; 19th C.] Source K-c.

> And this actually happened in the autumn of 1895. I remember that I was then passing through a dangerous illness in the French capital, when my longing to be in the bosom of my family overcame me to such a degree that I saw the inside of my house and for a moment forgot my surroundings, having lost the consciousness of where I was. I was really there behind the piano as I appeared, and the imagination of the old lady had nothing to do with the matter.[39]

"Now it's one thing to be seen as a 'virtual image' of yourself – by another person," I said to myself. "And it's another thing to see your own body – from outside yourself – when it's lying on a bed. But it's quite another thing if you find yourself outside your own body – and you watch it carry on with doing something that's active and intelligent – when you're not in the body yourself!" And I turned to a book by Alfred Douglas that I was reading, and re-read this remarkable passage:

> 8:40. In many ... cases subjects reported that they found themselves observing their bodies from the outside, while the body, curiously, was seen to continue with whatever it was engaged in at the time of separation as if nothing unusual was happening.
>
> In one example ... a woman found herself sitting on the roof of a car watching her body inside the vehicle as it attempted to pass its driving test. In another example a dentist stood three feet outside his body and looked on while it was pulling a patient's tooth.
>
> People who have had [out of body experiences] ... during traumatic situations – such as being blown up during battle – generally report having felt unaffected by the situation and, indeed, to have been notably detached from any concern about the fate of the physical body.[40]

8:39. Strindberg, Johan August: *Legends*. pp. 85-86.
[Swedish writer; 19/20th C.]

8:40. Douglas, Alfred: *Extra Sensory Powers*. p. 324.
[American writer; 20th C.]

And this sense of detachment is mentioned again in some other accounts:

> 8:41. I was trapped underwater, wearing scuba-gear, in the cod-end of a trawl net. ... The trawl was travelling faster than I could swim or claw my way out of it; I had lost my face mask and was immersed in a slimy, spiny mass of struggling fish; and I went into a panic. ... at once I slipped out of my body and was outside the net, rear end up, watching myself lapse into senseless struggling. ... 'I' felt a total dispassion, no discomfort, worry or fear. ... 'I' thought of the heavy knife in 'its' belt, and watched as the automaton reduced its frantic struggling, reached for the knife, unsheathed it and sawed a hole in the net through which it was able to get out. 'I' saw it head toward the surface. ... The next thing I knew, I was spluttering and gasping on the surface, watching the trawler recede.[41]

So the scuba-diver had 'slipped' from his body when his predicament was too frightening; and similarly, some prisoners of the Second World War described how they escaped from their bodies when life was too 'intolerable':

> 8:42. "The work was so hard and the fear so dreadful, I'd be removed from my body completely. I'd be working or walking along and I'd be able to see myself, all of me, standing next to me. I could watch myself."
>
> Other [ex-prisoners of war] confirmed that such 'out-of-body' experiences were commonplace; 'escapes' one man called them, as if grateful that his mind had contrived a means of removing him from the intolerable. ... "Coming back to camp some evenings, you'd be completely gone. You felt like you'd come to the very end of yourself, and you knew the other men around you felt the same.

8:41. In Watson, Lyall: *Beyond Supernature.* p. 172.
[W. Travis: private letter quoted by Lyall Watson; 20th C.]

"But then someone - and you could hardly believe it - someone would start whistling, usually *Colonel Bogey*, and you'd come back into yourself."[42]

Now Kübler-Ross was a specialist who worked for very many years with people who were dying, and with their loved ones, and she says:

> 8:43. Many people have shared with us during our lectures and workshops around the world a fact that ... people in a life-threatening and painful situation ... have the ability to leave their physical body ...
> [This shows that a person can] ... "simply slip out of its cocoon," as one assault victim later described it. She was able to describe the assaults on her body, the repeated stabbings; she watched them happen with what she described as "no bad feelings, almost a sense of compassion and grief" for [her assailant.] ... She was later found unconscious and on the verge of death, with over fifty stab wounds all over her body.[43]

> 8:44. Several young people who have been critically injured, molested, or raped shared similar experiences. ... [These were] 'out-of-body experiences' to avoid the pain and anguish of their helpless predicament.[44]

8:45. The spirit Seth says that "your consciousness, as you think of it, may of course leave your body entirely before physical death".[45]

And descriptions of this have been found amongst some ancient accounts of the crucifixion of Jesus. The scholar, Kurt Rudolph, introduces these passages – which are taken from these Gnostic Gospels:

8:42. In *Sunday Times Magazine*, Nov. 8, 1992. p. 50.
[Article by Peter Martin.]

8:43. Kübler-Ross, Dr Elisabeth: *On Children and Death* p. 103.
[American specialist for the dying; 20th C.]

8:44. Ibid. p. 219.

8:45. In Roberts, Jane: *Seth Speaks.* p. 145.
[Seth: spirit teacher, through medium, Jane Roberts; 20th C.]

8:46. ... in the gnostic *Acts of John* ... the Lord, [Jesus,] already risen from the body, gives to the disciple John – who has fled to the Mount of Olives – a vision and interpretation ... while below them the actual crucifixion is in process:

> "John, for the men below I am crucified in Jerusalem and pierced with lances and with reeds and given to drink of vinegar and gall...
>
> "I am not the one on the cross, I whom now you do not see but whose voice you only hear. ... I have thus suffered nothing of that which they will say about me...
>
> "You hear that I have suffered – and yet I have not suffered –, ... that I was pierced – and yet I have not been struck –, that blood flowed from me – and yet it did not flow –, in brief that I have not had what those men say of me."

A similar situation ... is described in the *Revelation of Peter.* Here the Saviour [Jesus] reveals to Peter, who sees everything before him as in a vision, his own fate upon the cross – [saying] –

> "... only that which is capable of suffering (the body) will suffer, in that the body is the substitute (or: the ransom). He however who was set free is my bodiless body; for I am (only) perceptible spirit which is full of radiant light, he whom thou hast seen."[46]

But the disciple, Peter, does not understand what Jesus is saying – and he questions this vision of 'radiant light':

8:47. "What do I see, O Lord, is it you yourself ... and (who is) the other whom they strike on feet and hands?"

8:46. Rudoph, Kurt: *Gnosis.* pp. 169-171.
[Gnostic Gospels, introduced by Kurt Rudolph.] Sousrce D-f.

The redeemer said to me: "He whom you see ... is the living Jesus. But he in whose hands and feet they drive nails is his fleshly likeness ... whom they put to shame. ... But look on him and me (for comparison)!" But when I had looked (sufficiently) I said: "Lord, no-one sees thee, let us flee from this place!" And he said to me: "I have told you that they are blind. Let them alone! And see how they do not understand ..."[47]

There has been so much misunderstanding since Jesus' death – And there still is. – Yet the following lines from the *Holy Quran* are remarkably close to these Gnostic accounts, saying:

8:48. [As to] their saying: "We slew the Messiah Jesus, son of Mary: ... They slew him not nor crucified, but it appeared so unto them."[48]

And in a third Gnostic Gospel, *The Apocalypse of James*, I found Jesus saying:

8:49. "James, be not concerned for my sake nor for this people (the Jews). I am the one who was in me. Never have I experienced any kind of suffering, nor was I (ever) tormented. ... This (suffering) was however reserved for ... (the body)."

Then in the Gospel, *Logos of the great Seth*, Jesus is really emphatic:

"I was not delivered up to them as they thought. I did not suffer at all. They sought to punish me, and I died, (but) not in reality but (only) in appearance, that I might not be put to shame through them. ... I suffered (only) according to their view and conception. ... For my death, of which they think that it is accomplished, consists (only) in their

---

8:47. Ibid. p. 170.

8:48. *Holy Quran*: Surah IV. v. 157.
[Islam's Holy book, through Prophet Muhammad; 7th C.] Source E-a.

> error and their blindness, when they nailed their man to the death. Their insight … did not see me, for they were deaf and blind ...
>
> "O you who do not see, do not see your blindness, that he whom they did not recognize has never been recognized nor understood."[49]

"Oh, Jesus, dear Lord Jesus," I prayed, "we never understood. But please, *please* help us now - to understand." And as I spoke I felt an overwhelming sense of misery for our misunderstanding, and then a surge of sweet relief for the sake of Jesus Christ. "Why have we never known of this before?" I went on. "Why don't we understand?" But the Gnostic disciples – who were loving and beloved – could not really understand, and they kept these sacred visions of the living Christ – the Christ freed from his body *before* it suffered on the Cross – to themselves alone.

And as I studied further, I saw that a certain Roman citizen would never have accepted the evidence of these Gnostic disciples. He had, at first, hated all the followers of Christ, and he strove to persecute them – until he was struck by a vision of blinding light, and heard Jesus calling him. Thereafter he became extremely influential and was known as Paul the Apostle, and was later sainted.

Paul was clearly one of the most dedicated and sincere followers of the crucified Christ; yet despite his sincerity, I feel that Paul interpreted the death of Jesus in a sacrificial light that fitted his own theological argument. For example, Paul says:

> 8:50. "I am ready to preach the gospel to you. ... For I am not ashamed of the gospel of Christ: for it is the power of God unto salvation to every one that believeth ... [that] –
>
> "Jesus our Lord ... was delivered for our offences, and was raised again for our justification ...
>
> "Therefore being justified by faith, we have peace with God through our Lord Jesus Christ: …

8:49. Rudolph, Kurt: *Gnosis*. pp. 167-168.
[1 Apocalypse of James: Gnostic Gospel found in Egypt.]
[2 Logos of the great Seth: Gnostic Gospel found in Egypt.] Source D-f.

> "For when we were yet without strength, in due time Christ died for the ungodly. ... While we were yet sinners, Christ died for us.
>
> "Much more then, being now justified by his blood, we shall be saved from wrath through him.
>
> "For if, when we were enemies, we were reconciled to God by the death of his Son, much more, being reconciled, we shall be saved by his life.
>
> "And not only so, but we also joy in God through our Lord Jesus Christ, by whom we have now received the atonement."[50]

It is somehow difficult to disagree with Paul's interpretation of the crucifixion since our Christian philosophy has really been shaped by his argument. But Nicholas Wright – while Dean of Lichfield and a Canon Theologian of Coventry Cathedral – wrote a really impressive book, *Jesus and the Victory of God*, in which he says:

> 8:51. There was ... no such thing as a pre-Christian Jewish version of ... Pauline atonement-theology.

Wright then explains that Jesus had lived at a time when the Jews believed that they – as a nation – had offended God so much that they were '*in exile*' from His favour, and that –

> ... the present evil exilic age ... could be brought to an end through certain persons embodying in themselves the sufferings of Israel. Jesus, therefore, was not offering an abstract atonement theology; he was identifying himself with the sufferings of Israel.

And Wright goes even further, stressing the fact that "Christian atonement-theology is only fully explicable as the post-Easter rethinking of Jesus' essentially pre-Easter understanding." This means that Jesus was not offering himself as 'The Atonement' for the personal sins of his individual followers. And Wright suggests that Jesus –

8:50. *Holy Bible*. Romans. Ch. 1. vs. 15-16. Ch. 4. vs. 24-25. Ch.5. vs. 1; 6; 8-11.
[St. Paul's interpretation of the crucifixion; 1st C.] Source D-c.

> … deliberately drew on himself the whole tradition of Jewish expectation and hope. He saw himself as Messiah, the focal point of the great divine act of liberation. ... The final meal, which he celebrated with his followers, … gained its significance from his own entire life and agenda, and from the events which, he knew, would shortly come to pass. It was Jesus' chosen way of investing those imminent events with the significance he believed they would carry.[51]

The early Christians, however, accepted Paul's post-Easter view that Jesus had been sacrificed to take their sins upon himself. Their more primitive, traditional sacrifices had been the slaughter of animals – as they believed that the blood would wash away their sins – and they were therefore prepared to interpret Jesus' apparent sacrifice as their ultimate Atonement.

8:52. And Wright continues now, saying that Jesus had clearly understood the importance of his life and work – and knew that he would be betrayed – and he shared his foreboding with the disciples at their last meal, the Last Supper.

Wright analyses the statements that were made at this meal, as described in three of the Synoptic Gospels in the Bible's New Testament:

> Jesus' blood will be shed 'on behalf of the many' (Luke has 'on behalf of you'). ... To this, Matthew has added 'for the forgiveness of sins.' Once again we must stress: in its first-century Jewish context, this denotes, not an abstract transaction between human beings and their god, but the very concrete expectation of Israel, namely that the nation would at last be rescued from the 'exile' which had come about because of her sins. Matthew is not suggesting that Jesus' death will accomplish an abstract atonement.[52]

8:51. Wright, N. T: *Jesus and the Victory of God.* pp. 592; 558.
[While Dean of Lichfield and a Canon of Coventry Cathedral, UK. 20th C.]
8:52. Ibid. pp. 560-561.

But Myers – in an afterlife communication – gives a very different view on the meaning of Jesus' death:

> 8:53. Paul [the Apostle] made it clear that the blood of Christ could redeem man and obtain for him forgiveness of his sins. But human beings cannot thus be magically saved by the blood of Christ. They can only save themselves through courageous effort extending over a long period of time. A man is a responsible being, responsible to himself, ... and responsible also to God. So he must, as any artist, labour, strive, in tears, misery, joy and love with his own nature, until, at last, it assumes form and loveliness and is truly in the image and likeness of Absolute Beauty.[53]

"But this is Karma," I said to myself. "This is nothing but Karma. We are responsible for our own sins and we, ourselves, must put them right. But how can we find the way by which we can form ourselves into 'the image and likeness of Absolute Beauty'?" And I turned to Jesus's words in the Bible – seeking his guidance and advice – and found the following passage:

> 8:54. Jesus saith, ... "I am the way, the truth, and the life. ... If ye love me, keep my commandments ...
>
> "Thou shalt love the Lord thy God with all thy heart, and with all thy soul, and with all thy mind.
>
> "This is the first and great commandment.
>
> "And the second is like unto it, Thou shalt love thy neighbour as thyself.
>
> "On these two commandments hang all the law and the prophets."[54]

"Amen."

8:53. In Cummins, Geraldine: *Beyond Human Personality.* p. 183.
[F. W. H. Myers: afterlife communication; 19/20th C.] Source J-d.

8:54. *Holy Bible.* John. Ch. 14. vs. 6; 15. Matthew. Ch. 22. vs. 37-40.
[Jesus Christ's guidance and advice; 1st C.] Source D-b.

9

Tasting Death and Dying

"I seem to have come a long way," I said to myself, accepting the words of Jesus. "It's a way that I never expected; a way that has led me to change inside myself, so that life – and even death – now seem to be so different. But it's also the way that leads me on to more questions.

"So – where are the boundaries now, between life and death? I mean how does life – go through death? Or when does death – end this life?

"Oh, that doesn't really make sense now!" I exclaimed, and went off to make some more coffee. Then I remembered reading a book by Dr George Ritchie, in which he describes his own near death experience.

9:1. Ritchie was quite a young man at the time, and he was very confused when he found himself lying in a bed that was not his own bed. He tried to work out why he was there, but could only remember that he had been feeling strangely light-headed. – So was he ill? Or had he fainted? – Something like that must have happened, but he knew that he had to get up. So he slipped out to look for his clothes – and then saw that a body was still in the bed. He stared at it in surprise, and with increasing horror.[1]

9:2. A sheet had been pulled up over the face of the body, but an arm was partly exposed, and there was a black onyx ring on the hand - an unusual ring that Ritchie recognised was his own. He struggled to understand this as he stared at the flaccid hand: – "Did that mean that

---

9:1. Ritchie, Dr. George: *Return from Tomorrow.* pp. 36-37.
[First experiences while clinically dead; 20th C.]

I was ... ? But I wasn't dead! How could I be dead and still be awake? ... Death was different. Death was – I didn't know."[2]

This was how his near death experience started – and Ritchie was lucky to survive, as he was desperately ill with typhoid. When he had recovered he decided that he should be a doctor, and was eventually taught all the medical aspects of clinical death – in which a person loses the classic signs of life: the pulse, breathing and all brain activity. But Ritchie had not really died as he lay in his hospital bed – and although his account is somewhat dramatic, it is also convincing, and one in a range of well-documented near death experiences.

9:3. Olga Adler, for example, was extremely unhappy when she had her own experience. Her marriage had been a dreadful disaster as she and her baby were repeatedly threatened with violence, and she reached the point when she felt she could not go on – and said:

> I was especially worn-out and went to bed with a death-wish in my mind. ... I was mulling over the day's events when a wave of coldness ... began at my feet and slowly swept over me. ... I was completely immobile. ... It was as if I had become mysteriously paralysed. Then I had the sensation of falling and of being very dizzy. ... There was a buzzing and a crackling noise inside my head. ... I knew I was awake and not dreaming and ... either my mind had become unhinged from worry ... or I was about to die. ... I must have 'blacked out' for a moment, because the next thing I knew was that the dizziness ... was over and I was hovering or floating up near the ceiling. I was very frightened: I thought I was dead.

But Olga had not died – and was surprised to see that the room was less dark than usual. Her husband and the little girl were both asleep, but she could not bring herself to look at her own bed as she was afraid that she would see her body lying there. As she looked away, she found that her view had somehow 'expanded' to include the sky and the

---

9:2. Ibid. pp. 46-48.

scene outside her house, and it all looked quite wonderful. It was so lovely that she began to enjoy her freedom, despite her concern about leaving her baby, and as she rose towards the night sky she glanced down, and saw her own body –

> ... sprawled face-down on the bed. There it was and there was no pretending – I was quite sure I had died.
>
> Suddenly I was travelling at tremendous speed out into space. Now there was no more fear, only exhilaration and freedom, and never a thought of what I had left behind.

So Olga was free from her troubles, and free to discover a different level of peace and happiness. She saw various scenes of life and activity, and even watched some carefree children laughing and playing there – and she sensed the love around them. She also described her own feelings, saying:

> I had now completely accepted the fact that I was dead and was enjoying every marvellous minute. ... It made me happy ... [until I thought] of my baby back on earth and I began to fall back as though I were being reeled-in on a tremendously long fishing-line. I returned with incredible speed and must have 'blacked out' again for an instant because the next thing I knew I landed in my bed with a tremendous repercussion. ...
>
> I fell asleep. When I awoke the remembrance of this experience was very vivid, – not vague and muddled as a dream would be. To this day I remember all the details clearly and accurately. ... I thought of it as 'the night I died'.[3]

Now the Swedish mystic, Swedenborg, explains how some people 'were taken into heaven' in the course of similar experiences:

> 9:4. Certain spirits ... were taken into heaven as to the interiors of their minds; for ... spirits can be taken into

---

9:3. In Crookall, Dr. Robert: *What Happens When You Die*. pp. 48-50.
[Olga Adler's experience; 20th C.]

> heaven and be taught about the happiness of those there. I saw them in the quiescent state for about half an hour, and afterwards they relapsed into their exteriors in which they were before, and also into a recollection of what they had seen. ... Thus they are permitted to learn what truly spiritual and heavenly good is.[4]

But Lorimer asks the question that was niggling in my mind – and his substantive answer explains certain aspects of the near death experience:

> 9:5. Is all this just hallucination or wish-fulfillment? Such is the immediate reaction of many people who have not closely studied the Near Death Experience, and are influenced by a mental climate that hypnotizes us into supposing that only the physical world really exists. Research opinion agrees that [this Experience] ... does occur, but there is no general consensus of theoretical interpretation. Some investigators favour physical explanations such as seizure of the brain's temporal lobe or cerebral anoxia; ... some put forward psychological explanations such as the psychological defence mechanism of depersonalization; a few evangelical Christians denounce the experiences as satanic deception because we are meant to sleep until the last trump, while others believe that the Near Death Experience points to a life beyond death.[5]
>
> 9:6. Some of the more sophisticated have denounced the spiritual world-view as an infantile superstition quite outmoded by the wizardry of modern technology, ... so that human life is stripped of any metaphysical context and purpose: we are born, we live, we perish at death. Or do we?
>
> Modern resuscitation techniques are capable of reviving many people who would have died twenty years ago. Up to 40 per cent of such people report that their conscious

---

9:4. Swedenborg, Emanuel. *Heaven and Hell.* paras. 411-412.
[Swedish scientist/mystic; 17/18th C.] Source J-a.

9:5. Lorimer, David. *Whole in One.* pp. 8-9.
[British, Director of the Scientific and Medical Netwok; 20th C.]

> experience continued in the absence of any outward signs of life such as breathing, heartbeat and measurable electrical brain activity. Such people are clinically dead, although by definition not biologically dead since they return to physical life.[6]

9:7. One person, who had appeared to be dead, was able to provide some evidence – after the event – which proved that her memories of the experience were remarkably accurate:

> A middle-aged woman, apparently dead from a heart attack, found herself floating out-of-body near the ceiling of the ward and watched doctors and nurses working frantically to save her. She drifted out of a window and around the back of the hospital, where something odd caught her eye – a tennis shoe on a window ledge.

When she had been resuscitated, the woman described what she had seen, 'and the shoe was' retrieved from the ledge! Now the writer, Jeffrey Iverson, explains that she 'was a stranger to the city' and had not been near the hospital before her serious heart attack. She was extremely ill on arrival and could not possibly have seen the shoe. So Iverson suggests that this experience proves that there is "an extra dimension of personal reality, a form of consciousness existing outside the brain of the dying person."[7]

Raymond Moody has recorded and studied many near death experiences that developed even further – as in the following examples:

> 9:8. "I stayed around for a while and watched the doctor and nurses working on my body, wondering what would happen. ... I was at the head of the bed, looking at them and at my body...

9:6. Ibid. pp. 7-8.
9:7. Iverson, Jeffrey: *In Search of the Dead.* p. 67.
[British writer; 20th C.]

"And after I floated up, I went through this dark tunnel ... and came out into ... a beautiful place. There were colors – bright colors – not like here on earth, but just indescribable. There were people there, happy people; ... some of them gathered in groups. Some of them were learning. –

"Off in the distance – I could see a city. ... A city of light I guess would be the way to say it. – It was wonderful. There was beautiful music. Everything was just glowing, wonderful. – But if I had entered into this, I think I would never have returned. – I was told that if I went there I couldn't go back, – that the decision was mine."[8]

9:9. "I knew I was dying, ... because I could see my own body there on the operating room table. My soul was out! All this made me feel very bad at first, but then, this really bright light came. ... I just can't describe it. ... I could see clearly, and it wasn't blinding.

"At first, when the light came, I wasn't sure what was happening, but then, it asked, it kind of asked me if I was ready to die. It was like talking to a person, but a person wasn't there ...

"Now, I think that the voice that was talking to me actually realized that I wasn't ready to die; ... it was just kind of testing me more than anything else. Yet, from the moment the light spoke to me, I felt really good – secure and loved. The love which came from it is just unimaginable ..."[9]

9:10. "When the light appeared, the first thing he said to me was 'What do you have to show me that you've done with your life?'... And that's when these flashbacks started. ... The things that flashed back came in the order of my life, and they were so vivid. The scenes were just like you walked

---

9:8. In Moody, Dr. Raymond: *Reflections on Life After Life.* pp. 16-17. [Near death experiences; 20th C.]

9:9. In Moody, Dr. Raymond: *Life After Life.* pp. 63-64. [Near death experiences; 20th C.]

outside and saw them, completely three-dimensional, and in color. And they moved. ... It wasn't like I was watching it all from my perspective at the time. It was like the little girl I saw was somebody else, in a movie. … Yet it was me. I saw myself doing these things, as a child, and they were the exact same things I had done, because I remember them.

"Now, I didn't actually see the light as I was going through the flashbacks; ... yet I knew that he was there with me the whole time … because I felt his presence, and because he made comments here and there. He was trying to show me something in each one of these flashbacks. It's not like he was trying to see what I had done – he knew already – but he was ... putting them in front of me so that I would have to recall them.

"All through this, he kept stressing the importance of love. The places where he showed it best involved my sister. … He showed me some instances where I had been selfish, … but then just as many times where I had really shown love to her and had shared with her. He pointed out to me that I should try to do things for other people, to try my best. There wasn't any accusation. … When he came across times when I had been selfish, his attitude was only that I had been learning from them, too.

"He seemed very interested in things concerning knowledge, too. He kept on pointing out things that had to do with learning, and he did say that I was going to continue learning. ... I think that he was trying to teach me, as we went through those flashbacks."[10]

'Flashbacks' are often described by those who have tasted death – and the Theosophist William Judge offers an explanation as to how the phenomenon arises, saying:

9:11. The whole mass of detail of a life is preserved in the inner man to be one day fully brought back to the conscious memory. ... And even now, imperfect as we are and little as we

---

9:10. Ibid. pp. 65-68.

> know, the experiments in hypnotism show that all the smallest details are registered in what is for the present known as the subconscious mind. The theosophical doctrine is that not a single one of these happenings is forgotten in fact, and at the end of life when the eyes are closed and those about us say we are dead every thought and circumstance of life flash vividly into and across the mind.[11]

9:12. One patient described this experience – when he discussed the accident in which he had virtually died. He told Dr Moody that he had been caught in a terrible 'explosion' at his workplace, and he immediately left his body and watched the scene from above as people rushed to save him. And then, the patient explained, –

> ... his physical surroundings seemed to disappear entirely and a review of his entire life came before him, while he 'discussed' it in the presence of 'Christ'. When asked how long the review seemed to take, he remarked ... that it took an hour at the very least. Yet, when he was told he must return and the review disappeared, he again saw his physical surroundings. The persons he saw coming to rescue him seemed frozen ... in the same positions they had been [in] just as the review started. When he seemed to be returning to his body, the action speeded up again.[12]

Now the Swedish writer, Strindberg, describes his own life review in the most unpleasant terms, saying –

> 9:13. ... in a second the record of my whole past life is enrolled. ... Everything is there! – all the horrors, the most secret sins, the most loathsome scenes in which I have

---

9:11. Judge, William: *The Ocean of Theosophy.* p. 76.
[American Theosophist; 19th C.] Source I-a.

9:12. In Moody, Dr. Raymond: *Reflections on Life After Life.* p. 101.
[Near Death Experiences; 20th C.]

played the chief part. ... I review my whole life from early childhood to this day ...[13]

Strindberg's horror on reviewing his life would not surprise David Lorimer – who defines the process of 'reviewing' very well, and points to the value of these experiences:

> 9:14. Reviewing literally means looking again, achieving a fresh perspective, which may give rise to reflections and the reassessment of values.[14]
>
> 9:15. The deeper the panoramic memory becomes – the more it includes an element of self-judgement and emotional reaction to it, so it more closely resembles the medieval idea of a post mortem encounter or judgement of one's deeds.[15]

This is clearly illustrated by Elaine Winner, who speaks of her own judgemental experience during a life review, and says that –

> 9:16. ... you realize the injustices that you as a person have created in the lives of other people. For me, it was *feeling* those injustices. I *felt* the pain I had caused. You *feel* your iniquities, your shortcomings. You feel it all. You feel yourself judged. But at the same time, you feel loved and forgiven.[16]

And several others have described their judgemental reviews to Dr Moody, as in the following example, –

> 9:17. "... everything in my life just went by for review, you might say. I was really very, very ashamed of a lot of the

---

9:13. Strindberg, Johan August: *Legends*. pp. 203-204.
[Swedish writer; 19/20th C.]
9:14. Lorimer, David: *Whole in One*. p. 16.
[British, Director of the Scientific and Medical Network; 20th C.]
9:15. Ibid. p. 16.
9:16. In Flynn, Charles: *After the Beyond*. p. 83.
[Elaine Winner: near death experience; 20th C.]

things that I experienced because it seemed that I had a different knowledge, that the light was showing me what was wrong, what I did wrong. And it was very real...

"It was like there was a judgement being made and then, all of a sudden, the light became dimmer, and there was a conversation, not in words, but in thoughts. When I would see something, when I would experience a past event, it was like I was seeing it through eyes with (I guess you would say) omnipotent knowledge guiding me, and helping me to see.

"That's the part that has stuck with me, because it showed me not only what I had done, but *even how what I had done had affected other people.* And it wasn't like I was looking at a movie projector because I could *feel* these things; there was feeling, and particularly since I was with this knowledge – I found out that not even your thoughts are lost. – Every thought was there. – Your thoughts are not lost."[17]

The realisation – that our inmost thoughts will be exposed – made Michael Perry exclaim:

> 9:18. How terrifying a prospect! The thoughts of all our hearts will be revealed; they will know what we are *really* like! Could we *bear* to be in a world where everyone would know the secret thoughts of everyone else? Could we bear to be in a world where our *own* secret thoughts and desires came to reality? Could we bear the truth about ourselves?[18]

"Oh no!" I said to myself. "The truth will embarrass and shame us!"

But the heart specialist, Maurice Rawlings, has seen some near death experiences that were even more terrifying. In fact, he had been an atheist before he witnessed the horror of these particular experiences, but he changed his views when he saw what was happening to these patients, and noted the impressive long-term effect that was left with them.

9:17. In Moody, Dr. Raymond: *Reflections on Life After Life.* p. 34-35.
[Near death experiences; 20th C.]

9:18. Perry, Archdeacon Michael: *Psychic Studies: A Christian's View.* p. 129.
[English theologian; 20th C.]

9:19. His first case was that of a postman who collapsed whilst undergoing investigations for a heart problem: his heart had just stopped beating, so the doctor and his assistant went into action. They tried to resuscitate the patient in the usual way, and he seemed to respond quite well, but then there were further problems as his heart was too weak to work properly. Rawlings explains that he had to feed a tiny pacemaker into a vein and up into the heart:

> This takes time, and meant several intervals of a few seconds from the heart massage.
>
> The patient's reaction to his stopping the massage was remarkable. Fully conscious and aware of the pain of severe and repeated pressure on the chest wall – to the extent that ribs might be broken – the usual reaction of a patient is to protest loudly and ask to be left alone. This man screamed for the doctor to continue, because he was in hell! He 'died' several more times in the next hour, and each time he apparently returned to hell, and the terror and distress he experienced was worse than anything in Rawlings' long associations with the dying.
>
> In the end the patient asked Rawlings, the unbeliever, how he could stay out of hell. The doctor had no alternative but to pray with him, foolish as it felt at the time.
>
> The postman recovered, and two days later had forgotten his brush with the infernal regions. Rawlings had not. ... [So his] conclusions about the process of death are the same as those of Moody and Kübler-Ross, with one major difference. He alone of the three was with most of his patients during their death experience and spoke to them in the seconds immediately after the crisis. The others based their reports on interviews conducted ... after the event, and were only informed of good after-death experiences. There is no trace of hell in their books.
>
> Rawlings explains this very simply. The hell-bound patients have such a terrifying time during their out-of-life period that on return their consciousness could not retain the memory without making them insane. The memory is therefore suppressed deep into the sub-conscious ...

Now it would be possible to hypnotise these patients, and awaken their terrible memories; but Rawlings is convinced that this would be a mistake, as the crucial thing about these near death experiences is that they seem to change the patients' lives for the better. For example, Rawlings' postman became a sincere and active Christian after his horrifying experience, and when he had a second heart attack he had a good experience that did not fade from his memory. It resembled the good experiences that are described now by an increasing number of doctors.

Rawlings believes that his patients have, in fact, as many bad as good experiences. But he stresses the fact that the central feature of many good experiences is the vision of a 'being of light', and says: "The 'being of light', identified by patients of the other doctors with Christ or, in those of other religions, with Krishna, Buddha or Mahomet, ... [is] very much part of the 'good' episodes ..."[19]

9:20. The American social scientist, Charles Flynn, suggests that the near death experience should be studied carefully from the viewpoint of other cultures, and he explains that this –

> ... may provide a validation of certain common threads that run through most, if not all, major world religions and many minor ones. In particular, each seems to include – as a central value orientation and belief – a strong concern for others ...[20]

9:21. Certain Hindu beliefs, for example, are quite similar to the views of Westerners who have had near death experiences – and Flynn points out the fact that the most obvious similarity is the ideal of non-violence towards all living creatures. And there are parallels in Buddhist teaching too. For example, the first Buddha was motivated by his extraordinary empathy with all the suffering that he saw about him – whereas those who have experienced the emotions of the life review are filled with a 'new-found compassion and empathy for others'. There are, in addition, certain Buddhist concepts of the nature of the afterlife

---

9:19. Cooper, Wendy and Smith Tom: *Beyond our Limits*. pp. 208-210.
[British, journalist and doctor; 20th C.]

9:20. Flynn, Charles: *After the Beyond*. p. 77.
[American social scientist; 20th C.]

– as described in *The Tibetan Book of the Dead* – which are similar to the understanding of those who have had fully developed near death experiences. Flynn now makes a further comparison, saying –

> ... there appear to be certain similarities between the values and beliefs of Islam and the [near death experience]. ... Throughout the Koran, Allah, the compassionate, the merciful, emphasizes the importance of helping the poor, the widowed, and orphans, and of avoiding selfishness. ... This basic belief in the supreme importance of caring for others is the most striking affirmation that NDErs report.[21]

9:22. 'NDErs' – as Flynn calls them – tend to be more sensitive than they were before their near death experiences, and they seem to have a greater respect for all living things and dislike any form of aggression. For example, one of them said:

> "When I watched violence on the television after the experience, I'll never forget what happened. I couldn't stand it. I had to turn it off. ... The needless loss of life bothered me terribly. ... I think I used to be a little reckless before."[22]

9:23. So 'NDErs' may change, to a greater or lesser extent, as the result of their experiences; and Flynn published an account that demonstrates this change – as it is a tough lad's description of his friend, who had virtually died in a serious accident:

> "When I went in, I expected that, if he wasn't hurt too bad, we'd be kidding around, you know, trade insults and whatnot. But when we came in, he just – had a smile. ... We talked a little bit, and I'm thinking, 'What's happened to him? 'Cause this ain't him.' From knowing him before, you know, there'd have been insults and threats and accusations about whose fault the accident was. ... But there was not one bit of bitterness. ...

9:21. Ibid. pp. 76-77.
9:22. Ibid. p. 39.

> "Before, he'd talk, and he wouldn't really listen to you. But after, he would really listen to you and show a real concern for what you were saying. ...
>
> "Before the incident, I never knew him to be religious; he never showed the least bit of interest. After, he didn't 'get religion', so to speak, but he did do quite a bit of off-duty work with the chaplain. ... Everything he did in that regard was either making life easier for people or looking after their health or well-being. If you had a problem and you'd want to talk, they'd help you out ...
>
> "Now this (change) was immediately after that incident. The day before that incident, if you'd looked at him cross-eyed, he'd have punched you in the mouth. That's one of the reasons it's so significant to me ...
>
> "There was a conversation with a couple of us around, and at the time we asked him, you know, 'What's wrong with you? What's happened to you? You used to be one of the guys.' ... And he said, 'Well, it's still me. There's no difference.' ... And then he did say, 'I saw a light.' That was the word, 'a light' At the time, if you said, 'I saw *the* light', you'd associate it with religion right away. ... So then we said, 'Oh, God, now he's got religion!' That was kind of how we evaluated it at the time. ... But that wasn't it at all. ... I just have never been able to rationalize it."[23]

The change in this boy's character was truly dramatic! But this is not too unusual, and the doctors who work with such patients are often affected by the spiritual significance of their experiences. For example, the American specialist, Elisabeth Kübler-Ross, has spent most of her life in working for the dying – and she says:

> 9:24. I have been criticized for 'getting involved in spiritual matters,' as some people put it, since I was trained in the 'science' of medicine. Others, in reacting to a growing spiritual awareness on my part, have dismissed all my work. ... But it is impossible to ignore the thousands of

---

9:23. Ibid. pp. 45-48.

> stories that dying patients – children and adults alike – have shared with me.

Kübler-Ross has always listened to their descriptions of dying – and to those who have had near death experiences – and she found that she could verify a number of their experiences. She describes all this in some detail:

> I have studied thousands of patients all around the world who have had out-of-body or near-death experiences ...
>
> They often described the very desperate efforts the medical team made during a resuscitation to bring them back and their own attempts to convey that they were really OK, so the would-be rescuers could cease all efforts. They then began to realize that they could perceive everything, but the others present could not hear or perceive *them.*
>
> The second awareness they shared in these experiences was the fact that they were whole again: amputees had their legs again, those who were in wheelchairs could dance and move around without any effort, and blind people could see. We, naturally, checked these facts out by testing patients who had been blind with no light perception for years. To our amazement, they were able to describe the color and design of clothing and jewelry the people present wore [at the scene of the experience]. ... When asked how they could see, people described it with similar words: "It is like you see when you dream and you have your eyes closed."
>
> The third event they shared was an awareness of the presence of loving beings, who always included next of kin who had preceded them in death. ...
>
> How does a critical and skeptical researcher find out if these perceptions are real? We started to collect data from people who were not aware of the death of a loved one, and who then later shared the presence of that person when they themselves were ... [dying].[24]

9:24. Kübler-Ross Dr. Elisabeth: *On Children and Death.* pp. 206-208.
[American specialist for the dying. 20th C.]

> 9:25. Shortly before children die there is often a very 'clear moment', as I call it. Those who have remained in a coma since the accident or after surgery open their eyes and seem very coherent. Those who have had great pain and discomfort are very quiet and at peace. It is in those moments that I asked them if they were willing to share with me what they were experiencing.
>
> "Yes, everything is all right now. Mommy and Peter are already waiting for me," one boy replied. With a contented little smile, he slipped back into a coma from which he made the transition we call death.
>
> I was quite aware that his mother had died at the scene of the accident, but Peter had not died. He had been brought to a special burn unit in another hospital. ... [But] I accepted the boy's information and determined to look in on Peter. It was not necessary, however, because as I passed the nursing station there was a call from the other hospital to inform me that Peter had died a few minutes earlier.[25]

Death is described in gentle terms by the spirit of Myers, who sees it now from beyond this world, saying –

> 9:26. ... death is an incident or a mere episode which we regard with a certain tenderness and not with any pain. To human beings, however, death should seem as a night at an inn, as a halt on the long road home.
>
> It may be a night of feverish insomnia, or heavy with fear; a night full of strange dreams, or a period of almost undisturbed peace. Always there is, contained in it, a time of stillness, of sinking gloriously into rest. Nevertheless, the soul eventually wakens to a new day. And, in dawn and dark alike, he is surrounded by certain of his discarnate kindred, by some of those who are woven into the pattern of his destiny.[26]

9:25. Ibid. p. 210.

9:26. In Cummins, Geraldine: *The Road to Immortatlity*. p. 78.
[F. W. H. Myers: afterlife communication; 19/29th C.] Source J-d.

> 9:27. For, wherever he may journey after death, always will he be caught again into the design of which he is a part, always will he find again, however deep his temporary oblivion or however varied his experience, certain human souls who were knit into his earth life, who were loved deeply ... in those bygone days.[27]

So death can be a natural, simple process – a 'passing on' within a continuing life that has its meaning, and direction, and is usually shared with loved ones.

9:28. And now another spirit – the spirit of Helen Salter – describes the ease of her own death, saying –

> ... it was so incredibly easy and painless. There was only one very brief nightmare, when I wanted to get back into my body in order to return to you. An instant's bad dream. That's all death was to me. After it, almost immediately, there came the unimaginable moment – a welcoming mother and father. Oh, just as they were in a long gone past. ... You can't imagine what a feeling of safety they gave me. Freedom at once from that inert thing, my body – freedom from the fear of the unknown ...
>
> In the past we, you and I, have wondered what our arrival to this level would be like. But nothing we supposed came up to that beautiful ... feeling I had with these two protectors waiting for me. That's why I have called it the unimaginable moment.[28]

9:29. And a third spirit, Hilda, carefully explains that –

> ... at the moment of death there was no pain. When I knew I was dying I ... wasn't unhappy or frightened or lonely; for I saw my father, my sisters, my brother, whom I had thought of as dead – and by dead, I meant asleep till Judgement Day.

9:27. Ibid. p. 89.

9:28. Cummins, Geraldine: *Swan on a Black Sea.* p. 139.
[Helen Salter: afterlife communication; 20th C.] Source J-d.

But Hilda's family were all still alive, and waiting in 'a pale mist' to welcome her. And Hilda carries on, stressing the point that –

> ... one of the happiest moments of my earth-life was the moment of death. Of course, it was much longer than a moment, but the wonderful freedom from pain, the feeling of peace and security when I saw my loved dead alive, smiling, waiting for me, drove away loneliness [and] fear.[29]

In contrast to Hilda's experience, the spirit of Julia was quite alone when she died – as she says:

> 9:30. I found myself free from my body. It was such a strange new feeling. I was standing close to the bedside on which my body was lying; I saw everything in the room just as before I closed my eyes. I did not feel any pain in 'dying'; I felt only a great calm and peace. ...
>
> I waited about a little; then the door opened and Mrs H. came in. She was very sad; she addressed my poor body as if it was myself. I was standing looking at her, but all her thoughts were upon the poor old body I had left behind. It seemed so absurd. ...
>
> Then I felt as though a great warm flood of light had come into the room, and I saw an angel. She ... gently touched me and said: "We must go."[30]

"But where do we go?" I asked myself quietly. "Where do we *really* go to – when we die?" And I turned to a wonderful book that was inspired by the spirit of Frances, and found a conversation – between Frances and a child spirit, Jeannie – which led me into the life that lies before us:

9:29. In Cummins, Geraldine: *They Survive.* p. 139.
[Hilda: afterlife communication; 20th C.] Source J-d.

9:30. In Stead, W. T: Letters from Julia. pp. 1-2.
[Julia: afterlife communication; 19th C.]

9:31. "I've just realised something. … I'm dead," [said Jeannie]. Her gaze held mine. "We're all dead. That's true, isn't it?"

"Yes. It's true, Jeannie," I answered her, "but you see, we're really more alive than ever. You've only got rid of your sick old body and found a new one." ...

She accepted this.

"I suppose this is ... Heaven."

"It's the *beginning* of Heaven, Jeannie."

"You mean we're only *starting*? ... We're not *there* yet?"

"Not in the Heaven you mean. … But we're on our way there." …

"But it's so beautiful here. Everyone's so kind and ... angelic."

"We're certainly not angels," I retorted and we both laughed at that. She was quiet suddenly.

"Then where's God?" she demanded.

"Much too far away for us even to see Him. We're not ready for His Glory yet. But we're all going forwards, on towards His Heaven." ...

"You mean, His Heaven could be better than this?"

"Oh, much, much better! Far more beautiful and full of Light, and angels, Angels of Light." ... She smiled ...[31]

9:32. "I suppose this is Life Everlasting?" – [Jeannie continued]. ... I had to think out my reply.

"We have always been in Life Everlasting, Jeannie, even when we were on earth. Our souls, our true Selves, always lived from experience to experience. This is only another *part* of experience."

She took this very seriously. "And Heaven will be another experience?"

"There will be many experiences I believe, my dear, even before we reach Heaven," – [said Frances.][32]

9:31. In Greaves, Helen: *Testimony of Light.* p. 92.
[Frances Banks: afterlife communication; 19/20th C.] Source K-a.
9:32. Ibid. p. 94.

10

To Judgement and Connection

Frances was undoubtedly a very wise soul, as she explained the meaning of 'death' and 'life everlasting' in a straightforward and simple way that satisfied Jeannie's curiosity; but we, like Jeannie, are curious about these concepts while we are living in this world, and we puzzle over them from time to time without finding the simple answers.

Now the common Christian view is that we may pass on, somehow, to 'a life after death'. But Raynor Johnson describes our difficulties in understanding what this really means, – saying:

> 10:1. The majority of people who accept the Christian teaching of a life after death appear to have few ideas about its nature and characteristics. The subject has been clothed in vague symbolic language, and by and large, the Churches have made very little effort to enlighten people. All too often, when bereavement comes, people are assured that their loved ones are "with Christ" ... or are "serving God with fuller powers." These things may be true, but those who wish to bring their minds to bear upon the problem of human destiny must feel profoundly dissatisfied with such answers. It is easy for the Church to say, "We know very little, and must be content to have faith in God until he chooses to unveil these mysteries to us." This attitude of making a virtue out of pious ignorance is so out of tune with today's scientific spirit that it does not commend itself to men. ...

> With death a certainty for everyone, men rightly wish to know all they can about their future journey.[1]

10:2. "That's very true," I said to myself. "We should look at death in some other ways – to help us to understand." So I scanned through the pages of *Seth Speaks*, and came across his suggestion that we are, in fact, dying while we are still alive, as our bodies are in –

> ... a state of becoming, and death is a part of this process of becoming. You are alive now, a consciousness knowing itself, sparkling with cognition amid a debris of dead and dying cells; alive while the atoms and molecules of your body die and are reborn, ... and you scarcely give the matter a thought. So you are ... alive despite, and yet because of, the multitudinous deaths and rebirths that occur within your body in physical terms.[2]
>
> 10:3. What you want to know, therefore, is what happens when your consciousness is directed away from physical reality.[3]

"You really do die," I thought – and remembered that one of Dr Fiore's patients had described this happening. Fiore had hypnotised him in the usual way, and asked him to recall the details of his last death, and he said –

> 10:4. "... my foot slips from under me ... and I'm hanging there ... from the rope. ... I'm beginning to scream. ... I can see way, way down. It's all ... rocks and water. ... I'm falling ... I'm just falling. ... I'm ... I don't know. ...
>
> "I can see my body falling but I'm ... not afraid any more. It's as though I were floating. ... It falls onto the rocks ... my face is down on the rocks but I don't – I don't feel anything. I was very afraid, but now ... I'm just surprised. ...

10:1. Johnson, Dr. Raynor: *A Religious Outlook for Modern Man*. p. 164.
[British physicist; 20th C.]

10:2. In Roberts, Jane: *Seth Speaks*. p. 138.
[Seth: Spirit teacher, through medium, Jane Roberts; 20th C.]

10:3. Ibid. pp. 140-141.

I don't know where I am. ... The body was falling but I stopped falling."[4]

This patient's inmost, conscious self had apparently left his body *before* it hit the rocks! And I found some other communications in which spirits explained that they had left their bodies without suffering the 'pangs of death' – as in this soldier's account:

> 10:5. We seemed to go down on all sides, British and German alike, tanks and guns and planes. ... I prayed for help, ... and I knew we couldn't escape; but prayer seemed to strengthen me and I felt that nothing really mattered so desperately, excepting the feeling of evil. ... I could not name it or explain it in words. It seemed to meet us from the sand and hang all around the tank battle. I felt sick and miserable, and then it passed off and I found myself standing outside the tank talking to my Colonel. He seemed unconscious of the bullets that were raining down upon us ... and said: "Don't you see, Kit, we are dead."[5]

In another account, a spirit explained how he had been mystified by his own death. He could only remember that he had been crossing a street:

> 10:6. "It all happened so sudden. ... I saw a crowd of people all standing looking down at something. I 'ad a look with the crowd and saw someone who looked exactly like me! ...
>
> "I thought, 'That's a coincidence. That fellow looks the same as I do.' ... Then I realized that my wife was there, crying her eyes out. She didn't seem to realize I was standing beside her.
>
> "They put [the] body in an ambulance, and the wife got in, and some nurse. I got in and sat with my wife and she

---

10:4 In Fiore, Dr. Edith: *You have been here Before.* pp. 235-236.
[Death memory, recounted under hypnosis; 20th C.]

10:5. In Dowding, Lord Air Chief Marshall: *Many Mansions.* pp. 32-33.
[Afterlife communication; 20th C.]

> didn't seem to realize I was sitting there at all. Then gradually it came on me that that was me lying down there.
>
> "I went to the hospital. Of course they put me in the mortuary. I didn't like that at all. So I got out quick and went home. There was the wife, [and] Mrs Mitchen ... trying to comfort her. I think that was the worst time. ... Nobody took any notice."[6]

It must be very disappointing when your wife fails to notice you under these circumstances. On the other hand, it is somehow disturbing to think that a newly-freed spirit could be hanging around with those who are still alive; yet this is clearly described in *The Tibetan Book of the Dead* – which says:

> 10:7. About this time (the deceased man) can ... hear all the weeping and wailing of his friends and relatives, and, although he can see them and can hear them calling upon him, they cannot hear him calling upon them, so he goeth away displeased.[7]

Now an army officer, who was killed in the Second World War, was less disconcerted when his own men failed to notice him – saying:

> 10:8. I got back to our fellows and I soon realised what had happened when they didn't see me; but I was so interested in finding myself unchanged that I hadn't time to think of anything else. I wanted to tell them not to fear death and all that, but I couldn't, ... so I wandered off wondering what to do next.
>
> I didn't exactly want to leave them to it, but there didn't seem to be any alternative, so I did.[8]

10:6. In Randall, Neville: *Life after Death*. p. 35.
[Ted Butler: afterlife communication; 20th C.]

10:7. In Evans-Wentz, Dr: *Tibetan Book of the Dead*. pp. 101-102.
[Tibetan Buddhist/Bon Teaching; pre-8th C.] Source B-b.

10:8. In Dowding, Lord Air Chief Marshall: *Many Mansions*. p.33.
[Afterlife communication; 20th C.]

Another spirit mentions the very same problem – amongst some others:

> 10:9. "I was going round to various people that I had known, trying to tell them that I was alive and well, and they just didn't realize I was there. ... I had to adjust myself to the fact that I had a body which … was not a real body from the point of view of Earth. Therefore I was in what I suppose one would term a spiritual body, and yet I was not particularly spiritual. I was puzzled and bewildered."[9]
>
> 10:10. "I just couldn't understand it. ... There was a terrible lightness about myself. ... I remember vividly sitting beside a river and looking at myself, and not seeing myself. I could see no reflection. I thought, 'That seems most extraordinary. I have a body and yet it has no reflection.' "[10]

The ancient Buddhist-Bon teaching in *The Tibetan Book of the Dead* describes this phenomenon too, explaining that –

> 10:11. ... if thou lookest into water, or into mirrors, thou wilt see no reflection of thy face or body; nor doth thy body cast any shadow. Thou hast discarded now thy gross material body of flesh and blood.[11]

The Tibetan lamas like to read their sacred *Book of the Dead* to those who are dying – and even to those who have recently died – to guide them through a good death, and to help them understand, in Eastern terms, the experiences of the afterlife. We have no such guidance in the West; but we do have an increasing number of spirit communications that explain our transition into the afterlife. For example, a spirit – who communicated through the medium, Miss Wingfield – explained that the stream of our conscious awareness is not

---

10:9. In Randall, Neville: *Life after Death.* p. 34.
[Afterlife communication; 20th C.]

10:10. Ibid. p. 34.

10:11. In Evans-Wentz, Dr: *The Tibetan Book of the Dead.* p. 177.
[Tibetan Buddhist/Bon teaching; pre-8th C.] Source B-b.

interrupted by a sudden death, whereas there is usually a period of 'rest' from conscious awareness when the death has followed a long illness:

> 10:12. If [the body] is suddenly cast off, consciousness never seems to be lost. They that pass thus suddenly from that life into this are sometimes even unaware that the change they feared has taken place. It is when the spirit has struggled and struggled to be free – wearing its rest away with pain and suffering, not to itself but to the body it inhabits – that rest is needed for a while.[12]

10:13. The spirit of Frances had suffered a slow and distressing illness that culminated in her death, and she had made no contact with her friend, Helen Greaves, for several weeks; she then explained, telepathically, that she was resting from the illness that had destroyed her body, and that her life was now very peaceful. She was quite content to rest, though she was aware that some other 'souls' were arriving from the world – and from 'other places' – to be tended gently after difficult transitions.[13]

Frances also described her earliest stage of recovery, – saying:

> 10:14. As soon as I was able to bring myself to a conscious state of mind, after my withdrawal from my worn-out body, I knew I was the *same in essence.* True, I felt light, and there was a new sense of freedom that was bewildering. ... It was a strange, almost eerie experience. ... I found that I was lying in an open porch with a vista of blue and silver before me. – This was beautiful beyond words and calming to my spirit. Trouble, anxiety and all sense of loss abated; a great feeling of peace enwrapped me.
>
> "*This is it,*" I kept assuring myself in wonder, "I have made the Change!"[14]

10:12. Wingfield, K: *More Guidance from Beyond.* p. 41.
[Spirit guidance, through medium, K. Wingfield; 19/20th C.]

10:13. In Greaves, Helen: *Testimony of Light.* p. 27.
[Frances Banks: afterlife communication; 19/20th C.] Source K-a.

10:14. Ibid. pp. 29-30.

'The Change' is the term that Frances used to describe the transition from an earth-life to the afterlife. But when the elderly die, their transition is often preceded by a period of preparation so that they are led gently towards their death, – as explained by the spirit, 'E.K.'

> 10:15. The normal experience is neither unhappy nor difficult. As old age comes on the two forms of being represented in the body begin to draw apart. Failing health and failing senses are the symptoms of this withdrawal. … When the final breath is drawn the process of severance is practically complete and is rounded off by unconsciousness. Where death comes gradually and naturally like this, one wakes quietly in the new conditions after an interval of a few days. One is fully through, as we say, and although the newcomer has to be cared for and kept quiet until the new rhythms of his [spirit] body are fully established, he soon becomes strong and vigorous and ready to begin his new life. The transition, like all natural processes, should not be interfered with by violence or haste. Death is a kind of birth and it should proceed with a quiet inevitableness and not be accompanied by pain or distress. Much of the apparent suffering of a death-bed is not consciously felt by the sufferer. His real life is already half retired from the mortal body, and neither experiences nor records its pangs.[15]

This description of 'the Change' may seem too good to be true; but the Reverend Charles Thomas published many spirit communications, and several of them suggest that a soul can pass very gently from this world. For example, one communicator says:

> 10:16. Before finally leaving earth I seemed to be dreaming, and yet it was not wholly a dream. It seemed as if I had come here before the final separation from my physical body. I was only partly conscious towards the last, only half within the body; for my soul was already freeing

---

10:15. In Sherwood, Jane: *The County Beyond*. pp. 60-61.
['E. K.': afterlife communication; 20th C.]

itself. Nor did it seem wholly strange to me when I found myself here. I must have frequently come during sleep; for I could now remember that I had been here previously.[16]

This gentle, dreamy account stands in contrast to a somewhat analytical discussion between the spirit of G.F. Scott and his medium, Jane Sherwood. Scott starts the ball rolling, by saying, –

10:17. "… let us go on examining the facts. ... I have here the things which escaped from my body. Taking the crudest first, there is life, just the sheer power of feeling, moving and being in a body; then there is emotion – desires and purposes, to drive the body on its various occasions; then thought, the power to understand, to reflect, to plan, to reason; and lastly, there is a mysterious co-ordination of all these activities which is I myself, a personality which can look on at all these other activities and approve or criticise them. I give you that wretched [physical] body because I have most of the other things here and they are still in bodily form. Remember what was lost from earth-life, emotion, thought and the ego itself. These were all in the body of escape which detached itself from my injured physical body...

"Go back now to my abandoned body. Apparently it has all the chemical elements within it as before, yet they all begin to function differently. The only possible inference is surely that from each of the atoms forming my erstwhile body something has escaped." ...

"Then life," I said, "is not some mysterious spiritual essence which leaves the body at death?"

"No. What leaves the body is the facsimile of the familiar earth body, built up atom upon atom on that body, but functioning in a different world of movement; at a more rapid rate, if you like, or in another dimension of being. What death does is to set this body free from its dependence

---

10:16. In Thomas, Rev. Charles D: *Life Beyond Death with Evidence*. p. 61. [Afterlife communication; 19th C.]

> on physical atoms, molecules and cells so that it can lift into an invisible form of activity. Do you follow?"
> "I think so," I replied.[17]

Now the spirit of Sir Donald Tovey joins, as it were, our present discussion, saying:

> 10:18. Death, after all, is like another birth into another world, excepting that one's new body is a counterpart of the lately vacated physical body. When you are born on earth, you enter a body provided by your parents; when you are born into the World of Spirit, you emerge in the counterpart of that body at whatever stage it has reached, excepting that it is without defect for defects are characteristics of the world of matter and not of the world of spirit. Does that sound too far-fetched? ... You will understand one day...[18]

Some of us may find it difficult to understand these concepts, while others have not even heard of them. And Polhem – who was a friend of the mystic Swedenborg – had yet another problem, as he was confused at his own funeral by the discrepancy between certain Christian beliefs and the reality of his own experience. – Swedenborg describes this dilemma:

> 10:19. Polhem ... saw his coffin, and those who were there, and the whole procession, and also when his body was laid in the grave; and, in the meantime, he spoke with me, asking why they buried him when he was still alive; and he heard, also, when the priest said he should be resuscitated at the last judgement, and yet he had been resuscitated for some time; and he marvelled that such a belief should exist, as that men should be resuscitated at the last judgement, when he was still alive; and that the

---

10:17. In Sherwood, Jane: *The Country Beyond.* pp. 49-50.
[G. F. Scott: afterlife communication; 20th C.]

10:18. In Brown, Rosemary: *Immortals at my Elbow.* p. 104.
[Sir Donald Tovey: afterlife communication; 20th C.] Source J-e.

> body should rise again, when yet he himself was sensible of being in a body.[19]

Polhem clearly understood that he had survived his own death.

10:20. But many souls remain bewildered – and I was interested to learn that some ancient funereal rites in Tibet were specifically designed to help the departing souls understand that they had 'died'. Evans-Wentz describes these rites, explaining that –

> ... there is much interesting ritual. Thus, when the officiating *lama* is preparing to assist at the removal of the corpse from the house, he presents a 'scarf of honour' to the corpse and, addressing the corpse as the deceased, ... warns it that it is dead and that its ghost must not haunt the place or trouble living relatives, saying in conclusion, ... "Come this way!"
>
> Then, as the *lama* begins to lead the funeral procession, he takes hold of one end of the long scarf, the other end having been tied to the corpse, and begins to chant a liturgy. ... From time to time the chief *lama* looks back to invite the spirit to accompany the body and to assure it that the route is in the right direction. ... Such priestly guiding of the deceased's spirit is for the laity alone, for the spirits of deceased *lamas*, having been trained in the doctrines, ... know the right path and need no guidance.[20]

When I read these words I felt that the spirit, Frances, would have needed little or no guidance as she passed through her death and into the afterlife. She had trained herself in the paths of service and dedication while she was on earth, working primarily as a nun - and also as the principal of a teachers' training college in Africa, then as a lay tutor-organiser in a large prison in England, and finally with the Churches' Fellowship for Psychical and Spiritual Studies. She had also

---

10:19. Swedenborg, *Emanuel: Minor Spiritual Diary*. 5. para. 4752.
[Swedish scientist/mystic; 17/18th C.] Source J-a.

10:20. Evans-Wentz, Dr: *The Tibetan Book of the Dead.* pp. 24-25.
[British anthropologist; 19/20th C.] Source B-b.

developed her spiritual and psychic skills to such an extent that she was an understanding and true teacher.

10:21. Then after the period of rest that followed her death, Frances described her early afterlife experiences – through Helen Greaves – in their book, *Testimony of Light.* She explained that she had somehow sensed that her cremation was taking place on earth, and she yearned to be with 'those friends' who had been so dear to her – and who were so affectionate in return – and she found that she was transported in thought to be with them at the service:

> I was grateful to those who ... [were] present at these last rites. I gloried in the beautiful flowers. ... I longed to say 'thank you' to those who had made my last days on earth comfortable. ... I felt 'lifted up' in mind and soul because I was being missed, because there was so much affection and because Richard was wisely making this a hopeful farewell, [in his address,] without the heavy burden of emphasised sorrow ... which would have saddened and distressed me.
>
> Then, just as inexplicably as I had become a part of these scenes, it all faded. I was lying here, at peace.
>
> "So this is death!" I recall saying. ... "*Life separated by density* - that is all!"
>
> Elation filled me. I knew now that I could 'tune in' and even 'see' the earthplane, if desire was strong enough to loosen the barrier between your world and my new one. The possibility rested with me. ... Now I dwelt in a realm of Thought; and such thought Power, when rightly implemented, can penetrate the dense plane which is the world of human habitation. ... I could still keep in touch ...
>
> By the time the London Memorial Service was held I had 'progressed' sufficiently in this method of extension of consciousness to be able to make my presence known to those who could open their minds to this new dimension of thought. I felt that certain present 'saw' me or were 'aware' of my presence. ... To me this was uplifting and comforting.[21]

10:21. In Greaves, Helen: *Testimony of Light.* pp. 31-32.
[Frances Banks: afterlife communication; 19/20th C.] Source K-a.

10:22. Now the medium, Rosemary Brown, was a little startled when she 'saw' the spirit of her father standing close to his coffin at the funeral. She had been concentrating on her grieving mother – sending waves of comfort to 'enfold' her – when she first noticed him. And although she was very psychic, Rosemary found herself staring at him:

> "What's the matter?" he asked. "You look as if you are seeing a ghost, and I'm not a ghost, I'm your father."
>
> This made me a little worried, as it seemed he did not know he had passed over, [Rosemary explained], but his next words reassured me.
>
> "As for that," he said, pointing to his coffin, "Blow that! Thank God I'm out of that old body at last."[22]

"Well, he seems okay about leaving his body," I said to myself, "and it sounds as though he's the same old character – as when he died." And then I remembered that the spirit Julia – who communicated through William Stead in the 19th century – had said something about a soul retaining its 'apparent' personality after dying:

> 10:23. When the soul leaves the body it remains exactly the same as when it was in the body, ... [and the] extraordinary thing which came to my knowledge when I passed over was the difference between the apparent man and the real self ...
>
> [The real self] is built up ... more by the use it makes of the mind than by the use it makes of the body. There are here, [in the afterlife], men who had seemed to be vile and filthy to their fellows, who are far, far, far superior, even in purity and holiness, to men who in life kept an outward veneer of apparent goodness while the mind rioted in all wantonness. It is the mind that makes character. It is the mind that is far more active, more potent than the body, which is but a poor instrument at

---

10:22. Brown, Rosemary: *Immortals at my Elbow.* p. 159.
[British medium/musician; 20th C.] Source J-e.

> best. Hence the thoughts and intents of the heart, the imaginations of the mind, these are the things by which we are judged.[23]

Our judgement in the afterlife is now described by the spirit 'E.K.' – in a way that suggests that the self-judgement, in a near death review, is only a foretaste of what we will experience after death. 'E.K.' explains that our –

> 10:24. ... thoughts begin to be much concerned with the life on earth which has been left behind. The [memory] ... grows in strength, the scenes and events of the past life begin to come vividly back in terms of their *feeling* content and in a manner never experienced before. In the course of one's life on earth, experiences are reflected in consciousness and one never doubts that one has realized the whole of them. But the impressions of people, events and acts which now come crowding back are far more real and comprehensive than when they were actually experienced ...

The spirit 'E.K.' then says that it is 'difficult to explain' this.[24]

But Paul Beard – who was the President of the London College of Psychic Studies – would be able to understand, as he has studied a number of spirit communications which deal with this subject, and says:

> 10:25. Communicators clearly find difficulty in conveying this experience of judgement in all its depth, so they frequently make use of simplified pictures and symbols to help us to understand; ... and in some manner the traveller is shown every single event in his life as it really was and not as he thought it had been. The record is made straight wherever he misunderstood it.[25]

10:23. In Stead, W. T: *Letters from Julia.* pp. 9-10.
[Julia: afterlife communication; 19th C.]

10:24. In Sherwood, Jane: *The Country Beyond.* p. 135.
[E. K': afterlife communication; 20th C.]

10:25. Beard, Paul: *Living On.* p. 99.
[British, President of the College of Psychic Studies; 20th C.] Source K-b.

Now the gifted seer, Swedenborg, was able to observe and describe the details of several judgement scenes:

> 10:26. There were some who had deceived others by wicked arts and had committed thefts. The deceits and thefts of these were ... enumerated in detail, many of which had been known to scarcely any in the world except themselves. These deeds they confessed, because they were plainly set forth, with every thought, intention, pleasure and fear which occupied their minds at the time.
>
> There were others who had accepted bribes, and had rendered venal judgements, who were similarly explored from their memory, and from it everything they had done from the beginning to the end of their office was reviewed. Every detail in regard to what and how much they had received, as well as the time, and their state of mind and intention, were brought to their recollection ...
>
> Others who had enticed maidens to shame or had violated chastity were called to a like judgement; and the details of their crimes were drawn forth from their memory and reviewed. The very faces of the maidens and women were also exhibited as if present, with the places, words and intentions, and this as unexpectedly as when an apparition is seen...
>
> In a word, to each evil spirit all his evils, villainies, robberies, artifices, and deceits are made clear, and are brought forth from the very memory of them, and his guilt is fully established; nor is there any possible room for denial, because all the circumstances are exhibited together. Moreover, I have learned from someone's memory, when it was seen and inspected by angels, what his thoughts had been ... as they arose from day to day. From these examples it can be established that man carries with him all of his memory, and that nothing can be so concealed in the world as not to be disclosed after death, which is done in the company of many, according to the Lord's words:

> There is nothing concealed that shall not be uncovered, and nothing secret that shall not be known; therefore what ye have spoken in the dark shall be heard in the light and what ye have spoken in the ear shall be proclaimed on the housetops.
>
> *Luke. Ch.12: vs.2–3.*

> Let no one believe, then, that there is anything that a man has ever thought in himself or done in secret that can be concealed after death; but let him believe that all things and each single thing are then laid open as clear as day.[26]

Paul Beard explains that in addition to a man's –

> 10:27. ... own deeds and the thoughts and feelings connected with them, he is also now obliged ... to experience within himself the thoughts and feelings, the pains and pleasures which his actions caused in the lives of other people; exactly what he caused them to feel he, in turn, feels in himself now. This is a surprising and very disconcerting event.[27]

10:28. Now the Rosicrucian, Max Heindel, agrees that 'everything is remembered'.[28]

And he says that –

> 10:29. ... the man has all the feelings that it is possible for him to have as, one by one, the scenes pass before him. ... When he comes to a point where he has injured someone, he himself feels the pain as the injured person felt it. He lives through all the sorrow and suffering he has caused to

---

10:26. Swedenborg, Emanuel: Heaven and Hell. paras. 462[b]-463.
[Swedish scientist/mystic; 17/18th C.] Source J-a.

10:27. Beard, Paul: *Living On*. p.99.
[British, President of the College of Psychic Studies; 20th C.] Source K-b.

10:28. Heindel, Max: *Rosicrucian Cosmo-Conception*. p. 101.
[American Rosicrucian; 19/20th C.] Source H-b.

> others and learns just how painful is the hurt and how hard to bear is the sorrow he has caused.[29]

This clearly relates to the Oriental concepts of Karma, as Paul Brunton writes:

> 10:30. For the first time, perhaps, he sees himself not only as others see him but also as the impersonal power of karma sees him. During this time he comes face to face with the *consequences* for other persons of his acts whilst on earth, consequences of which he was often quite unaware or in which he was often egotistically uninterested. ... A great remorse overwhelms him.

"Overwhelms '*him*'," I muttered to myself. "These writers treat us all as males! But 'remorse' will clearly overwhelm us all. So I must find out more about it."

Brunton now explains that every soul must overcome its 'remorse', and its wayward emotions and habitual 'self-deception', so that it can truly understand its recent life. This will enable the soul to see its own mistakes and sins, which it had failed to recognise on earth, and it will come to understand the true nature of all the people with whom it was associated. They, too, will have been projecting their own self-images and actions into the world, and the soul will have been deluded by them as well as by itself. Taking this all into account, the world and its happenings – as experienced by the soul – was really a world of the soul's own fabrication, with all its sad mistakes and misunderstandings.[30]

There is still more to be considered on this subject, as Brunton says –

> 10:31. ... although we may certainly blame man himself for some of the evil and suffering in the world, ... understand that this whole world and not merely a part of it – the part which pleases us – is a divine manifestation. ... We must face facts bravely and realize that the divine will is ultimately behind the whole universe and consequently

10:29. Ibid. p. 108.

10:30. Brunton, Dr Paul: *The Wisdom of the Overself.* p. 128.
[British writer on ancient philosophy; 19/20th C.] Source A-d.

> must even be behind its horror and agony and wickedness too. Not that these things have been deliberately created but that they have indirectly been made inevitable through the inner necessity, the karmic continuity of ... a succession of finite incarnate lives.

When these 'incarnate' beings were evolving on earth – Brunton continues – it was inevitable that they would compete for their individual wants by 'struggling' against each other. And we, too, were with them. As we evolved, we increasingly recognised our individuality and were fully prepared to get what we wanted by fair means or foul. We chose – and now choose – how we want to live our own lives, however sinful they are. But our 'sin' leads us on to further 'suffering' – to karmic training, as it were – so that we learn that the better paths will lead us to a greater peace and happiness. If our behaviour were to be controlled from some external source, we would be nothing more than mindless puppets.

Brunton then suggests that we will understand why our world is a world of conflict if we remember that countless beings are all struggling for themselves at their own levels. We have found it all too easy to choose the evil ways of selfishness. Over time, however, we will evolve through our experiences and develop our better traits; we will understand ourselves, and find increasing peace as our 'strife' and conflicts lessen; and then we will realise that our problems with ourselves – and with others – arose from our failure to understand the purpose of living our lives on the earth plane.[31]

And Brunton has more to say on these vital topics, as he feels that our understanding has been so limited. We are, he explains, actually living in –

> 10:32. ... a regulated world-system, an orderly cosmos, and hence one in which things are related to other things and beings to other beings in a vast network that stretches through all time and across all space. The universe is both a collection of forces which are unable to exist separately but act and interact upon each other, and a collection of things which do not stand by themselves but are intrinsically linked as parts of the whole.

10:31. Ibid. pp. 174-176.

We are wrong – Brunton says – when we think that anyone or anything is really on its own. It may look as though we are separate beings, and that there is separation between all things; but this is not so in the underlying reality:

> Human life, particularly, is like a gigantic moving wheel which contains within itself countless tiny cogged wheels revolving continuously against each other. The great wheel is God, the World-Mind, whilst the little ones are individual men. And just as the imperfect or irregular working of a single wheel affects the working of its neighbouring ones, which in their turn pass on something of the trouble to their neighbours, so does the daily life of mankind feel the benefits and disadvantages of its own inter-dependence. The to-and-fro flow of exchanges – mental, emotional and physical – between a man and his human environment is constant and unavoidable. He literally shares life with others. The belief in the existence of a completely separate person is really a superficial one ...
>
> Physically we are all so inter-dependent on each other in the present, so intimately related with the entire procession of all mankind in the past; mentally, we are all so constantly inter-changing our ideas and so frequently inter-circulating our feelings; and karmically, all our historic lives are so inter-penetrating and linked in such a large network of circumstances, that it is more correct to view the person as being only one particular aspect of the total unified existence out of millions. ... Just as all the countless cells in a human body really belong to its single existence, so all the countless creatures in the cosmos really belong to the One Existence ...
>
> If therefore we wish to think truly of our self we must think of it in terms of the Whole.[32]

David Lorimer now takes up the subject, saying:

10:32. Ibid. pp. 218-221.

> 10:33. Our customary state is one of limited and contracted self-consciousness. We set up boundaries between the inside and the outside, self and other, thus tending to isolate and alienate ourselves from the oneness of reality ...
>
> Individual self-consciousness ... might be said to arise out of unitive consciousness and erect protective barriers around itself; nevertheless, ... it remains semi-permeable and can interact with other individual selves. ... When, however, unitive consciousness is experienced, the boundaries dissolve and there dawns the realization that one's ground is the unitive consciousness ... out of which other individual self-consciousnesses also arise: the many arise out of the One and are linked to each other through participation in that One.
>
> This was the theory of the greatest Neo-Platonist, Plotinus. ... The Universal Soul is undivided, individuals being linked in a sympathy bearing witness to underlying unity behind the apparent separateness. ... Thus when awareness is focused in this higher sphere, the transcendent unity will be directly experienced. ... In other words, empathetic resonance naturally arises between souls united in the same universal field of consciousness. The common ground of being provides the immediate conductor of such resonance, thus enabling us to enter empathetically into the experiences of other self-consciousnesses.[33]

The Indian Sufi, Hazrat Inayat Khan, would support these views – as he gives further details on the way in which we share conscious experiences through the 'universal field of consciousness', saying:

> 10:34. To put it plainly, ... the first thing that we must understand is that the soul is an individual portion of the all-pervading consciousness.

The 'individual soul' may appear to be completely on its own – Khan continues – but it is, in reality, connected with the over-all consciousness,

---

10:33. Lorimer, David: *Whole in One*. pp. 89-91.
[British, Director of the Scientific and Medical Network; 20th C.]

and is therefore bound within the 'universal spirit' – which some might call God. Despite this, the soul is usually unaware of this connection:

> So long as the soul has not awakened to its majesty, it is full of poverty, which is caused by its limitations; ... it disconnects itself from the things and beings around it, concentrating upon the limited vehicles, the mind and body ... through which it experiences life. It calls these 'my individual self', thus limiting its far-reaching power and intelligence.[34]
>
> 10:35. [Yet when] we think of another thing or being, forgetting our self, that thing or being becomes reflected in our soul. ... By focusing our soul with responsive mind on the mind of another we read his thought; by focusing our soul with expressive mind we send a telepathic message. When a spirit focuses his soul with expressive mind upon the mind of another, it obsesses another. When we focus our soul with expressive mind, we communicate with and help the spirit on the other side; when we focus our soul with responsive mind to a spirit, we get spirit messages.
>
> We can learn from our ... [spirit guide], be inspired by a prophet, or become illuminated by the light of God without study, practice, or any effort on our part, if we only know how to focus our soul rightly in any direction desired ...
>
> When the soul awakens, then no being, no thing is far from its reach, ... for the soul perceives feeling, thought, memory, reason, and identity, and identifies itself with them.[35]
>
> 10:36. Thought-reading, knowing the feeling of another, receiving sympathetic impressions upon oneself, all these things are the experiences of our soul through the spirit of another.[36]

10:34. Khan, Hazrat Inayat: *The Sufi Message*: Vol. 5. pp. 240-241.
[Indian Sufi teacher; 19/20th C.] Source E-b.
10:35. Ibid. pp. 241-242.
10:36. Ibid. pp. 245-246.

"But 'these things' are all paranormal happenings!" I said to myself in amazement. "Mind reading. – Telepathy. – Communications to and from the spirits. – Obsession, or possession. – And even mysticism, reaching up into the higher levels! – These happenings are all made possible through the interconnections of each soul with every other soul, and with every other thing, through the universal spirit. This is the most incredible and yet the most straightforward explanation of so much that I never, ever understood! But can it really be so simple?"

Then I found that Lorimer had tied these ideas together by discussing the concept of shared consciousness and empathy:

> 10:37 What exactly is the basis of such empathetic resonance? The very possibility presupposes an underlying web of interconnectedness and interdependence among human beings, perhaps even linking the whole of creation. Without an inner connectedness such 'co-feeling' would be impossible in principle.[37]

10:38. And Lorimer adds the fact that this 'co-feeling', or empathy, is felt by those who have experienced a near-death 'life-review', when they "found that they received back what others had experienced of an event in which they had participated. An underlying unity of being implies empathetic resonance, and empathetic resonance implies an underlying unity of being."[38]

10:39. Paul Beard suggests that the concept of empathetic resonance can explain the 'consequences of actions carried out on earth'. And he moves on to summarise some further aspects of the judgement, saying:

> The past is irrevocable, certainly; however, its consequences are not final, they can be overcome. Therefore it would be equally true to regard the judgement as a stocktaking, as a result of which a man discovers limitations created by past acts or omissions which have put part of him into a self-prison. It must not be supposed, of course, that all the factors

---

10:37. Lorimer, David: *Whole in One.* pp. 73-74.
[British, Director of the Scientific and Medical Network; 20th C.]
10:38. Ibid. p. 117.

> in his judgement are negative ones. A man finds there his positive qualities too and, just as the negative factors make for limitation, the positive ones make for him a free pathway into his future; they are expansive and liberating.
>
> Thus there is this important difference from the once-for-all judgement pictured in so many world religions. Though it is none the less decisive, its meaning is very different. Its purpose is not punishment, but education.[39]

10:40. Now the spirit, Frances, says that her own judgement was especially helpful in teaching her the 'meaning' that lay behind the experiences of her recent life. She saw everything that had happened during this life, not as a simple life review, but in a way that enabled her to compare this life with her original life-plan. She describes it all in detail, saying –

> ... in the deeps of my mind two 'blue-prints' are brought forward into my consciousness. ... One is the Perfect Idea with which my spirit went bravely into incarnation. The other is ... my life as it was actually lived.
>
> It was a shock to me, and a very salutary experience, to find that these two plans differed exceedingly. And yet, one learns so much by facing the results ...
>
> First of all the mind looks at the whole comparison. ... This is the first shock; a true humbling of yourself to find that you did so little when you would have done so much; that you went wrong so often when you were sure that you were right.
>
> During this experience the whole cycle of your life-term unfolds before you in a kaleidoscopic series of pictures. During this crisis one seems to be entirely *alone*. ... You stand at your own bar of judgement. ... You take your own blame. ... You are the accused, the judge and the jury ...
>
> The second stage of this recapitulation starts when the soul feels strong enough and calmed sufficiently to take

---

10:39. Beard, Paul: *Living On*. pp. 97-98.
[British, President of the College of Psychic Studies; 20th C.] Source K-b.

the earth life, round by round (so to speak), ... only this time the start is made from the moment of [death]. ... The mind works slowly, oh! so slowly, backwards through one's experiences. (I am not confessing where I have reached in this exercise!) But I will tell you that now you seem *no longer alone.*

'Someone' is beside you. Whether it is your own High Spirit or a Great Helper I have yet to discover. Only now, as you ponder, work out, go over, tabulate and judge what you did AND WHY AND WHAT WERE THE RESULTS (good or bad) you are gloriously 'aware' of this great Being beside you, giving strength, peace, tranquillity and helping with constructive criticism. This is a wonderful experience, though harrowing at times. But very cleansing and bringing new hope.[40]

10:41. It's wonderful. ... I've learned so much. Why, oh, why couldn't I have known of this when I lived on earth? What a marvellous Purpose and Plan there is to Life! And how small, almost insignificant, the struggles, fallacies and failures of the last earth life appear now.[41]

10:40. In Greaves, Helen: *Testimony of Light.* pp. 34-35.
[Frances Banks: afterlife communication; 19/20th C.] Source K-a.
10:41. Ibid. p. 67.

11

Extensions of Existence

"It's wonderful. ... I've learned so much. Why, oh, why couldn't I have known of this when I lived on earth?" These were the words that inspired and strengthened me – as they made me realise that Frances had explained the nature and purpose of our judgement-to-come before the time of my own death. I also realised that I should try to understand how our lives would continue in the afterlife, and as I turned to search even further through the books I felt that Frances would approve of my efforts. I was clearly not alone in my search – as Paul Beard, amongst others, had studied a number of communications in which spirits described their existence between their incarnations. And he says:

> 11:1. The key to understanding discarnate life is that we are concerned with a number of different levels of consciousness, and that what is true at one level is not necessarily true in the same way at deeper levels. It is often considered necessary for the sake of clarity to describe post-mortem experiences as if they take place in separate areas or 'spheres' ... divided off from one another. The real difference, however, has to be seen in terms of expanding consciousness.

While we are living on the earth – Beard continues – we can experience differing levels of consciousness, as 'a man can advance or retreat within his own consciousness with a motion like a wave on a beach'. Now these differing 'levels of consciousness' continue after death. Certain experiences will enable our souls to develop and mature in the afterlife, so that they advance in terms of consciousness; but then they retreat for a while. And Beard explains that they have varying levels of understanding too – both before and after they die – and yet they know so little of what they really are:

> This is partly because they imprison themselves in various illusions, and partly because they succeed in expressing only a comparatively small part of their full being. Many sense that this is so whilst they are still on earth. The purposes of the early, or comparatively early, stages of the next life are ... to enable a man to recognise and shake off his illusions, often by continuing to live within them until their illusion becomes clear to him.[1]

Now Evans-Wentz says that we are imprisoned by our illusions while we are living in this world:

> 11:2. As a man is taught, so he believes. Thoughts ... [are] planted like seeds in the mind of the child and completely dominate his mental content. Given the favourable soil of the will to believe, whether the seed-thoughts be sound or unsound, whether they be of pure superstition or of realizable truth, they take root and flourish, and make the man what he is mentally.

These beliefs 'flourish' to such an extent that we usually experience, after death, what we were anticipating before we died. And people of other faiths will usually experience the afterlife in other ways. For example –

> ... the Buddhist's or the Hindu's thought-forms, as in a dream state, would give rise to corresponding visions of the deities of the Buddhist or Hindu pantheon; a Moslem's, to

---

11:1. Beard, Paul: *Living On*. pp. 72-73.
[British, President of the College of Psychic Studies; 20th C.] Source K-b.

visions of the Moslem Paradise; a Christian's, to visions of the Christian Heaven. ... And, similarly, the materialist will experience after-death visions as negative ... and as deityless as any he ever dreamt while in the human body.[2]

Frances would clearly support these views, as she says that souls are often surprised when they discover the true nature of their existence. They –

11:3. ... are either completely over-whelmed by the fact of a further existence, or disillusioned because in their narrow creeds, they have envisaged a heaven of utter delight which, to such crude imaginations, included the joyful inference that from henceforth no efforts would ever be needed by them. In fact, a blessed state of negativity, of passive acceptance, of paradise, a kind of super-Welfare State where they would dream away Eternity.

But this is certainly no super-Welfare State.

It is, indeed, a state of welfare, which has a different meaning altogether, and super, yes, if by that adjective we describe an existence where beauty is manifest, where negative or unkind thoughts are prohibitive because such thoughts are visible and audible, where help and love are always at hand to help the traveller, and where every circumstance points to a greater Life, a wider understanding and the glorious certainty of progress after effort and exertion.

This is an existence in another dimension of thought.[3]

Now the spirit, Silver Birch, joins the discussion, saying:

11:4. Here essentially is a world of thought, where thought is reality. And, being a thought world, thought moulds every

---

11:2. Evans-Wentz, Dr. W. Y: *Tibetan Book of the Dead.* pp. 33-34.
[British anthropologist; 19/20th C.] Source B-b.

11:3. In Greaves, Helen: *Testimony of Light.* p. 85.
[Frances Banks: afterlife communication; 19/20th C.] Source K-a.

expression of its life and its activity. Being so near to your world, and peopled by men and women who are naturally still very material in their outlook on life, the expression of their thought is very gross and so whatever they think is in terms of physical things. ... [But] gradually as awakening comes the grossness slowly disappears and becomes more refined. And life, they begin to see, is something beyond its material aspect. When spiritual realisation dawns they ... begin to live in the world of spirit...

You must always remember that ours is a mind world, a spirit world where consciousness is king. The mind is enthroned and the mind rules. What mind dictates is reality.[4]

"But how can a 'mind world' – a 'spirit world' – be any sort of a *real* world?" I asked myself, puzzling over this concept. Then I found that the spirit of Myers had formulated an answer which contained something like quantum physics. He explained that –

11:5. ... this world beyond death, which at first seemed empty space, actually consists of electrons differing only in their fineness or increased vibratory quality from those known to earthly scientists. These very subtle units are extremely plastic and, therefore, can be moulded by mind and will. In other words, on earth matter cannot, as a rule, be altered by the power of thought acting directly upon it. But human beings, in the After-death, control substance through their freed ... imaginations.[5]

11:6. Understand, however, that ... you do not consciously create your surroundings through an act of thought. Your emotional desires [and] your deeper mind manufacture these without your being actually aware of the process. For still you are the individualised soul caught within the

---

11:4. In Ortzen, Tony (Ed.): *Siver Birch Companion*. pp. 35-37.
[Silver Birch: spirit teacher, through medium, Barbanell; 20th C.]

11:5. In Cummins, Geraldine: *Beyond Human Personality*. p. 46.
[F. W. H. Myers: afterlife communications; 19/20th C.] Source J-d.

> limitations of your earthly self and caught also within the fine etheric body which now is yours.[6]

Frances would clearly support this view – as she says that her afterlife body is of a very 'fine' nature:

> 11:7. Here I have a body, certainly, but it is of finer composition than my late physical body. Here I look as I did on earth, or relatively as I looked, but here I am free to refashion this body by thought.[7]

"How I would love to 'refashion my body by thought'," I said to myself, remembering a passage from Swedenborg – which I had read with approval:

> 11:8. Women who have died old and worn out with age ... advance with the succession of years more and more into the flower of youth and early womanhood.[8]

And the spirit, Seth, describes the same thing:

> 11:9. You may die at eighty and after death think of the youth and vitality that you had at twenty, and find then that your form changes to correspond with this inner image.
>
> Most individuals after death choose a more mature image that usually corresponds to the peak physical abilities, regardless of the age when the physical peak was reached. Others choose instead to take the form they had at the particular point when the greatest mental or emotional heights were achieved, regardless of the beauty or age that characterized the form.

11:6. In Cummins, Geraldine: *The Road to Immortality*. p. 41.
[F. W. H. Myers: afterlife communications; 19/20th C.] Source J-d.

11:7. In Greaves, Helen: *Testimony of Light*. p. 107.
[Frances Banks: afterlife communication; 19/20th C.] Source K-a.

11:8. Swedenborg, Emanuel: *Heaven and Hell*. para. 414.
[Swedish scientist/mystic; 17/18th C.] Source J-a.

Although you usually 'take the form' that represents you best – Seth adds – you may select another of your 'forms' to be recognised in other situations.[9]

11:10. And as an example of this, Helen Salter describes how she was able to recognise her parents when they came to welcome her, while she was dying. She knew them immediately, as they were just the same as they had been when she was a child, and they had even formed her first home again – in the way that was possible within their world of thought:

> They brought with them my very old-fashioned home of long ago and its dear, comfortable ugliness, its books, its papers and its flowers, even the photographs that figured in numbers in Victorian sitting-rooms. ... I was very tired, and it has been so restful to me – imbued as it is with the fragrance of many distant memories.[10]

In contrast to this description, the American, Emmet Fox, writes:

> 11:11. People naturally wonder whether they will see again those whom they loved who have passed out of sight; and to tell the truth, many are quite apprehensive of having to renew their contact with people whom they have disliked – members of the family perhaps whom they would much prefer never to meet again. The fact is that where there is a strong emotional link either of love or hatred there is likely to be a meeting. ... [But] the relationships of parents and children, brothers and sisters, uncles and nephews, husbands and wives, are but temporary arrangements for this life only. If two brothers, or a parent and child, have a strong bond of sympathy in this life, they will meet again and perhaps be closely associated on the

---

11:9. In Roberts, Jane: *Seth Speaks*. pp. 155-156.
[Seth: spirit teacher, through medium, Jane Roberts; 20th C.]

11:10. In Cummins, Geraldine: *Swan on a Black Sea*. pp. 139-140.
[Helen Salter: afterlife communication; 20th C.] Source J-d.

next plane. ... When a marriage is satisfying to both partners here, the partnership can continue by mutual consent on the other side.[11]

The Reverend Stainton Moses takes this even further, saying:

> 11:12. The loving bonds which encircle such souls are the greatest incentive to mutual development, and so the relations are perpetuated, not because they have once existed, but because ... they minister to the spirit's education. In such cases the marriage tie is perpetuated, but only in such sort as the bond of fellowship between friends endures, and is strengthened by mutual help and progress. ... [When] it is more profitable for them to separate they go their way without sorrow, for they can still commune and share each other's interests ...
>
> Spirits filled with mutual love can never be really separated. You are hampered in understanding your state by considerations of time and space. You cannot understand how souls can be far apart, as you count space, and yet be, as you would say, intimately united.[12]

Now Swedenborg explains how these 'separated' souls can be reunited:

> 11:13. Whenever anyone in the other life thinks about another he brings his face before him in thought, and at the same time many things of his life; and when he does this the other becomes present, as if he had been sent for or called. This is so in the spiritual world because thoughts there are shared, and there is no such space there as in the natural world. So all, as soon as they come into the other life, are recognized by their friends, their relatives, and

---

11:11. Fox, Emmet: *Power Through Constructive Thinking*. p. 215. [American writer; 19/20th C.]

11:12. Stainton Moses, Rev. William: *Spirit Teachings*. pp. 45-46. [Founder: London Spiritualist Alliance; 19th C.] Source J-c.

> those in any way known to them; and they talk with one another, and afterwards associate in accordance with their friendships in the world.[13]

11:14. The spirit of Myers makes the point that it is natural to want to be with those whom one has loved, and although people are afraid that they will be separated by death, they will be together again. Myers also reminds us that it is the energy of thought that creates the environment and conditions of the afterlife, saying –

> ... we work together in small communities, building up our little worlds, expressing our many unsatisfied human desires in a manner that is at last adequate and sufficient for our needs.
>
> I describe in this instance, of course, the fate of the average human being when he has passed through the gates of death. ... Men, women and children bask in the satisfaction of earthly illusions which, through the imaginative processes, are satisfactorily fulfilled. The absence of struggle and effort from such lives gives to them a dream-like quality ... suggestive, in its aspect, of the peaceful character of a still, summer day. This may be said to be particularly the case when the dream is fading. Eventually the collective desire for progression shatters this community life. The units that sustain it seek either the way back to earth, or choose the more difficult path that leads to ... [a higher] level of consciousness.[14]

So this gentle, recuperative phase of the afterlife comes to an end, and every soul must make its own decision as to whether it would like to move on within the higher planes or return to this world.

11:15. Seth says that the returning souls should consider their options very carefully:

11:13. Swedenborg, Emanuel: *Heaven and Hell.* para. 494.
[Swedish scientist/mystic; 17/18th C.] Source J-a.

11:14. In Cummins, G: *Beyond Human Personality.* pp. 37-39.
[F. W. H. Myers: afterlife communication; 19/20th C.] Source J-d.

> When most people think of reincarnation, they think in terms of a one-line progression in which the soul perfects itself in each succeeding life. This is a gross simplification. There are endless varieties of this one theme, individual variations. The process of reincarnation is used in many ways, ... [and] individuals must decide on the unique way in which reincarnation will be of use.

Seth then explains how these incarnations can be used, in terms of developing the souls who do return to earth. He says that each soul should select a life that will enable it to work on certain aspects of its character:

> In one life the intellect may purposely by very high, and those powers of the mind carried as far as the individual can take them. These abilities are then studied thoroughly by the entire personality, both the benefits and the detrimental aspects of the intellect weighed carefully. Through experience in another life this ... individual might specialize in emotional development, and purposely underplay intellectual abilities.

From an earthly viewpoint, such incarnations would appear to be above the norm in intellectual or emotional terms; but further incarnations can be used to develop other traits, thereby rounding and maturing the soul through the course of its 'development'.[15]

Now the Rosicrucian, Max Heindel, says that –

> 11:16. ... the desire for new experience and the contemplation of a new birth ... conjures up a series of pictures before the vision of the spirit – a panorama of the new life in store for it. But, mark this well – this panorama contains only the principal events. The spirit has free will as to detail ...

11:15. In Roberts, Jane: *Seth Speaks.* pp. 178-179.
[Seth: spirit teacher, through medium, Jane Roberts; 20th C.]

> The pictures in the panorama of the coming life, of which we have just spoken, begin at the cradle and end at the grave ... to show the returning Ego how certain *causes* or acts always *produce* certain *effects*. ...
>
> But it may be asked, Why should we be reborn? Why must we return to this limited and miserable earth existence? ...
>
> Such queries are based upon misunderstandings of several kinds. In the first place, let us realize ... that *the purpose of life is not happiness, but experience ...*
>
> Experience is 'knowledge of the effects which follow acts.' This is the object of life, together with the development of 'Will', which is the force whereby we apply the results of experience. Experience must be gained, but we have the choice whether we gain it by the hard path of personal experience or by observation of other people's acts, reasoning and reflecting thereon, guided by the light of whatever experience we have already had ...
>
> The choice is ours, but so long as we have not learned all there is to learn in this world, we must come back to it. We cannot stay in the higher worlds and learn there until we have mastered the lessons of earth life. That would be as sensible as to send a child to kindergarten one day and to college the next. The child must return to the kindergarten day after day and spend years in ... school before its study has developed its capacity sufficiently to enable it to understand the lessons taught in college.[16]

Heindel's argument is both clear and logical, so one can understand the need for repeated incarnations.

11:17. But Seth says that certain souls may sometimes take a break – a 'sabbatical' –

> ... a side trip so to speak, to another layer of reality, and then return. Such cases are not common, however. ... Those

---

11:16. Heindel, Max: *Rosicrucian Cosmo-Conception.* pp. 129-132. [American Rosicrucian; 19/20th C.] Source H-b.

> who choose to leave this system, whose reincarnational cycles are finished, have many more decisions to make.[17]

So Seth had made me realise that Frances could be planning to move on from the 'system' of repeated incarnations, as she described her feelings about taking the 'next step' in her 'journey', saying:

> 11:18. I'm on a journey; ... when the Spirit in me rises and seems to take flight towards the next step, I become uplifted and eager, so very eager, for that succeeding stage. ... What joy it will be, going forwards, gravitating (even though slowly) to one's true Place! ... Yet I am content here and happy. As one must be! You can't *push* yourself into heavens beyond ...
>
> But I *am* trying to shed some of the clutter of the personality. We all have to do that. – And there are three ways in which to carry it out here. By self-judgement, and true assessment of experiences; by service to one's fellows; and by aspiration. ... This, I begin to comprehend, is the law of progress. By it we advance onwards into realms of incredible beauty and wonder. How can I make this clear?
>
> The 'subjective' or inner contents of my thoughts, aspirations and desires here and now will fashion the 'objective' place to which I will pass on the next stage of my journey, just as the inner life of the soul within the body-mind on earth decides the first future 'home' on this level.

So Frances believes that 'meditation and contemplation' are increasingly helpful in preparing ourselves for our lives beyond death.[18]

11:19. Seth, however, suggests that we should not attempt to force the pace of our spiritual progress; but we should allow ourselves to

---

11:17. In Roberts, Jane: *Seth Speaks.* p. 181.
[Seth: spirit teacher, through medium, Jane Roberts; 20th C.]

11:18. In Greaves, Helen: *Testimony of Light*. pp. 59-61.
[Frances Banks: afterlife communication; 19/20th C.] Source K-a.

develop our levels of 'consciousness' quite naturally, as we are using our 'intuition' to 'receive inner knowledge' and we have 'the freedom to understand ... [our] own reality'.[19]

11:20. Frances is fully aware that her 'reality' – in the afterlife – is empowered by her mind, as she says: "Therefore, by thought and will, we can travel far out beyond what constitutes our immediate circumstances." On one such occasion, Frances travelled to 'another mansion in this world' and found herself in a 'great atmosphere of learning'. She could sense that she was in some kind of 'university', in which there was –

> ... a pervading atmosphere of Thought which thrilled my soul and satisfied a deep yearning in me ...
>
> Here, here I told myself, is my University of the Spirit. ... I felt I was in some ecstatic dream, so uplifted and transported in my mind was I. *This is heaven indeed.* Always this has been my objective, like some half-forgotten vision of reality.[20]

11:21. In his detailed account of a near death experience, George Ritchie describes how he had perceived –

> ... a whole new realm! Enormous buildings stood in a beautiful sunny park and there was a relationship between the various structures, a pattern to the way they were arranged, that reminded me somewhat of a well-planned university. ...

Ritchie had ventured into 'one of the buildings' and was fascinated to find that there were 'people' there, who were –

> ... caught up in some all-engrossing activity. ... I sensed no unfriendliness between these beings, rather an aloofness of total concentration...

11:19. In Roberts, Jane: *Seth Speaks.* p. 199.
[Seth: spirit teacher, through medium, Jane Roberts; 20th C.]
11:20. In Greaves, Helen: *Testimony of Light.* pp. 72-73.
[Frances Banks: afterlife communication; 19/20th C.] Source K-a.

Through open doors I glimpsed enormous rooms filled with complex equipment. ... I'd prided myself a little on the beginnings of a scientific education. ... But if these were scientific activities of some kind, they were so far beyond anything I knew, that I couldn't even guess what field they were in ...

We entered a studio where music of a complexity I couldn't begin to follow was being composed and performed. There were complicated rhythms, tones not on any scale I knew. "Why," I found myself thinking, "Bach is only the beginning!"

Next we walked through a library the size of the whole University of Richmond. I gazed into rooms lined floor to ceiling with documents on parchment, clay, leather, metal, paper. "Here," the thought occurred to me, "are assembled the important books of the universe."

Immediately I knew this was impossible. How could books be written somewhere beyond the earth! But the thought persisted, although my mind rejected it: "The key works of the universe ..."[21]

11:22. Now Seth explains that knowledge and learning are of the greatest importance in the higher realms. There are many learned souls who use their abilities in teaching others, having been trained in 'multidimensional teaching' – which is, somehow, more complex than any form of teaching that we have in this world. But other souls are of a different inclination, and some –

... may begin the long journey leading toward the vocation of a creator. On a different plane, this can be compared to geniuses in creative fields within your own physical reality.

Instead of paints, pigments, words, musical notes, the creators begin to experiment with dimensions of actuality, imparting knowledge in as many forms as possible – and I do not mean physical forms. What you would call time is

11:21. Ritchie, Dr. George: *Return from Tomorrow*. pp. 68-70.
[An experience while clinically dead; 20th C.]

> manipulated as an artist would manipulate pigment. What you would call space is gathered together in different ways...
>
> Such an art is impossible to describe in words. The concept has no verbal equivalent. These creators, however, are also involved in inspiring those in all levels of reality available to them. For example, inspiration in your system is often the work of such creators ...
>
> There are also those who choose to be healers, and of course this involves far more than healing as you are familiar with it. These healers must be able to work with all levels of the entity's experience. ... The healing involved is always psychic and spiritual, and these healers are available to help each personality in your system as you know it, in your present time, and in other systems.[22]

"Seth is obviously a teacher in his own right," I said to myself. "And he really explains these things in a way we can understand – by using a stretch of imagination, that is! But Frances is brilliant too, and she's worked so hard in describing our life-to-come." So I turned again to her book with gratitude, and found her gentle description of caring for some of the souls who had recently come from the earth's plane without understanding much of the 'mysteries of life'. She says:

> 11:23. Our work is to be on hand when ... [they] awake to awareness. Sometimes their friends and loved ones already in these realms have been 'alerted'. Then we wait in the background until the greetings are over. In other cases ours are the first 'countenances' they see; ours are the words of comfort, assurance and welcome.
>
> Our 'patients' stay with us until they have adjusted to this new life and are ready to join their dear ones or their special Groups. This may be only a short passing phase or a longer 'period' according to their state of development. According

---

11:22. In Roberts, Jane: *Seth Speaks*. pp. 196-198.
[Seth: spirit teacher, through medium, Jane Roberts; 20th C.]

> to the reactions after [reviewing] … their earth lives, so is our method of helping them, with understanding, extreme gentleness and certainly no hint of censure…
>
> I suppose you could call this a hospital, a home of rest upon the Way ... [for the] weary souls, the frightened souls, the ignorant and 'fallen' souls ...[23]

Now a spirit communication – which was received by the Reverend Stainton Moses – describes how a 'fallen' soul comes into the afterlife with the same 'low' character that it had developed on earth:

> 11:24. The soul that on earth has been low in taste and impure in habit does not change its nature by passing from the earth-sphere, any more than the soul that has been truthful, pure, and progressive becomes base and bad. ... The one is no more possible than the other. The soul's character has been a daily, hourly growth, ... a weaving into the nature of the spirit that which becomes part of itself, identified with its nature, inseparable from its character. ... The soul has cultivated habits that have become so engrained as to be essential parts of its individuality. The spirit that has yielded to the lusts of a sensual body becomes in the end their slave. It would not be happy in the midst of purity and refinement ...
>
> There are many such.[24]

These enslaved and unhappy souls are described by Swedenborg too, who says:

> 11:25. An evil man - [on earth] - who in externals takes on the semblance of a good man may be likened to a vessel shining and polished on the outside and covered with a lid, within which filth of all kinds is hidden ...

11:23. In Greaves, Helen: *Testimony of Light*. p. 86.
[Frances Banks: afterlife communication; 19/20th C.] Source K-a.
11:24. In Stainton Moses, Rev. William: *Spirit Teachings*. pp. 13-14.
[Spirit communication, via Rev. Stainton Moses. 19th C.] Source J-c.

> When such in the other life – [the afterlife] – come into the state of their interiors, and are heard speaking and seen acting, they appear foolish; for from their evil lusts they burst forth into all sorts of abominations, into contempt of others, ridicule and blasphemy, hatred and revenge; they plot intrigues, some with a cunning and malice that can scarcely be believed to be possible in any man. For they are then in a state of freedom to act in harmony with the thoughts of their will, since they are separated from the exterior things that restrained and checked them in the world...
>
> When in this ... state, spirits become visibly just what they had been in themselves while in the world, what they then did and said secretly being now made manifest ...[25]
>
> 11:26. ... [Now] every man, as regards his spirit, is conjoined to some society, either infernal or heavenly, the evil man to an infernal society and the good man to a heavenly society, and to that society he is brought after death. The spirit is led to his society gradually, and at length enters it. When an evil spirit is in the state of his interiors, [his true nature], ... he is turned by degrees towards his own society, and ... he himself casts himself into the hell where those are who are like himself.[26]

"He 'casts himself into hell'? – But what is hell? – What is it, really?" I asked myself in horror, remembering some medieval paintings of fearsome fires and frightful devils that could not possibly be real. Then I found an answer that might be plausible – which came from the spirit of Private Dowding, who was killed in the First World War. In his communication, he says:

> 11:27. I have looked into hell! ... Evil dwells there and works out its purposes. ... It is not a place; it is a condition. The human race has created the condition. It has taken millions of years to reach its present state.

11:25. Swedenborg, Emanual: *Heaven and Hell.* paras. 505-507.
[Swedish scientist/mystic; 17/18th C.] Source J-a.
11:26. Ibid. para. 510.

When I first read this, I was not at all sure that Dowding would be able to describe hell; but he caught my attention when he explained that he had been asked to support his brother in trying to rescue a soldier's spirit:

> A soldier had been killed who had committed very evil deeds. ... He was a degenerate, a murderer, a sensualist. He died cursing God and man. An awful death. This man was drawn towards hell by the law of attraction. My brother had been told to rescue him. ... An angel of light came to protect us, otherwise we should have been lost in the blackness of the pit. This sounds sensational, even grotesque. ... [But the] power of evil! Have you any idea of its mighty strength, its lure? Can that power be an illusion too? The angel said so. The angel said the power of hell ... drew its power from man! As man rose toward spiritual life the powers of darkness would subside and finally become extinguished. 'Extinguished' is my word. The angel said 'transmuted'. That conception is quite beyond me.
>
> We descended gloomy avenues. The darkness grew. There was a strange allurement about the atmosphere. Even the angel's light grew dim. I thought we were lost. At moments I *hoped* we were lost. So strong is the attraction. I cannot understand it. Something sensual within me leaped and burned. ... I should have been lost but for the angel's and my brother's help. I felt the giant lusts of the human race. They thrilled through me. I could not keep them out.

"But this is really horrible," I said to myself as my skin crawled on my back. "And how can Dowding - and the others - have the nerve to go on?"

> As a matter of fact, I never reached the point where the rescue was attempted. The angel and my brother went alone. I waited for their return...
>
> All this my brother told me afterwards: Those who die filled with thoughts of selfishness and sensuality are attracted down the grey avenues toward this hell of the

> senses. ... At last, light is seen ahead. It is not the light of heaven, it is the lure of hell. These poor souls hasten onwards, though not toward destruction; there is no such thing. They hasten down into conditions that are the counterpart of their own interior condition. The Law is at work. This hell is a hell of the illusions and is itself an illusion. ... It consists in the lure of the senses without the possibility of gratifying them. ... Hell, apparently, or that part of it we are speaking about, depends for its existence on human thoughts and feelings. ... All the thoughts of lust and passion, greed, hatred, envy, and, above all, selfishness, passing through the minds of men and women, generate the 'condition' called hell ...
>
> We all must pass through a purging, purifying process after leaving earth life. ... [But a] minority refuse to relinquish their thoughts and beliefs in the pleasures of sin and the reality of the sense life. They sink by the weight of their own thoughts. No outside power can attract a man against his will...
>
> Some of these thoughts came to me whilst I waited. ... Then the angel and my brother returned. They had found him whom they sought. He would not come away. They had to leave him there.[27]

It is hard to understand how any soul would want to stay within these regions; but Dowding's unpleasant account is supported by the following communication – which was received through Stainton Moses:

> 11:28. Such are they who gravitate ... [to the regions of hell] where they live in hope of gratifying passions and lusts, which have not faded with the loss of the means to satisfy their cravings.
>
> In these spheres they must remain subject to the attempted influence of missionary spirits, until the desire for progress is renewed. When the desire rises, the spirit

---

11:27. In Pole, Major Wellesley Tudor: *Private Dowding.* pp. 32-35.
[Private Dowding; afterlife communication; 19/20th C.]

> makes its first step. It becomes amenable to holy and ennobling influence, and is tended by those pure and self-sacrificing spirits whose mission it is to tend such souls ...
>
> So amongst us there are spirits who give themselves to work in the sphere of the degraded and abandoned. By their efforts many spirits rise, and when rescued from degradation, work out long and laborious purification in the ... care of the pure and good.[28]

11:29 Frances is clearly one of the 'pure and good' as she cared for some spirits who had been rescued from hell. (She was working at this stage in a 'hospital, a home of rest upon the Way', with Mother Florence and Father Joseph – with whom she had worked on earth.) Now Mother Florence warned her that one of the rescued spirits was in an dreadful state – although he "was conscious of his terrible cruelty, and filled with remorse" – and she advised Frances "to draw a web of protection" around herself when they went to help him. Frances, however, felt 'apprehensive' as the atmosphere about him was vile, but as she became accustomed to the murk she saw the hideous but very tragic figure of their 'patient'.

And Francis continues, describing her perception of their work:

> "Now," I heard Father Joseph say, although there was no *apparent* sound in the room. "This poor unfortunate creature needs all our care and compassion. He has come to us to be healed and to be enabled to face himself and judge his deeds when he wakens from his terrible ordeal of darkness. Let us together concentrate our thoughts and blessings on him. Let us *feel* a gentle soft healing Light, God's healing Force of the utmost sweetness and gentleness, pour out from our souls to his. Let us ask that Light may come into this place that it may touch him, comfort him and give him sweet sleep." ...
>
> Slowly, as I sank deeper into concentration, I felt myself swept up into a great joy and strength and power.

11:28. In Stainton Moses, Rev. William: *Spirit Teachings*. p. 28.
[Spirit communication, via, Rev. Stainton Moses. 19th C.] Source J-c.

> The poor creature moaned but I scarcely heard him. The ward had been dark. Gradually Light grew in it; in one corner an intense shimmer of Light became clearly visible; a Light that condensed into a white-hot Flame, like a pillar of fire.
>
> Then I knew that a Celestial Being had added His Ray of Spirit Force. I found myself praying, not only for this tormented soul but also for the souls of his victims. ... Then a Voice echoed in my mind – and the words were similar to those of the Master Jesus.
>
> "Father, forgive him. He knew not what he did ..."
>
> I found myself on my knees gazing at the Light, now slowly diminishing. ... I felt my whole self tremble. At that moment I had been *at one* ... with this small band of dedicated and devoted Servers of the Light; and at the same moment *at one* with the penetrating white Light of a great healing Angel.
>
> There is no separation. We are all one.
>
> "Neither heaven nor earth nor hell can separate us from the love of God," I murmured to myself as the realisation flooded me that the patient had literally come from hell to us.[29]

11:30. And further on in her account, Frances describes her first impressions of hell, and explains that it is "a terrible region, or regions, of semi-gloom, of unwholesome 'sticky' emotions, of utter distortion of all that is beautiful." Yet she felt 'compassion' for all who were there 'in their self-darkness', and says:

> There are wonderful Helpers in these regions. These have to be advanced souls, strong in themselves and firm in the Light before they can choose to do such work. Whilst I was there on a visit, I saw the face of a Being of such beauty that I was arrested in my progress onwards and had to stop

---

11:29. In Greaves, Helen: *Testimony of Light.* pp. 49-51.
[Frances Banks: afterlife communication; 19/20th C.] Source K-a.

> awhile just to be in the aura of this Great One. I learned afterwards that he had been almost a saint on earth. He was a great mystic, though an unlettered philosopher. Now he is the Leader of a Band of Helpers here and the Light of his countenance, though toned down for his patients to the potency they can stand, is glorious. ... [I was told] that this is his final training work and is a preparation for a high mission on which this great Soul will embark. I was not sure whether this presaged a return to earth conditions as a Great Teacher or Seer, or whether this is a prelude to undergoing further initiation into greater mysteries. I asked as many questions on the subject as could be answered, and was informed that he was indeed a Master of Wisdom and a most saintly soul, devoted to the Christ and one of a great band of potential World Redeemers. He has ... 'passed through' many of the Higher Planes, being a Member of a Brotherhood of Light. His selfless service here is an unspoken lesson.[30]

11:31. Frances then discovered that there is a significant relationship – a banding together, as it were - of certain souls in the afterlife. These are the souls, she says –

> ... to whom we instinctively and immediately react with affection, admiration, union. I used to believe that these were souls with whom we had been in contact in other incarnations and to whom we owed karmic debts or who owed us reparation for wrongs inflicted. Now my understanding is widening. What I believed may still be true in part, but now I realise that those souls who attract us are *part of ourselves.* They belong to the same Group, the same Spiritual Family, the same Group Soul. Their connection with us is deeper and far more permanent than mere earth contacts could make it.[31]

11:30. Ibid. pp.81-82.
11:31. Ibid. p. 119

Now the spirit of Winifred Willett gives a more detailed description of Group Souls, saying:

> 11:32. The human being's soul belongs to, or is derived from, a Group Soul, which is inspired by one spirit. If we make progress in the after-death, we become more and more aware of this Group Soul. It is more than a brotherhood, it is organic, an organized psychic or spiritual structure. Its spirit is the bond that holds together a number of souls. The spirit might be described as a thought of God … connected with a Group Soul.
>
> As we evolve in the Hereafter, we individual units enter into the memories and experiences of other lives that are derived from the earthly and other existences of the souls that preceded and are of our Group. It is not, therefore, necessary to reincarnate, as Buddhists and Theosophists – I believe – claim, hundreds of times on earth.[32]

"Does this mean that we will be able to live through other people's experiences – the experiences that they had had on earth – by being involved with them in a group soul?" I asked myself. "I mean – can we *actually experience* these additional lives through these other souls – learning more from them, and sharing more with them – maturing our own selves in this way, without having to be reincarnated time – after time – after time?"

Now this extraordinary concept would seem to be beyond the realms of possibility. But the spirit of Myers came to my rescue, saying –

> 11:33. ... it is well agreed that, even if we run the race of life on earth … [many] times, we touch but on the fringe of human experience. We have obtained only a certain discipline. We have not plumbed the depths or scaled the heights of being; we have not covered all the space of human consciousness, of human feeling. Yet I can assure

---

11:32. In Cummins, Geraldine: *Swan on a Black Sea.* p. 106.
[Winifred Willett: afterlife communication; 20th C.] Source J-d.

you that until we have harvested many times the fruits of lives spent on earth we shall not, save in exceptional cases, live on the higher planes beyond death.

It is not necessary for us to return to earth to gather into our granary this manifold variety of life and knowledge. We can reap, bind and bring much of it home by participating in the life of our group-soul. Many belong to it, and ... enter into every act and emotion in their past chronicles.

Through our communal existence I perceive and feel the drama in the earthly journey of a Buddhist priest, of an American merchant, of an Italian painter, and I am, if I assimilate the life thus lived, spared the living of it in the flesh.

You will recognise how greatly power of will, mind and perception can be increased through your entry into the larger self. You continue to preserve your identity and your fundamental individuality. But you develop immensely in character and in spiritual force. You gather the wisdom of the ages ... through love which has a gravitational pull and draws you within the memories of those who are akin to your soul, however alien their bodies may have been when they were on earth.

This existence within the memories of others is a form of experience scarcely understood by human beings. The soul resembles a spectator caught within the spell of some drama, that is strange to its actual life. ... It perceives, however, all the consequences of acts, moods, and thoughts in detail in this life of a kindred soul and so it may ... win the knowledge of all typical earth-existences.[33]

Now Paul Beard questioned – as I did – the fairness of gaining vital knowledge and experience through such vicarious techniques. "It's using other people's lives – without experiencing things for yourself," I thought, "or being a Peeping Tom!" But after some discussion, Beard concludes that this is quite all right:

11:33. In Cummins, G: *Beyond Human Personality*. pp. 77-78.
[F. W. H. Myers: afterlife communication; 19/20th C.] Source J-d.

> 11:34. At first sight it might seem unfair to be able to claim the spiritual advantage of experiences which someone else has carried out. But is this really a concealed selfishness, based on a sense of possession? Possession is the very thing that is subdued within the group relationship. After all, at everyday level, we feel no scruple in using the roads and walls, fields and buildings created by the sweat of our forebears. In the group it could be irrelevant which members have won certain experiences. Once absorbed, they belong to the group as a whole. Thus there could be an overlapping and interblending, a sharing of the essence of various experiences, ... [and the] self comes to recognise that it is less itself when alone, and more itself – only really and truly itself – when it is operating as part of this team.[34]

11:35. "Mind becomes communal in the last stages", the spirit of Myers explains –

> ... for the spirit, the unifying principle, is tending all the time to produce greater harmony, and therefore greater unity. The various individuals are merging more and more, becoming one in experience and in mind, and thus attaining to undreamt-of levels of intellectual power.
>
> On the lower rungs of this ladder of consciousness dwell those souls who still cling to human habits of thought, to the earthly personality, to their own individual line of thought; ... they are caught in its dream, and are snared in the many errors thereof. For instance, ... [some] may still seek only to follow the aspiration of their particular religion or philosophy, the freeing of the soul from matter, ecstatic contemplation of the universe.
>
> They appear to gain their aspiration; but in consequence they abide merely on one of the lower rungs of the ladder.

11:34. Beard, Paul: *Living On*. pp. 147-148.

[British, President of the College of Psychic Studies; 20th C.] Source K-b.

> They believe that they have ... entered into the Mystery of God. But they have done nothing of the kind; for they are still individualised, still clinging to their blissful little dream created when they were on earth, ... and their state of alleged ecstatic contemplation narrows and limits experience, [and] confines them still in the prison of their own ego.
>
> I remarked before that when souls reach to the higher rungs of the ladder they became merged in the unifying Spirit, and might at last ... enter into the Mystery of God. In so doing they slough form and no longer express themselves in an outward appearance. But those spirits who pass out Yonder do not dwell in ecstatic contemplation as does the sage or the Yogi; they are, though formless, in contact with the whole of the material universe: an incredible activity of a spiritual and intellectual kind is theirs. For now they share in the timeless Mystery, ... [and] they know and experience the alpha and omega of the material universe. The chronicle of all planetary life, the history of the earth from the beginning to the end are theirs. Truly they are not merely heirs, they have become inheritors, in deed and in truth, of eternal life. You are, as you climb the long ladder of consciousness, a sum in arithmetic. When you pass out Yonder you become the Whole.[35]

When we become the 'Whole' – or even part of the 'Whole' – we will be as One with all others; but we will not lose our own selves completely, as the Rosicrucian Max Heindel explains that –

> 11:36. ... there will be no 'I' nor 'Thou', but all will be One *in reality*, ... each having access to all the knowledge garnered by each separate individual. Just as the single facet of a diamond has access to all the light that comes through each of the other facets, is one with them, yet bounded by lines which give it a certain individuality

---

11:35. In Cummins, Geraldine: *The Road to Immortality*. pp. 51-53.
[F. W. H. Myers: afterlife communication ; 19/20th C.] Source J-d.

without separateness, so will the individual spirit *retain the memory of its particular experiences*, while giving to all others *the fruits* of its individual existence.[36]

And Myers carries on again - by saying:

11:37. We are at the opening of a new chapter in our evolution ... [when] we become sensible of the company of souls, the psychic tribe, who are all more than brothers to us. We recognise the universe as our friend, gradually discovering the multitude of the strands that binds us to it intimately and beautifully. We perceive as well as feel our fundamental relationship to the planets, the sun, the moon, and all the vast stellar system.

These subtle strands are but memories dating back through aeons of time – the scars of sinister struggles, the marks that indicate old painful wounds, the coloured kaleidoscopic brightness of remembered joy, the brilliant radiance of recollected ecstasy. All this stored up experience belongs to the psychic tribe; and to the group such gathered harvest is priceless in the spiritual sense. For it contains not merely earthly recollections, ... it contains also the sum of experiences contributed by those members of the Tribe who have incarnated on planets in the various solar systems. ... Widely dissimilar are the offerings of all the psyches when they begin to pool knowledge, to share divinely, to draw the universe within their own beings and thus destroying division, loneliness, terror and solitariness, seek and find their integral kinship with the one universe before they start on their last adventure, the discovery of universes external to our own, and the discovery of our harmony with God, our entry into the Mystery of the Cosmic Creative Imagination.[37]

11:36. Heindel, Max: *Rosicrucian Cosmo-Conception*. pp. 435-436.
[American Rosicrucian; 19/20th C.] Source H-b.

11:37. In Cummins, Geraldine: *Beyond Human Personality*. p. 100.
[F. W. H. Myers: afterlife communication; 19/20th C.] Source J-d.

12

The Ultimate Expression

"'Our harmony with God, our entry into the Mystery,'" I repeated to myself. "Are you 'the Mystery of the Cosmic Creative Imagination'? But what does that mean? What are you, really? –

"Who are You – really?" –

I waited. But there was no reply. A heavy silence lay about me – a silence that told me that I had not yet reached the end of the path, and that I should search even further in trying to understand.

12:1. So I turned again to the library shelves, and discovered that the medium, Elsa Barker, was asking her spirit guide the same questions: "What is God?" - and "Where is God?"

"God is everywhere. God *is*," her guide replied. But this failed to satisfy Elsa, and she persisted by asking if he had ever wondered about God in the way that she did, when he had been living in this world.

"Yes," her guide said, –

> "I thought of little else. ... Sometimes when praying, for I prayed much, there would come to me suddenly the question, 'To what are you praying?' And I would answer aloud, 'To God, to God!' But though I prayed to Him every day for years, only occasionally did I get a flash of that true consciousness of God. Finally, one day when I was alone in the woods, there came the great revelation. It came not in any form of words, but rather in a wordless and formless wonder, too vast for the limitation of thought. I fell upon the ground and must have lost consciousness, for after a

> while – how long a time I do not know – I awoke, and got up and looked about me."

At first Elsa's guide had remembered nothing; but then the "revelation" came back to him – and he found himself repeating the phrase, "All that is, is God":

> "'All that is, is God.' That must include me and all my fellow beings, human and animal; even the trees and the birds and the rivers must be a part of God, if God were all that is.
>
> "From that moment life assumed a new meaning for me. I could not see a human face without remembering the revelation – that that human being I saw was a part of God. When my dog looked at me, I said to him aloud, 'You are a part of God.' When I stood beside a river and listened to the sound of its waters, I said to myself, 'I am listening to the voice of God,' ... and the realisation nearly took my breath away. Life became unbelievably beautiful. ... Sometimes I tried to tell others what I felt, but they did not understand."[1]

And I could not understand; but as I walked with my dog each day I tried ideas in my mind. "God is everywhere, everywhere," I thought with increasing emotion, "and God is in everything too." This concept then became wonderful – though I still could not understand! But at last I found that the writer, Elisabeth Haich, had explained how one can become truly aware of God, – saying, –

> 12:2. ... to become conscious in God, to understand God completely ... [is] to become completely one with one's divine self, the God dwelling within. That is easy to say but very hard to do! Because man has fallen out of his divine consciousness he can only imagine God in accordance with

---

12:1. In Barker, Elsa: *Letters from a Living Dead Man.* pp. 83-85.
[Afterlife communication; 19th C.]

> his own personal power of understanding. How can he know what the real, living divinity is like in its perfection when his power of imagination only corresponds to the level he personally stands on, separated as he is from unity, and having fallen as he has from divinity? How can the finite understand the infinite, the mortal the immortal, the temporal the eternal?[2]

"Oh, this is so true," I said to myself – and remembered reading a passage in which the spirit, Seth, suggests that we might find it easier to seek God within ourselves rather than pursue Him with more intellectual approaches. – And Seth says:

> 12:3. God can only be experienced, and you experience Him whether or not you realize it, through your own existence. He is not male or female, however, and I use the terms only for convenience's sake. In the most inescapable truth, He is not human in your terms at all, nor in your terms is He a personality. Your *ideas* of personality are too limited to contain the multitudinous facets of His multidimensional existence.
>
> On the other hand, He is human, in that He is a portion of each individual. ... He literally was made flesh to dwell among you, for He forms your flesh in that He is responsible for the energy that gives vitality and validity to your private multidimensional self. ... This private multidimensional self, or the soul, has then an eternal validity. It is upheld, supported, maintained by the energy, the inconceivable vitality, of All That Is.[3]

Now the Hindu philosopher, Shankara, describes the 'unity' of the all-encompassing God as being within us too:

12:2. Haich, Elisabeth: *Initiation*. p. 227.
[Swiss writer/yoga teacher; 19/20th C.]

12:3. In Roberts, Jane: *Seth Speaks*. pp. 245-246.
[Seth: spirit teacher, through medium, Jane Roberts; 20th C.]

> 12:4. By recognizing that pure consciousness is the essential character both of the Eternal and of the Self, their unity of being is perceived by those who are illumined. Thus in a hundred holy texts is set forth the oneness of the Eternal and the Self, their undivided being ...
>
> That Eternal, which transcends birth and rule and race and clan, having nor name nor form nor quality nor fault, dwelling beyond space and time and all things objective, "That thou art"; bring it to consciousness in thy Self.
>
> That Eternal, which cannot be attained by any speech, yet is attained by the pure vision of illumination, a realm of pure consciousness, beginningless substance, "That thou art"; bring it to consciousness in thy Self ...
>
> That Eternal, which, being One, is the cause of many, the Cause that sets aside all other causes, itself apart from cause and what is caused, "That thou art"; bring it to consciousness in thy Self ...
>
> That Eternal, which shines alone, beyond the highest, hidden, of single essence, of the character of the supreme Self, eternal substance, wisdom, joy, endless, everlasting, "That thou art"; bring it to consciousness in thy Self.[4]

'That Eternal' is *brahman* in Hindi, whereas the soul is *atman.* And Professor von Stietencron describes the interwoven relationship between the two, explaining that –

> 12:5. ...*brahman*, is consciousness, because consciousness is the prerequisite for any sort of knowing, willing, and creating. *Atman* too, the individual self, is consciousness, and as a result, consciousness in man establishes the connection with the deity ...[5]

12:4. Shankara, Acharya: *The Crest Jewel of Wisdom.* pp. 44-45.
[Hindu Teacher; 5th C. BC.] Source A-c.

12:5. In Kung, Hans: *Christianity and the World Religions.* p. 190.
[Prof von Stietencron: German professor of theology; 20th C.] Source A-e.

12:6. Von Stietencron takes this even further, saying that "the individual self, called *atman*, is identical to universal consciousness, to *brahman*, the primordial absolute One".[6]

And the *Bhagavad Gita* describes this relationship in simple yet beautiful terms:

> 12:7. I, [Brahman, am] the Atman that dwells in the heart of every mortal creature ...
>
> I am the mind: I am consciousness in the living ...
>
> I am the knowledge of things spiritual ...
>
> I am the strength of the strong: I am triumph and perseverance: I am the sattwa – [the purity] of the good. ...
>
> I am the sceptre and the mastery of those who rule, the policy of those who seek to conquer: I am the silence of things secret: I am the knowledge of the knower. ...
>
> I am the divine seed of all lives. In this world, nothing animate or inanimate exists without me.
>
> There is no limit to my divine manifestations, nor can they be numbered. ... What I have described to you are only a few of my countless forms.[7]

This concept of Brahman, von Stietencron says, –

> 12:8. ... is, historically speaking, the most abstract idea of God that has ever been conceived. It is completely unencumbered by anthropomorphic images and functional ties. *Brahman* is neuter, neither god nor goddess, without attributes, without form, without task – omnipresent and yet imperceivable. It is a transcendent being that penetrates, vivifies, and supports the world. An immortal principle within and beyond a transitory world.[8]

12:6. Ibid. p. 189.

12:7. *Bhagavad Gita: The Song of God*. pp. 114-117.
[Krishna's teaching; pre-5th C. BC.] Source A-b.

12:8. In Kung, Hans: *Christianity and the World Religions*. p. 189.
[Prof von Stietencron: German professor of theology; 20th C.] Source A-e.

This concept is apparently so simple and yet so very complex, and was accepted by the primitive Aryan invaders of Northern India, around 1500 BC. Their ancient religion then spread amongst the peoples of the subcontinent – and their amazing concepts of God still form the core of Brahman Hinduism to this day.

12:9. Now, von Stietencron describes how the 'Vedic poet' of those early times visualised the creation of our world:

> He saw the world as an emanation, as procreation, and as sacrifice. He also saw it ... as the work of a craftsman, somewhat like the Bible's account of how God fashioned man from the earth. But this raises the question – as it did in India also – of where the ... craftsman got the material for his work. Was it already there at his side, without beginning or source? Was there some sort of primeval stuff out of which the world could have been made? Or is [it] ... right to say that in the beginning there was only the One, and nothing else? ... For in that case the world has not been created by the One, but the One has brought forth the multiplicity of things through an unfolding of itself; and there is nothing in the world, no animal, plant, or stone, that is not still related in this way to its origin and hence does not participate in the one absolute Being. ...
>
> Can there be alongside the absolute One a Nothing, that is, a realm not penetrated by the all-encompassing fullness of the One? That would be to restrict and limit God, and hence an argument against his claim to absoluteness.
>
> Christians had to wrestle with this problem. But Hindus could avoid it, because with the rise of monotheism they referred back, with perfect consistency, to the passages in the Veda where the genesis of the world is ultimately thought of not as creation but as an evolutionary unfolding, and because they therefore accepted in advance the essential identity of the world as a fragment of God.[9]

12:9. Ibid. pp. 187-188.

And the beautiful Bhagavad Gita gives expression to this concept of 'unfolding' – as if from God's perspective:

> 12:10. I am the birth of all cosmos:
> It's dissolution also.
> I am he who causes:
> No other beside me.
> Upon me, these worlds are held
> Like pearls strung on a thread.
>
> I am the essence of the waters,
> The shining of the sun and the moon;
> *OM* in all the Vedas,
> The word that is God.
> It is I who resound in the ether
> And am potent in man ...
>
> Know me, eternal seed
> Of everything that grows:
> The intelligence of those who understand ...[10]

> 12:11. Know ... that I exist, and that one atom of
> Myself, sustains the universe.[11]

This ancient universe is now described by Maclaine - but in her very modern terms:

> 12:12. The universe is a gigantic, multidimensional web of influences, of information, light particles, energy patterns,

---

12:10. *Bhagavad Gita: The Song of God.* pp. 89-90.
[Kristna's teaching; pre-5th C. BC.] Source A-b.
12:11. Ibid. p. 117.

> and electromagnetic 'fields of reality'. Everything it is, everything we are, everything we do, is linked to everything else. There is no separateness.[12]

A further description of the interrelated, unified energy of the universe comes from the teaching of a Spirit Master of Wisdom, 'The Tibetan', who says that –

> 12:13. ... the whole Universe, with all it embraces, consists of *Energy* – energy in its myriad forms of manifestation; energy freely moving in space, supporting the celestial bodies, and at the same time the carrier of those powers and forces which interrelate everything in the universal system, synthesising it all into the *One Whole.*[13]

12:14. And 'The Tibetan' stresses the importance of our understanding 'the One Whole', saying that –

> ... no form of whatever description, whether a galaxy, a planet, a man or an atom, can ever lead a separated or detached existence. Each and every form is part of the One Life, and each form is but a fraction or component of a greater form, and every form in turn is again an aggregate of subsidiary forms or lives. All these forms are the expression of the indwelling or ensouling Life – that quality which interrelates and binds each and every form ... into the ONE WHOLE.[14]

Now the writer, Gary Zukav, is fascinated by the nature of this interrelated energy that constitutes the 'Whole' – and by the Eastern understanding of the make-up of our world:

12:12. Maclaine, Shirley: *Going Within.* p. 85.
[American filmstar/writer; 20th C.]
12:13. Jurriaanse, Aart: *Bridges.* p. 17.
[A Master's teaching, as explained by Jurriaanse; 20th C.] Source I-d.
12:14. Ibid. p. 49

> 12:15. In the East ... [the] world of matter is a relative world, and an illusory one: illusory not in the sense that it does not exist, but illusory in the sense that we do not see it as it really is. The way it really is cannot be communicated verbally, but in the attempt to talk around it, eastern literature speaks repeatedly of dancing energy and transient, impermanent forms. This is strikingly similar to the picture of physical reality emerging from high-energy particle physics.[15]
>
> 12:16. It is in this realm, the subatomic realm, that ... quantum mechanics is required to explain particle behavior.
>
> A subatomic particle is not a 'particle' like a dust particle. ... A dust particle is a *thing*, an object. A subatomic particle cannot be pictured as a thing ... [as it] is a quantum, which means a quantity of something. What that something is, however, is a matter of speculation. Many physicists feel that it is not meaningful even to pose the question. It may be that the search for the ultimate 'stuff' of the universe is a crusade for an illusion. At the subatomic level, mass and energy change unceasingly into each other, ... mass becoming energy and energy becoming mass ...[16]

12:17. Dr Brunton takes up the discussion now, saying that quantum physics has shown us that the whole world – and even the whole universe – is a 'sum of dynamic processes', as the atoms are forever changing and interchanging their energy:

> The world's stuff is not a stable one but a process of happenings. The universe is a 'becoming' – not a thing, and certainly not a material thing, – but an ever-active force which, astonishing but true, appears as though it were a thing.

12:15. Zukav, G: *Dancing Wu Li Masters: Overview of New Physics.* p. 155.
[American writer on new physics; 20th C.]

12:16. Ibid. p. 32.

> Thus the scientists who have discarded belief in matter still believe in energy. The latter has become their ultimate 'stuff'. But the energy out of which they would derive the world is as uncertain as matter. ... Scientists have never perceived it. All that they have perceived of it are its *appearances* of sound, light, heat, etc., but never the isolated energy itself. As a detectable reality, it is still as uncatchable as matter ...
>
> The science of the nineteenth century boasted that it alone dealt with the real world. The relativistic science of the twentieth century has begun ruefully to admit that it can deal only with a world of abstractions. For it has found that it is handling only some particular characteristics of a thing – nothing more – and certainly not the thing in itself. It is steadily moving in a particular direction which will compel it ... to see, through its own facts and its own reasoning, that the world-stuff is of the same tissue as that out of which our own ideas are made. It will then be seen that energy is not the prime root of the universe, that ultimate reality being mental in character cannot be limited to it and that it is but one of the chief aspects of this reality and not an independent power in itself. Mind is itself the source of the energy to which science would reduce the universe. Energy will be found, in short, to be an attribute of mind. ... This is not of course that feeble thing which all we humans usually know of mind and which is but a shadow, but the reality which casts the shadow, the universal Mind behind all our little minds.[17]

"This really is mind-boggling stuff," I said with some excitement, "though I still don't understand." But Elisabeth Haich steadied me, saying:

> 12:18. Listen my child: There is only one eternal being – only one God. In everything alive there lives this one single

---

12:17. Brunton, Dr Paul: *The Wisdom of the Overself.* pp. 19-20.
[British writer on ancient philosophy; 19/20th C.] Source A-d.

> being, there lives this one single God. God is the indivisible unity, he is present everywhere, he fills the entire universe. The whole universe lives because God animates it with his own eternal being! Hence God is like a tree of life giving its own being to the created, recognizable world. ... All creatures, all plants, animals, man himself, all are fruits on the tree; ... all are alive because the vital flow from the tree of life streams through their veins, that is, because the tree of life lives within them.[18]

The American Indians could sense this unity of being as they could feel the energy that flows through everything; and Chief Seattle tried to explain this unity – in his letter to an American President – in the mid-19th century:

> 12:19. We know the sap which courses through the trees as we know the blood that courses through our veins. We are part of the earth and it is part of us. The perfumed flowers are our sisters. The bear, the deer, the great eagle, these are our brothers. The rocky crests, the juices in the meadow, the body heat of the pony, and man, all belong to the same family...
>
> All things are connected like the blood that unites us all. ... [And] our god is also your god. The earth is precious to him and to harm the earth is to heap contempt on its creator.[19]

Now the professor of theology, Hans Kung, ties together – as it were – all these threads of understanding:

> 12:20. ... the creator does not remain outside his work. Instead, creation can be understood as God's *unfolding* in the world, without the world dissolving into God or God into the

---

12:18. Haich, Elisabeth: *Initiation*. pp. 174-175.
[Swiss writer/yoga teacher; 19/20th C.]

12:19. In Campbell, Joseph: *The Power of Myth*. pp. 34-35.
[Chief Seattle: North American Indian; 19th C.] Source G-b.

> world, without the world surrendering its autonomy or God vanishing into the world. Thus we would have creation as a process of unfolding, or unfolding through creation ...
>
> *God* is to be thought of as the omnipresent, ineffable *mystery of this world*, a mystery that embraces the origin of its being, its becoming, its order, and its goal.[20]

"'It's being – its becoming – its order – and its goal'," I repeated to myself. "I like these ideas – especially the 'becoming', which can only mean God's 'unfolding' in the world and the universe, and '*experiencing*' through the universe and life. Experiencing, too, through all our lives. Yes, even through my own life! –

"But why?" –

So I turned again to the bookshelves, and found that the Theosophist, William Judge, had worked further on these lines, saying:

> 12:21. What then is the universe for, and for what final purpose is man the immortal thinker here in evolution? It is all for the experience and emancipation of the soul, for the purpose of raising the entire mass of manifested matter up to the stature, nature and dignity of conscious god-hood. The great aim is to reach self-consciousness ... through the perfecting, after transformation, of the whole mass of matter as well as what we now call soul. Nothing is or is to be left out. The aim for present man is his initiation into complete knowledge, and for the other kingdoms below him that they may be raised up gradually from stage to stage to be in time initiated also. This is evolution carried to its highest power; it is a magnificent prospect; ... there is strength and nobility in it, for by this no man is dwarfed and belittled, for no one is so originally sinful that he cannot rise above all sin ...
>
> As to the whole mass of matter, the doctrine is that it will be raised to man's estate when man has gone further on

12:20. Kung, Hans: *Christianity and the World Religions*. p. 207.
[German professor of theology; 20th C.] Source A-e.

> himself. ... It is all worked up into other stages, for as the philosophy declares there is no inorganic matter whatever but that every atom is alive and has the germ of self-consciousness, it must follow that one day it will all have been changed. ... This is perhaps a 'fanciful' scheme for the man of the present day, ... but for the disciples of the ancient theosophists it is not impossible or fanciful, but is logical and vast. ... [And] as to reincarnation and metempsychosis, we say that they are first to be applied to the whole cosmos and not alone to man.[21]

This grand view was intriguing; so I looked further through the books, and found that the Sufi teacher, Hazrat Inayat Khan, had also explained his concept of God as 'becoming' through His creation:

> 12:22. There is a saying of a dervish, "God slept in the mineral kingdom, dreamed in the vegetable kingdom, awakened in the animal kingdom, and realized Himself in the human race."[22]
>
> 12:23. Those parts of creation that do not have much activity we may call living-dead. The mineral does not feel itself alive because it has very little activity. We consider the insects, birds and animals to be the most alive because they have the greatest activity. ... [But the] manner of manifestation is the same all through, from beginning to end and from God to the smallest atom. ... The wheel of evolution is such that the consciousness gradually evolves through rock, tree, animal, to man. In man it evolves enough to seek its own way back to its eternal state of being. ... Man and animal are made from the same element, spirit substance, but man is the culmination of creation.[23]

12:21. William: *The Ocean of Theosophy*. pp. 60-63.
[American Theosophist; 19th C.] Source I-a.

12:22. Khan, Hazrat Inayat: *The Sufi Message:* Vol. 5. pp. 89-90.
[Indian Sufi teacher; 19/20th C.] Source E-b.

112:23. Ibid. pp. 96-97.

12:24. Now a clear definition of 'spirit substance' is provided by Aart Jurriaanse, who says that an –

> ... ancient adage states that 'matter is spirit at the lowest level of its cyclic activity, and spirit is matter at its highest.' Matter is therefore merely the densest manifestation of energy.
>
> All energy, of whatever nature, is in a constant state of movement, vibration or cyclic activity. Limited perception brings the human being under the illusion that a great deal of energy is permanently locked up in certain physical forms, and that energy in that state lies perfectly dormant. Take for instance a piece of rock which according to geologists may already have been formed many millions of years ago; to the uninitiated mind such a piece of rock is absolutely lifeless, inert and inanimate. But microscopic examination with present day equipment, and evidence by modern science will testify to the deceptive nature of this appearance, and that this rock is really constituted of myriads of live [active] atoms, differing considerably from the inanimate consistency so often ascribed to them in earlier days.[24]
>
> 12:25. The mineral kingdom represents the densest expression of the life of God in substance, and its outstanding characteristic – which has become so apparent with the development of nuclear physics – is the imprisoned or unexpressed power contained within its constituent atoms. ... Earth substance is therefore nothing but tangible etheric substance or energy that has been reduced or compressed into manifestation as dense and tangible objective matter. But this process of condensation represents only the involutionary part of the picture, and reflects only one cycle in an unending spiral of the evolutionary plan, because eventually this earth substance must again be progressively transmuted back into the

---

2:24. Jurriaanse, Aart: *Bridges*. p. 27.
[A Master's teaching, as explained by Jurriaanse; 20th C.] Source I-d.

> originating energy. This restoration or resolution ... [follows its own] course over the aeons.

Jurriaanse then describes the higher order of the vegetable kingdom, in which we can sense the living energy more easily than in the mineral kingdom. We can understand, for example, that everything in the vegetable kingdom grows, and that plants can also react to their environment.

And Jurriaanse explains this further – saying:

> Certain investigators have come to the conclusion that plants are not only extremely sensitive to vital factors of their environment, such as the relative position of the sun and moon, light intensity and colour, temperature, moisture, soil nutrients and atmospheric conditions, but that they will even react to music or at least certain ranges of sound. There are also indications that plants may show response to the human voice and to emotional and mental emanations directed even unconsciously towards them; this may be reflected as an attractive or positive reaction towards certain individuals, in contrast to a comparable negative response towards others. Does this not tend to confirm the old-fashioned belief that some people have 'green fingers' and a knack of handling plants with success, and others not? Yes, it should be realised that plants are living entities with a delicious sentiency, comparable with an early form of instinctive consciousness ...
>
> In considering the animal kingdom it should be pointed out that in common with the vegetable kingdom, an extremely wide range of types and species occurs, varying from unicellular to relatively highly developed forms. ... What is of importance for present purposes is that it should be realised that all of this realm also remains in a perpetual state of change and evolution, and that within each group or type representative specimens will be found at practically every stage of development, ... not only in bodily qualities, but also in intelligence or instinctive reaction within such species as dogs, cats, horses and ... elephants.

Some of the more outstanding members of these higher animals have, however, as a result of many ages of close association with man, developed such a relatively high form of intellect and awareness that they are already closely approximating the early stages of self-consciousness, and are therefore being prepared for eventual transfer to the lower levels of the human kingdom – towards which over the aeons the animal kingdom as a whole is slowly evolving.[25]

12:26. The main difference between man and animal lies in the respective degree of *consciousness* displayed. The human being is qualified with what is called *self*-consciousness, while the higher animals are generally guided by *instinctive* consciousness, or a consciousness controlled by natural instinct rather than by a *reasoning mind* as with mankind.

The degree of consciousness exhibited will be determined by the presence or absence of the soul, that vague spiritual quality, which because of its ephemeral nature cannot be pinned down and truly defined in human words. It is that divine spark with which *animal-man* was endowed and by means of which he was raised into the human kingdom. ...

The Sages estimate that it was some twenty-one million years ago when animal-man – [the prehistoric prototype of the human being] – first became distinguished in the animal world. These precursors of intelligent man cannot be described with any degree of certainty, but according to deductions based on archaeological research, these humanoids probably had an upright posture, but otherwise they still very much resembled present day man-apes – [the great apes]. It should be noted that these animal-men, being without self-consciousness, are not yet classified as human beings ... [who each have] a soul of their own, instead of having to share and be guided en masse by a common group-soul. Individualisation is regarded as the portal of entry into the human kingdom.[26]

12:25. Ibid. pp. 55-59.
12:26. Ibid. pp. 59-60.

Now the Rosicrucian, Max Heindel, explains the difference between the individual souls of people and the 'common group-souls' – the 'group-spirits' – of other creatures. He says that while –

> 12:27. ... a separate, self-conscious Ego is within each human body and dominates the actions of its particular vehicle, the spirit of the separate animal is not yet individualized and self-conscious, but forms part of ... a self-conscious entity belonging to a different evolution – the group-spirit.[27]
>
> 12:28. The animal has the dense body, ... but the group-spirit, which directs it, is outside. ... We hear of 'animal instinct' and 'blind instinct.' There is no such vague, indefinite thing as 'blind' instinct. There is nothing 'blind' about the way the group-spirit guides its members – there is Wisdom ...
>
> It is the spirit of the group which gathers its flocks of birds in the fall and compels them to migrate to the south, neither too early nor too late to escape the winter's chilly blast; that directs their return in the spring, causing them to fly at just the proper altitude, which differs for the different species...
>
> It is the wisdom of the group-spirit that directs the building of the hexagon cell of the bee with such geometrical nicety; that teaches the snail to fashion its house in an accurate, beautiful spiral; that teaches the ocean mollusk the art of decorating its iridescent shell. Wisdom, wisdom everywhere! so grand, so great that one who looks with an observant eye is filled with amazement and reverence.[28]
>
> 12:29. This group-spirit dominates the actions of the animals in harmony with cosmic law, until the virgin spirits in its charge shall have gained self-consciousness and become human. Then they will gradually manifest wills of

---

12:27. Heindel, Max: *The Rosicrucian Cosmo-Conception*. p. 82.
[American Rosicrucian; 19/20th C.] Source H-b.

12:28. Ibid. pp. 77-79.

their own, gaining more and more freedom from the group-spirit and becoming responsible for their own actions. The group-spirit will influence them, however (although in a decreasing degree), as race, tribe, community, or family spirit until each individual has become capable of acting in full harmony with cosmic law. ... [Each individual] will then enter a higher phase of evolution.[29]

12:30. Paul Brunton believes that our "evolution is guaranteed because some fragment of the cosmic mind is itself the life-force which strives upward through all the muffling veils of the four kingdoms of Nature, a striving to attain self-maturity which is inherent in every finite form, from that of a so-called dead mineral to that of a living man. Consciousness too develops along with the life-force, attaining conscious sensation in the lower animals, conscious thinking, that is intellect in the higher animal and lower human stages, and spiritual self-knowledge that is insight in the higher human stage. ...

"Thus the world evidences a hidden mainspring of life and mind, will and intelligence. ... There is true meaning, there is strict law, there is genuine coherence, there is a movement through stone to flower, through beast to man, through higher and higher levels of integration in this universal existence. When this is understood, it can then also be understood that karma is not merely a law of inheriting previous impressions or of self-reproduction or of moral retributive justice but is also something much larger. It is an eternal law which tends to adjust the individual operation to the universal operation. It works for the universe as a whole to keep its innumerable units in harmony with its own integral balance. Retribution merely falls inside this activity as a small concentric circle falls inside a larger one."

12:29. Ibid. p. 82.

As seen from our human level, our retributive karma may sometimes seem unpleasant and even quite unfair, but it realigns us in a way that enables us to evolve within the vast pattern of evolving life.

And Brunton stresses this again, – saying that –

> "... each individual's existence, his heritage of thought and action, have to be controlled so that they shall in the end obey the larger regularity of the cosmos itself. Every part is bound to the whole. Everything thus tends to ultimate rightness.[30]
>
> 12:31. Brunton then describes how God's creation continues – "... forever producing and perfecting out of its own substance, and under the necessary conditions of time and space, a universe whose members will grow in consciousness ... towards a sublime goal. The value of the cosmic activity consists in the general upward direction along which its individual centres move."[31]

But Brunton then surprises us, – explaining that the whole of God's creation is even more extraordinary:

> 12:32. Looked at from the outside, the universe comes forth out of nothingness and passes away into nothingness. But looked at from inside, there has always been an internal hidden reality in its background. This reality is Mind. The world is only its manifestation...
>
> We have already seen that the cosmos itself is continuous, and that its past is beginningless. But intervals of non-existence periodically interrupt its history. These are only temporary, however. There are no real breaks in its existence but there are apparent ones when it lapses into latency. For it rotates through changing phases. Each successive appearance of the remanifested universe follows inevitably after the one which had previously gone into a

---

12:30. Brunton, Dr Paul: *The Wisdom of the Overself.* pp. 251-253.
[British writer on ancient philosphy; 19/20th C.] Source A-d.
12:31. Ibid. p. 256.

latent state. When the collective karmas of all individual and planetary centres exhaust themselves, a cycle ... closes. The manifested universe then retreats and ... Mind rests from its labours. But dawn follows night and the cosmic dawn witnesses the re-imagining of all things once again. When the same karmas begin once more to germinate and to reproduce themselves a new cycle opens and the visible world comes into being once more as the heritage of all the existences which were to be found in the previous one. The characteristics of a previous cosmos determine the nature of the one which succeeds it.[32]

12:33. The gradual unfoldment or evolution of the universe is really a gradual manifestation of ... Mind itself, a mutual interplay of its own mental projections.[33]

12:34. The ceaseless procession of images, picturing forth suns and stars, lands and seas and all things visible emanate from the ... Mind under a divine immutable mysterious karmic law like water trickling from an inexhaustible fountain. ... Whether it be a planet or a protoplasm it has to inherit the characteristics of its own previous existence and thus adjust effect to cause ...

This antithesis of work and rest, of Becoming and Being, of a rhythm curiously like that of the in-breathing and out-breathing of living creatures, immediately confronts us when we try to understand the ... Mind's relation to the universe. The present universe is not the first which has manifested nor will it be the last. ... Each is a heritage from one that existed before, a precipitation of karmas which have succeeded in bringing about their own realization. ... The universe of forms ever returns to its starting point: it is without beginning and will be without end; this is why it is subject to birth and death, degeneration and renewal, that is to *change*. It is like an ever-rolling wheel moving onward through these alternating aeons ...[34]

12:32. Ibid. pp. 40-41.
12:33. Ibid. p. 268.
12:34. Ibid. pp. 40-42.

Brunton's concept from the East overwhelmed me as its philosophy was truly marvellous, but I wondered whether it could be supported in any way by any sort of modern science. So I turned to search through the books again, and found a heavy volume entitled *Astronomy, The Cosmic Perspective*; and I leafed through the pages of dense print, diagrams and photographs – and found the passage that was needed – and my heart leapt up within me. –

"This is all quite possible! This could be the answer," I whispered, as I read a discussion on the nature of our universe. "These scientists are saying that the universe *can* 'return to its starting point' over and over again – just as Brunton did, when he said:

> "'The universe of forms ever returns to its starting point: it is without beginning and will be without end. … It is like an ever-rolling wheel moving onward through these alternating aeons.'"

Then I turned back to the tome on astronomy, and re-read the passage in which the professors, Zeilik and Gaustad, give us their argument – saying,

> 12:35. Einstein preferred a closed universe. ... If closed, the universe expands until clusters of galaxies reach a maximum separation. ... Then the universe contracts. ... Eventually the universe ends in a crushing singularity ...
>
> A closed cosmos begins in a Big Bang and ends in a Big Crunch ...
>
> Can the cosmic crunch be avoided? We don't know. But one set of cosmological models does presume that a closed universe survives the singularity. In these models the universe bounces outward at the end of its contraction, its contents somehow missing the singularity. Then comes another phase of expansion, another contraction, another bounce, and so on. These are called the *oscillating models.* They not only have the appeal of symmetry, but also the beauty of no end or beginning for the cycles…

This model makes sense, in a strange way. If you accept the Big Bang, you've taken on the notion that the universe was *born out of a singularity*. Then its expansion is the mirror image of collapse. The evidence shows that the universe survives a singularity at birth, and this fact then implies that it can somehow survive a singularity at death. Expansion and contraction are just time-reversed sequences of the same physical process.[35]

Now the Hindu classic – the *Bhagavad Gita* – has put this into poetry:

12:36. There is a day, also, and night in the universe:
The wise know this, declaring the day of Brahma
A thousand ages in span
And the night a thousand ages.

Day dawns, and all those lives that lay hidden asleep
Come forth and show themselves, mortally manifest:
Night falls, and all are dissolved
Into the sleeping germ of life.

Thus they are seen, O Prince, and appear unceasingly,
Dissolving with the dark, and with day returning
Back to the new birth, new death:
All helpless. They do what they must.

But behind the manifest and the unmanifest, there is another Existence, which is eternal and changeless. This is not dissolved in the general cosmic dissolution.[36]

12:35. Zeilik, M; Gaustad, J: *Astronomy, The Cosmic Perspective.* pp. 943-945. [American astronomy professors; 20th C.]

12:36. *Bhagavad Gita: The Song of God.* pp. 97-98. [Krishna's teaching; pre-5th C. BC.] Source A-b.

The writer, Emily Brontë, sensed something of this – when she wrote:

12:37. Though earth and man were gone,
And suns and universes ceased to be,
And Thou wert left alone,
Every existence would exist in Thee.

There is not room for Death,
Nor atom that his might could render void:
Thou – Thou art Being and Breath,
And what Thou art may never be destroyed.[37]

So I turned, again, to the Bhagavad Gita - to its wonderful poetry and power of expression – and I knelt as I poured my soul, at last, into worshipping my beloved Lord, – my magnificent God, – and our great, great Creator:

12:38. I am the birth of all cosmos:
It's dissolution also.

I am He who causes:
No other beside me.
Upon me, these worlds are held
Like pearls strung on a thread.

I am the essence of the waters,
The shining of the sun and the moon:
OM in all the Vedas,
The word that is God.
It is I who resound in the ether
And am potent in man ...

12:37. In *The Oxford Book of English Verse*. pp. 895-896.
[Emily Brontë: English poet; 19th C.]

Know me, eternal seed
Of everything that grows:
The intelligence of those who understand. ...[38]

12:39. [For] I am the end of the path, the witness,
the Lord, the sustainer ...
I am the cosmos revealed, and its germ that
lies hidden.[39]

12:40. God be in my head, and in my understanding;
God be in mine eyes, and in my looking;
God be in my mouth, and in my speaking;
God be in my heart, and in my thinking;
God be at mine end, and at my departing.[40]

12:38. *Bhagavad Gita: The Song of God.* pp. 89-90.
[Krishna's teaching; pre-5th C. BC.] Source A-b.
12:39. Ibid. p. 105.
12:40. *In Songs of Praise.* No. 501.
[Horae B. V. Mariae; 16th C.]

The Sources of Information

The Sources provide some background information on the religions and philosophies that are mentioned in the main text, and give further details on their histories and relationships. They also add some details on certain authors and books, and a few concluding comments of my own.

The footnote codes below the main text – *e.g.* Source A-a – give access to the relevant appendices on the following subjects:

- SOURCE A – HINDUISM
- SOURCE B – BUDDHISM
- SOURCE C – GREEK and ROMAN PHILOSOPHY
- SOURCE D – JUDAISM, CHRISTIANITY and GNOSIS
- SOURCE E – ISLAM and SUFISM
- SOURCE F – AFRICAN BELIEFS
- SOURCE G – AMERICAN INDIAN BELIEFS
- SOURCE H – ROSICRUCIAN PHILOSOPHY
- SOURCE I – THEOSOPHY
- SOURCE J – MEDIUMSHIP
- SOURCE K – PSYCHICAL RESEARCH and CONCLUSION

- **SOURCE A – HINDUISM**

  Introduction: Hinduism is the oldest of the great living religions of the world. It evolved in India, from around 1500 BC, when the Aryan invaders brought their Vedic religion from the north to the peoples of the subcontinent. Their ancient beliefs merged with the local religions and traditions in many areas – and this explains why Hinduism is made up of several schools of thought. The Brahman school is closest to the original Vedic religion, and contains some wonderful and mystical interpretations of God, creation and life in the poetry of the Vedas; their concepts reach right back to the ancient Vedic oral tradition and are found in the earliest scriptures of the 2nd millennium BC.

- ***Source A-a.*** **– Brihadaranyaka Upanishad**
  Sections: 8:8–10. The Upanishads followed the ancient Vedas and date from around 700 BC. These poems interpret man's inmost existence as being both within and part of the universal all-pervading Spirit of God.
- ***Source A-b.*** **– The Bhagavad Gita**
  Sections: 1:19. 2:13–14. 12:7; 10–11; 36; 38–39. The *Bhagavad Gita* is the most spiritual section of an epic poem that describes the forces of good and evil, love and symbolic war. 'Bhagavad' is a title for the Lord Krishna, who is a great spiritual Avatar of the Hindus; his teaching in the *Gita* is wise beyond measure, and as relevant today as when it was first put into writing – before or around 500 BC. The *Gita* is the best-loved piece of Hindu literature, and it is read frequently by the devout and, when possible, to those who are dying.
- ***Source A-c.*** **– Acharya Shankara, *The Crest Jewel of Wisdom***
  Sections: 1:11–12. 12:4. Shankara was the leading Hindu philosopher who was given the title Acharya, which means 'he who causes others to go forwards'. Shankara's commentaries on the *Upanishads, Bhagavad Gita* and the *Brahma Sutras* are inspiring literature in their own right, and his most famous work is *The Crest Jewel of Wisdom.* There is some doubt as to when Shankara lived on the earth, but Hindus believe that it was probably in the 5th century BC.
- ***Source A-d.*** **– Brunton, *The Wisdom of the Overself***
  Sections: F:1. 1:6; 16; 30. 3:11; 19; 21–22. 7:6. 10:30–32. 12:17; 30–34. The philosophy and mysticism of Indian and Oriental religions fascinated Dr Paul Brunton, who was born in 1898. He worked at first as a travel journalist, and then as a philosophical writer – after studying Oriental wisdom and religion with some holy men, yogis and mystics. His interest in these subjects enabled him to write a series of profound and comprehensive books which interpret Eastern philosophies for Western minds.
- ***Source A-e.*** **– Kung, van Ess, von Stietencron and Bechert *Christianity and the World Religions***
  Sections: 3:5. 12:5–6; 8–9; 20. Hans Kung, Josef van Ess, Heinrich

von Stietencron and Heinz Bechert were professors of theology who were teaching at the same university in Germany when they collaborated to write their book. Their work is clearly expressed and intriguing, enabling the reader to follow the concepts and interrelationships of Hindu, Buddhist, Christian and Islamic religious philosophy and history.

- **SOURCE B. – BUDDHISM**
  Introduction: Buddhism stemmed from Hindu origins – as the founding Buddha, Prince Gautama, grew up in a royal Hindu palace in Northern India in the 6th century BC. The Buddha's personal experience of spiritual enlightenment, and his subsequent teaching and way of life, formed the base of Buddhist philosophy. He saw the world as being illusory and changeable, and also full of suffering caused by man's wrongdoing. His devout followers believe that the Buddhist Path of discipline and dedication will lead them, eventually, to karmic liberation from their cycles of earth lives. Their understanding is that Karma – the Law of Cause and Effect – is the driving force of our repeated incarnations on the earth.
- ***Source B-a.* – Rahula, *What the Buddha Taught***
  Cerminara, *The World Within*
  Sections: 2:15. 3:13–14. Buddhist philosophy may seem rather complex, but the Rev. Dr Rahula introduces and discusses the fundamental principles of ancient Buddhist texts very well. His deep understanding is explained by the fact that he is both a Buddhist monk and an erudite scholar.
  Section: 3:20. In this quotation, Cerminara gives a fine example of Buddha's teaching – which suggests that we should try to understand the Law of Karma so that we can work on the course of our own lives. Her book is a valuable tool in explaining karma and reincarnation.
- ***Source B-b.* – Evans-Wentz, *The Tibetan Book of the Dead***
  Sections: 2:29. 8:36. 10:7; 11; 20. 11:2. When Buddhism spread to other countries it usually accepted some of the local traditions, and in Tibet it absorbed several intriguing elements from the ancient Bon religion, and some Tantric practices that had come from Nepal. There was a period of religious persecution in the 9th century AD, and the Tibetan monks hid many of their sacred texts in rocky mountain

caves. Several of these texts may well have been lost, but one that was found was translated as *The Tibetan Book of the Dead,* and Lama Govinda wrote the fascinating and scholarly introduction.

- ***Source B-c.*** **– David-Neel, *Magic and Mystery in Tibet***
  Section: 4:26. Alexandra David-Neel was a French explorer of both Tibet and its unusual philosophy. She was given the extraordinary honour, as a foreign woman, of being trained and entitled as a Buddhist lama. Her detailed accounts of the beliefs, ceremonies and unusual practices of the Tibetan people are quite fascinating, and her book was first published in 1931, under the title: *With Mystics and Magicians in Tibet.*
- ***Source B-d.*** **– Blofeld, *The Wheel of Life***
  Sections: 2:17; 31; 6:4. John Blofeld was born into a Christian family in Europe, but he felt an instinctive affinity with Buddhism when he was only a child, and came to believe that he had been a Buddhist in the past. He travelled widely in Asia to study the ways and beliefs of these people, and was reconverted to Buddhism and wrote five intriguing books on this subject.

Buddhism's influence is very widespread. It originated in India and spread into Sri Lanka, then north and east across Central Asia to China, Japan and Korea, and south into Vietnam and through all of South East Asia. And there is increasing interest now, in the West.

- **SOURCE C. – GREEK and ROMAN PHILOSOPHY**
  Introduction: The ancient Greek philosophers explored many ideas that were, at times, remarkably similar to Buddhist and Hindu concepts. In the 6th century BC, Pythagoras was interested in the doctrine of the transmigration of souls from dead to new bodies; and two centuries later, Alexander the Great led his armies into northern India and became interested in their religious philosophies. His philosophical discussions were often recorded in detail, and some of these accounts were rewritten by Diodoros and Plutarch.
- ***Source C-a.*** **– Plato, *The Last Days of Socrates***
  Plato, *Protagoras and Meno*
  Sections: Pre:1. 4:15–17. Plato was an Athenian who lived *c.* 428–348 BC. He was a great admirer of his famous friend, Socrates, despite the fact that he was said to have matched Socrates in

philosophical debates. Socrates, however, was tragically executed for political reasons, and this made Plato give up his own ideas of pursuing a political career. He then became one of the most famous Western philosophers and a great writer, and he founded and administered his own university.

- *Source C-b.* – **Plotinus, *The Enneads***
  Plotinus, *Five Books of Plotinus*
  Sections: 1:24–25; 8:17. Plotinus lived *c.* 205–270 AD, and he studied philosophy in Alexandria for many years before settling in Rome to teach and write. He was very interested in the concepts of Indian and Persian religions – though his teaching was centred on the study of Plato and Aristotle, and on Stoic philosophy. He founded the Neo-Platonist school of thought – which has had an enduring influence on Western mystical philosophy – as he believed that we are able to experience our unity with the One Supreme Reality of God, Who is both within and beyond "All That Is". This concept is quite unlike the dualist concept of God in which He is above and beyond all His creation, as described in the Judaic scriptures.

- **SOURCE D. – JUDAISM, CHRISTIANITY and GNOSIS**
  Introduction: Judaism is the monotheistic religion of the Jewish people, and it reaches back to their tribal origins in Arabia and Syria, some time before the 2nd millennium BC. Their historical and religious scriptures are greatly treasured, and several of these scriptural books form the Old Testament of the Christian Bible. The first five books form the Pentateuch, and contain the Law – or Torah – in the tradition of Moses.
- *Source D-a.* – **Holy Bible**
  Sections: 6:2–3. The second section of the Old Testament is made up of the books of the prophets, including the Book of Samuel. These books are mainly historical narratives, but they also describe cultural traditions and mention some paranormal activities – like mediumship and precognition.
  Section: 1:21. The Book of Proverbs is set in the third section of the Old Testament. This section was apparently compiled in the 2nd century BC, and it contains some older books of beautiful religious poetry and thought.

- ***Source D-b. – Holy Bible***

  Judaism was the great foundation from which sprang Christianity and the religion of Islam. Jesus was born a Jew, and his religious training would have been based on the books of the Law and the Prophets.

  Sections: 2:3-5. 7:22-23; 8:54. The New Testament opens with the Gospels of Matthew, Mark, Luke and John – which describe the life and teaching of Jesus. It is therefore surprising to learn that these Gospels were written quite a time after Jesus' death – and that the Acts of the Apostles and the Epistles of Paul were written *before* the Gospels, and within thirty years of the crucifixion. According to the well-known Professor of Theology, Ninian Smart, the Gospel of Mark was written just after the Epistles and Acts, Luke 'toward the end of the first century', and Matthew and John quite soon after that.[1] These Gospels were based on the interwoven descriptions of Jesus' life, and they may have been written to support the propagation of Christian teaching.

- ***Source D-c. – Holy Bible***

  Section: 8:16. St Paul the Apostle was the leading evangelist in spreading the news about Jesus' life and teaching – and it is interesting to find that he included this description of an out of body experience in his work.

  Section: 8:50-51. Despite his obvious sincerity, Paul – who was a Jew but also a Roman citizen – may not have understood the Jews' belief that 'The Atonement' was made for their sin of exiling themselves from God's favour. And Paul was perhaps too ardent in pursuing his own ideas when he interpreted the crucifixion as being the sacrificial atonement for all the sins of repentant Christians.[2]

- ***Source D-d. – Catholic Encyclopaedia*, Vol.4; 11**

  Sections: 2:7-8. Some misunderstandings prevail in certain areas of religious philosophy, and this is clearly demonstrated by the question as to whether the concepts of pre-existence and rebirth were anathematised properly by the Fifth Ecumenical Council in 553 AD. This subject is discussed frankly, and in detail, in two volumes

---

1. Smart, N: *Religious Experiences of Mankind.* pp. 401-402.
2. Wright, N. T: *Jesus and the Victory of God.* ch. 12.

of the scholarly *Catholic Encyclopaedia*, and the quoted excerpt from Volume 11 suggests that Christians should weigh the arguments for and against reincarnation for themselves.

- ***Source D-e.*** **– Head and Cranston, *Reincarnation***
Sections: 2:6; 9. This impressive book is based on a great deal of careful research – and is most informative on the subject of reincarnation, and the misunderstandings about this subject.
The authors also discuss the fact that the New Testament of the Bible contains a small selection of the Gospels that were written after Jesus had died. (p.134.) The contents of the New Testament were almost certainly finalised by the Western Council of Hippo in 593 AD – which was forty years *after* the Fifth Ecumenical Council (See Sections 2:7–8 above). And research has shown that twenty-four Gospels, at least, were around at that time – and that the Council selected only four, omitting those that they thought undesirable. The four selected Gospels have also been altered since then, both in copying and translating new editions.
- ***Source D-f.*** **– Rudolph, *Gnosis: The Nature and History of Gnosticism***
Introduction: The Gnostic Gospels were omitted from the New Testament, despite the fact that the first Gnostic Christians were amongst Christ's closest companions. These disciples, however, were somewhat secretive in keeping what they heard of His teaching to themselves, and their Gospels – which included this teaching – were later considered heretical. Some of them may have been destroyed; but these Gnostic Gospels, to which I referred in my discussion on the Crucifixion, were discovered in 1947 in earthen jars that had been buried near Nag Hammadi in Egypt.
Sections: 8:46–47; 49. We should not ignore these Gnostic accounts of the crucifixion, for two reasons:
a) They bear a remarkable similarity to the modern near death experiences that have been studied very carefully, and this degree of similarity suggests that the spirit of Jesus Christ could have left his body during – or even before – the crucifixion.
b) These Gnostic Christians are thought to have written their accounts soon after Jesus had died. (And I have edited the accounts cautiously, to uncover the line of meaning that I see within their distressed and confused words; but please refer to Kurt Rudolph's book, *Gnosis*, so that you understand.)

These Gnostic accounts describe the disciples' perceptions of a spiritual Christ who was free from suffering on the cross. If Christ did not suffer this death, how can the crucifixion be the sacrificial Atonement to God whereby He will forgive the sins of those who have faith in this doctrine?

Jesus Christ had taught his followers that God forgives our sins in the way that we forgive those who sin against us, and that we will only reap what we have sown. This all agrees with the philosophy of karma: we must free ourselves from our pattern of sin, and work to become better souls, if we are to move on beyond our cycles of earthly experience.

Now I have come to believe that Jesus Christ's sacrifice was to give us his life on earth – and not his death. He descended to our level of strife, falsehood and misunderstanding, to teach and demonstrate how we should live our lives. When this mission was done, Jesus followed the course that led to the Crucifixion – which took place at the time of the Jews' traditional sacrifice of paschal lambs, thereby fulfilling the words of Judaic prophets. The fulfilment of this prophecy would have emphasised the importance and validity of Jesus' life and teaching, which strengthened his followers to spread his Gospel; but it later led them to accept Paul's view that Jesus had been crucified as the Atonement for the sins of the faithful, thereby ensuring their salvation. The most significant passages from these Gnostic Gospels, however, carry the comforting news that Christ did not suffer the terrible indignity and agony that was inflicted on his body.

The Gnostic Gospels, from which I quoted, had been buried for safety. Such burials took place when people had to flee from persecution – and Christians have often risked persecution for their beliefs through the centuries. But some Christians, in their turn, blamed the Jews for the death of Jesus.

- **SOURCE E. – ISLAM and SUFISM**

Introduction: During the years that followed Jesus' crucifixion, some Gnostic Christians – who were of Jewish descent – were apparently disliked and persecuted. So they left Jerusalem, taking their beliefs to the land where the Prophet Mohammed would be born in 570 AD.

The Prophet was a very religious and sincere man, and even as a young boy he was deeply influenced by monotheistic views. He had many ecstatic and spiritual experiences, and was recognised as a prophet by his people as he received spiritual revelations from an angel whom he identified as Gabriel. These revelations are held as being the sacred Word, and they form the Muslim's most treasured book, the *Holy Quran* – or *Koran*.

The religion of Islam, like Christianity, has its deepest roots in Judaism. It has retained the Judaic concepts of the One God, and the same prophets – amongst whom Jesus is especially revered as the prophet who preceded Mohammed – and the future judgement to come, and their religious history.

- ***Source E-a.*** **– Holy Quran**
  Section: 8:48. Some Gnostic Christians of Jewish descent settled in Arabia, having fled from persecution in the early years of Christianity. They had been among Jesus' closest followers, and as they got to know the Arabs they would have described the life, teaching and death of their beloved Christ. They may have discussed their understanding that he left his body before the crucifixion, and that he had not suffered death upon the cross – and this is described in the concise but meaningful words of the quoted Quranic text.
- ***Source E-b.*** **– Khan, *The Sufi Message***
  Sections: 1:14–15; 17–18. 10:34–36. 12:22–23. Sufism is the esoteric and mystical branch of Islam that has grown since the 8th century. Its origins are recognised as Islamic, though many believe that its roots are older than Islam. The Sufis may have been influenced by the mystical Gnostics who fled from Palestine to Arabia, as there are many strands woven into their Sufi philosophy. And Sufism has a widespread influence in other mystical movements, and is linked to the Kabala branch of Judaism and the Arabian and Zoroastrian schools. This is not surprising, as Sufism crosses the boundaries between our religions in sharing mystical experiences, enlightenment and understanding.

The author, Hazrat Inayat Khan, has taught Sufism in the West, and his descriptions of Sufi concepts are fascinating.

- **SOURCE F. – AFRICAN BELIEFS**
  Introduction: The orthodox Islamic faith and Sufism are established throughout North Africa, having been introduced by a constant flow of traders from the Arab states. But one of the oldest religions flourished in Egypt, long before these times.
- ***Source F-a.* – Head and Cranston, *Reincarnation***
  Section: 1:20. The ancient Egyptians developed a remarkable philosophy that included a firm belief in reincarnation and eternal life. Their best-known work describes the soul's journey beyond death, and is called *The Egyptian Book of the Dead.* Copies of this work have been found in important tombs, and a good papyrus copy was dated as around 1450 BC; and extracts from the book were carved on the monuments of kings, back to the first dynasty.
- ***Source F-b.* – Said-Ruete, *Memoirs of an Arabian Princess***
  Sections: 5:3–4; 7:26. Emily Said-Ruete was an Omani princess who grew up on the African island of Zanzibar in the 19th century, living the luxurious life of the Muslim rulers. Despite her pampered background, she eloped with the German Consul and became his wife, and then wrote her fascinating autobiography to explain her origins to her children. This work was published in 1889, and it includes descriptions of the beliefs and culture of her family, and of the Africans, Hindu traders and evangelising Christian missionaries.
- ***Source F-c.* – Maynard Smith, *Frank, Bishop of Zanzibar***
  Sections: 7:24–25. Bishop Frank arrived in Zanzibar in 1898 and died on the mainland of East Africa in 1924, having had a most interesting career. His biography contains some excellent accounts of local beliefs, witchcraft, and cases of possession. The shamans of sub-Saharan Africa are the witch-doctors, who use healing and magical skills – possibly utilising the powers of interconnected consciousness – for both good and evil; and other shamans are found in societies from Asia, the Americas and Europe. Animist and pantheistic beliefs still persist in parts of the African continent – and particularly in West Africa.
- ***Source F-d.* – Okri, *The Famished Road***
  Sections: 3:39; 4:3. The brilliant writer Ben Okri is from West Africa, and *The Famished Road* is an extraordinary and poetic novel, which describes a Nigerian child's heightened perception of the

spirits and animistic forms that abound in his life. Okri's work justifiably won the 1991 literary Booker prize.

- ***Source F-e.*** **– Lorimer, *Survival?***
  Van der Post, *The Lost World of the Kalahari*
  Section: 2:28. David Lorimer's excerpt is taken from a South African Hottentot myth that describes reincarnation – and this concept is accepted across much of sub-Saharan Africa.
  Section: 5:1. Laurens van der Post is a sensitive South African writer, and his books are alive with descriptions of African life, mysterious happenings, and the deeper levels of understanding amongst indigenous peoples.

- **SOURCE G. – AMERICAN INDIAN BELIEFS**
  Introduction: The historical traditions of the North American Indian tribes were founded on their strong spiritual and religious philosophies. Their customs were highly developed in caring for each other and their environment, as they believed that they lived many lives within an eternal Life, and that they should try to maintain everything for their future. They also kept in contact with the spirits of their dead, and with other spirits who could influence their lives. They believed that spirits, people, and all forms of life – and even inanimate forms – shared the supernatural power of consciousness.
- ***Source G-a.*** **– Seton, *The Gospel of the Redman***
  Section: 1:22. The American Indians took pride in preserving their mythology, which described natural and supernatural phenomena. Ernest Thompson Seton had a great respect for these people, and he collected examples of their teaching for this book. The Foreword describes how Seton was working rather casually - till he was summoned to meet an Indian woman, who accosted him with the words: "Don't you know who you are? You are a Red Indian Chief, reincarnated to give the message of the Redman to the White race, so much in need of it. Why don't you get busy? Why don't you set about your job?" Seton was deeply impressed by her reprimand, and he worked much harder to complete this interesting book.
- ***Source G-b.*** **– Campbell, *The Power of Myth***
  Section: 12:19. The North American Indians were quite unsettled by the colonisation of North America, and the great Chief Seattle

replied to the President's request to buy their tribal lands in 1852, explaining his people's feelings about their homeland. The quoted excerpt from the Chief's letter expresses their love for their sacred land and life, and describes their concept of the interconnected consciousness of all that lies within creation.

This concept of universal consciousness is found in the ancient teaching of many cultures, and it acts as the 'web' of mysticism and is fundamental to the understanding of several schools of thought – as in Rosicrucian and Theosophical philosophies.

- **SOURCE H. – ROSICRUCIAN PHILOSOPHY**
  Introduction: Rosicrucians study and practice an esoteric and ancient wisdom that combines their religious beliefs with occult mysteries. Some contend that their doctrines came from ancient Egypt – and were spread by Plato, Jesus, Philo of Alexandria, Plotinus and many others. In 1614, two pamphlets claimed that the German adept, Christian Rosenkreuz, had founded the Rosicrucian Mystery School. He had apparently studied Arabic and Cabalist philosophies and magic in Asia and Africa, and died in 1484. Other sources say that he began his work in Europe in the 13th century – but it is difficult to unravel their history, as Rosenkreuz is believed to be taking successive bodies as 'an Initiate of high degree' to this day.
  Unfortunately, the medieval Rosicrucians were sometimes thought to be impostors who were seeking gold – rather than the elixir of life – through their spiritual study of alchemy; but 'gold' was their term for the secret elixir! And there was renewed interest in the Cabalist order of the Society in Europe in the 19th century, when a group of Catholic Rosicrucians became established amongst other groups in Europe. In addition to this, there are four known sects of Rosicrucians now in the USA.
- ***Source H-a.*** **– Playfair, *The Indefinite Boundary***
  Section: 4:23. Some people believe that Paracelsus was the true founder of the Rosicrucians. He was a Swiss mystic and prophet who died in 1541, and his philosophy has also influenced the Theosophical movement, which was formed in the 19th century.
- ***Source H-b.*** **– Heindel, *The Rosicrucian Cosmo-Conception***
  Heindel, *The Rosicrucian Mysteries*
  Sections: 4:20; 34; 10:28–29. 11:16; 36. 12:27–29. 8:28.

Heindel gives us some fascinating details about Rosicrucian concepts and occult work in the 19th and early 20th centuries. Many of his explanations are complex, but they depend on the essential understanding that universal consciousness is everywhere, and that it affects everything.

- **SOURCE I. – THEOSOPHY**

Introduction: Theosophy is a combination of selected religious philosophies from both the East and the West; but it is not a religion in itself. Theosophy is a Greek word that means 'divine wisdom as it unfolds in the human spirit', and this philosophy was studied in the mystery wisdom schools of Alexandria – the greatest centre of learning in the 3rd century AD.

The Theosophical movement was revived during the 19th and 20th centuries, and its philosophy acted as a catalyst that stirred Western religious thought. It synthesised philosophies from the Indian subcontinent with those of China, Egypt and ancient Greece; and it included Gnostic, Neoplatonist, Jewish, medieval, Renaissance and German mystical concepts.

- ***Source I-a.* – Judge, *The Ocean of Theosophy***

Sections: 1:10; 3:6; 12; 17. 9:11; 12:21. William Judge was one of the founders of the Theosophical Society in New York in 1875, but their movement nearly fell apart when two of their founders left America to continue their work in India. William Judge, however, succeeded in keeping the Society alive, despite considerable problems. And in his book, *The Ocean of Theosophy*, he interprets many concepts of esoteric philosophy in his beautiful and clear style.

- ***Source I-b.* – Olcott, *The Buddhist Catechism***

Section: 2:16. Henry Olcott was the first president of the Theosophical Society in New York. He had worked and travelled for many years with Madame Blavatsky – as described below – while she studied, lectured and wrote her books. They then settled in America to found the Society, but they later returned to Madras to set up a second centre. Olcott died in 1907, six years after Madame Blavatsky.

- ***Source I-c.* – Blavatsky, *The Key to Theosophy***

Sections: 3:8; 15–16. Madame Blavatsky was widely known as 'H.P.B.' She was born in Russia in 1831, and was married to a nobleman for a very, very short time. She was a natural psychic and medium – and a powerful character – who travelled a great deal to study and work with Indian philosophers and some Masters of Wisdom. Blavatsky then lectured in Europe and the USA and became the most famous Theosophist, acting as the driving force behind the Society's Centres in both New York and Madras. Her abnormal lifestyle, behaviour and beliefs, however, aroused great jealousies and antagonism in certain people, which added controversy to her history. She finally died in 1891 in England – though she was only sixty at the time.

- ***Source I-d.* – Jurriaanse, *Bridges***

  Sections: 12:13–14; 24–26. Aart Jurriaanse has worked devotedly in running a School of Esoteric Philosophy in South Africa, and in writing his book called *Bridges*. His fascinating treatise outlines and explains the teaching of the spirit Tibetan Master, Djwhal Khul, which was received through Alice Bailey between 1919 and 1949. Bailey wrote a total of seventeen volumes of the Master's complex and esoteric philosophy – so Jurriaanse's *Bridges* is especially welcome as it is relatively concise and absolutely fascinating. Bailey also wrote *The Unfinished Autobiography*, in which she describes her interesting but taxing work as a medium for the Tibetan Master.

- **SOURCE J. – MEDIUMSHIP**

  Introduction: Mediums are found in every culture. They are sensitive people who are able to communicate with spirits, whom they perceive in various ways, and some can enable spirits to communicate with the living.

- ***Source J-a.* – Sigstedt, *The Swedenborg Epic***

  Swedenborg, *Arcana Caelestia*, Vol.1
  Swedenborg, *Heaven and Hell*
  Swedenborg, *The Minor Spiritual Diary*

  Sections: 5:17–18. Emanuel Swedenborg was born in 1688 and died in 1772. Sigstedt's excellent biography describes his life and work, and helps us understand that Swedenborg was a brilliant Swedish scientist, a gifted philosopher and theologian, a sensitive mystic, and a medium too. He understood all our spiritual aspects, and communed with a great number of spirits – as described in the following sections from his own books:

  Sections: 1:8–9. 5:16; 23–24. 7:12. 8:14–15. 9:4. 10:19; 26. 11:8; 13; 25–26. Swedenborg's major work, *Heaven and Hell*, is remarkably informative and most interesting.

- ***Source J-b.*** **– Kardec, *Experimental Spiritism: The Mediums' Book***
Sections: 5:6–7; 19–21; 27; 31. 6:1; 13–14; 17–18; 23; 27. 7:4–5; 20–21. 8:2; 18–20. Allan Kardec was born in Switzerland in 1804, and his real name was Léon Rivail. He proved to be dull and unimaginative as a Protestant schoolteacher, but he joined the current enthusiasm of his society – which was holding séances in Spirit Circles. He found that he could receive far more than the usual messages, and he came to understand – with the help of many spirits – a great deal about the spirit levels that interrelate with our own earth level. He compiled five books of extraordinary Spiritist philosophy, under the name Allan Kardec – which had been his name in a previous life – and he died in 1869.
- ***Source J-c.*** **– Stainton Moses, *Spirit Teachings***
Sections: 6:20; 29. 7:16. 11:12; 24; 28. The Rev. Stainton Moses was a sincere and learned man, who was ordained as a Minister in the Church in 1863 – having graduated from Oxford University – and was later appointed to be a master at the University College School. He joined a spiritualist circle in 1872 and discovered that he had considerable psychic powers as a medium. He received copious teachings – through automatic writing – in the following years, and his book, *Spirit Teachings*, was first published under the pseudonym, 'M.A. Oxon'. He also founded the London Spiritualist Alliance, and his books are regarded as classics by the Spiritualist movement.
- ***Source J-d.*** **– Cummins, *Beyond Human Personality***
Cummins, *The Road to Immortality*
Cummins, *Swan on a Black Sea*
Cummins, *They Survive*
Sections: 7:15. 8:26; 53. 9:26; 28-29. 11:5–6; 10; 14; 32–33; 35; 37. Geraldine Cummins was an Irish lady from a respectable and academic family – as described by Professor C.D. Broad, a Fellow of Trinity College, Cambridge. Cummins had discovered that she could receive detailed and informative scripts from various spirits through automatic writing. She explained that she was able to suspend her mind completely, allowing the spirits to communicate through her in their own individual script.

Several people – who had died – communicated through Cummins, and many of them described their lives beyond death, thus providing some of the most informative texts on the afterlife.

One of these spirits was called 'Mrs Willett' – which was the pseudonym that had been used by the medium, Winifred Coombe Tennant; she had been a magistrate, a Justice of the Peace and the first woman to be appointed as a British Delegate to the Assembly of the League of Nations. 'Mrs Willett' had been an impressive medium, and when she died she returned to describe her death and afterlife experiences in the characteristic style of her earth personality. She had been one of a group of mediums who received the cross-correspondences from F.W.H. Myers, as described in Section 6:19.

F.W.H. Myers had been one of the Founders of the Society of Psychical Research during his life, and he continued with his useful work after death by communicating – mainly through Geraldine Cummins – his remarkable accounts of life beyond death.

- ***Source J-e.*** **– Brown, *Immortals at my Elbow***
  Sections: <u>8</u>:25. <u>10</u>:18;22. Rosemary Brown was a remarkable psychic who was known for her ability to receive and write musical compositions that came to her from composers in the Afterlife. Despite her lack of a musical education, her scripts were in the composers' own style of notation. Her ability in communicating with spirits of the dead – including some very famous people – was so impressive that she was invited to a private lunch with the Bishop of Southwark and his chaplain to discuss and demonstrate her gifts as a medium. Brown's account then said: "The Anglican Church ... made a long and careful enquiry into Spiritualism, but suppressed its report which was favourable." (p.9.) And later on she said: "It is as long ago as 1937 when Dr. Cosmo Gordon Lang, then Archbishop of Canterbury, set up a commission on Spiritualism, which drew a highly favourable report. When a journalist asked Dr. Mervyn Stockwood, Bishop of Southwark, why the report of the commission was not published, he replied, 'They did not have the guts to publish it.' The official reason for non-publication was that 'the war made it inopportune'; but Dr Stockwood said that he thought the reverse would have been the case." (pp.41–2.)

  This was a tragic decision, as knowledge of this report would have comforted many aching hearts during and after the war; but the level of evidence of life beyond death and the existence of spirits will increase our understanding.

- ***Source J-f.*** **– Barrett, *Death-Bed Visions***
  Heindel, *The Rosicrucian Cosmo-Conception*
  ***The Times*, London, 4 April 1992**

  Sections: 4:33. 4:34. 4:35. Many young and innocent children are aware of spirits, and some have invisible playmates. But some spirit friends are not so friendly – and the psychologist, Dr Fiore, believes that there is a danger that these spirits can possess children.
- ***Source J-g.*** **– Fiore, *The Unquiet Dead***
  Langley, *Edgar Cayce on Reincarnation*

  Sections: 7:7–8; 10–11; 18–19; 27–29. Dr Fiore's book is discomforting at times, and an understanding of her work would enable the victims of possession – both children and adults – to receive better treatment. (Possession is described clearly in 7:17 and 7:20–26.)

  Sections: 3:10; 3:18. The healer and visionary, Edgar Cayce, was born in Kentucky in 1877 and died in Virginia in 1945. He was famed for his skill in entering deep trance states to give 'readings' on medical problems and their cure, and he stressed the vital importance of leading a balanced life in terms of body, mind and spirit. Cayce needed no more than the name and the place of a patient to enable him to give the 'reading' while in a trance state, and his diagnoses and cures were remarkably effective, and carefully documented as being 85% accurate.

  Cayce was able to help an amazing number of people in all kinds of difficulties. But paranormal happenings are still quite unusual, and they are often ignored or thought to be untrue, despite the evidence that they do take place under certain circumstances.

- **SOURCE K. – PSYCHICAL RESEARCH**

  Introduction: Paranormal happenings are not fully understood, but there are certain areas of research in which many are studying the subject, including the Churches' Spiritual and Psychic Study Group. The President of this study group, Lieut.- Col. R.M. Lester, wrote an interesting Foreword in 1969 to Greaves' *Testimony of Light*, and said that Frances Banks was held 'in the highest esteem by all who had had the privilege of meeting her'.
- ***Source K-a.*** **– Greaves, *Testimony of Light***
  Langley, *Edgar Cayce on Reincarnation*

  Sections: 9:31–32. 10:13–14, 21; 40–41. 11:3; 7; 18; 20; 23; 29–31.

Frances had been a remarkable woman when she was last on earth, working in both the spiritual and practical planes. She had worked as a teaching nun, and then as the principal of a teacher training college in South Africa for twenty-five years. During those years her inner life had deepened, and she moved back to England and worked as the tutor-organiser in a large prison, and wrote a useful book that stemmed from her work, called *Teach Them to Live.* Frances also gave lectures and worked for the Churches' Fellowship for Psychical and Spiritual Studies, and during this time she and the writer, Helen Greaves, found that they could communicate very well by telepathy. And then – *after* Frances had died – she transmitted her really wonderful book, *Testimony of Light,* through Helen. This book was acclaimed by many, and inspires its readers.

- ***Source K-b.* – Beard, *Survival of Death***
  Beard, *Living On*
  Sections: 5:32–33. 6:19. 10:25; 27; 39. 11:1; 34. Paul Beard joined the Society for Psychical Research around 1955, and was appointed as the President of the College of Psychic Studies in London in 1968. His books show that he was a deeply committed person who worked hard to help us understand the evidence of life beyond death.
- ***Source K-c. – Proceedings of the Society for Physical Research***
  Sections: 5:9; 12–15. 8:38. The Society for Psychical Research was founded in London in 1882 by a group of Spiritualists, scientists, and other leading scholars from America and Europe, including the Rev. Stainton Moses, Sir William Barrett and F.W.H. Myers. The aim of the Society was to carry out some thorough research on paranormal phenomena, and it published its findings in 4,000 pages of the *Proceedings of the Society for Physical Research* within the first ten years of its existence. These journals provide the most impressive and authoritative work in this field, and people are free to study them in the Society's headquarters in London.

The American Society for Psychical Research was set up three years later, in 1885. There has always been a close relationship between the two societies, but the American Society has a stronger financial and scientific base, which has enabled it to overtake the British Society for Physical Research in research and publications.

The quantity and quality of research that has been published by these societies is really quite remarkable, but I feel that their dedicated work has not been properly recognised. It is true that a critical approach is essential when investigating the more unusual avenues of our existence – but these paranormal areas can set our levels of assessment into a state of overdrive, which tends to block our understanding.

MY CONCLUSION

While I was working on this book I had to weigh and judge, criticise and delete, deny and yet pursue the compelling philosophies that led me ever onwards; and at the more doubtful stages of my work I was forced to open my mind to all that I was reading – though my suspicions still persisted, from time to time, about the reality of spirits. But then the proof came to me when I went to the medium.

- ***Source K-d. – The medium, London College of Psychic Studies***

Section: 5:34. My visit to the medium was the turning point of all my experiences, and I know that my guide knows me through and through. His gentle guidance and support have been quite wonderful and he has given me the strength to complete this book.

When I first received his encouragement I became more sensitive to the extraordinary guidance that arose within me. I felt it as a subtle comfort, an enthusiasm and an ability to keep working through endless hours when *Our Pathway* was going in the right direction; but an increasing discomfort and irritability would prevent me from writing whenever I strayed from the way. I gradually came to understand that these intuitive feelings and compulsions were directing me – I am sure – in this work.

I realise now that these compulsions have been with me since I felt I should work on this book; they have directed my research and thoughts, and encouraged or discouraged me when I became obstinate or wayward in pursuing my own ideas. I therefore know, quite simply, that this book has not been my own creation: I have only been the means – the earthly tool – by which the work has been built up in this way. I feel very grateful for all the help that I have received, and regret that I have been so slow in understanding! But my overwhelming feeling is that I have been very, very privileged to be a member of the dedicated team who have brought *Our Pathway of Being* to completion for you, and you – and you.

Index of Authors, Titles and Source Codes

Asch, Sholem.

The Nazarene.

2:32; 35.

Banks, Frances. – See Greaves.

Barker, Elsa.

Letters from a Living Dead Man.

12:1.

Barrett, Sir William, F.R.S.

Death-Bed Visions.

4:33.[Source J-F.]

Beard, Paul.

Living On.

10:25; 27; 39. – 11:1; 34. – [Source K-b.]

Survival of Death.

5:32-33. – 6:19. – [Source K-b.]

Bhagavad Gita, The Song of God.

(Krishna's teaching.)

1:19. – 2:13–14. – 12:7; 10-11; 36; 38-39. – [Source A-b.]

Bible. – See *Holy Bible.*

Blavatsky, Madame.

The Key to Theosophy.

3:8; 15-16. – [Source I-c.]

Blofeld, John.

The Wheel of Life.

2:17; 31. – 6:4. – [Source B-d.]

Bragdon, Claude.
Merely Players.
4:25.
Brihadaranyaka Upanishad.
8:8-10. [Source A-a.]
Brown, Rosemary.
Immortals at my Elbow.
8:25. – 10:18; 22. – [Source J-e.]
Brunton, Dr Paul.
The Wisdom of the Overself.
F.1. – 1:6; 16; 30. – 3:11; 19; 21-22. – [Source A-d.]
7:6. – 10:30-32. – 12:17; 30-34. – [Source A-d.]
Butler, Rev. Alban.
Lives of the Saints.
4:28.
Campbell, Joseph and Moyers, B.
The Power of Myth.
12:19. [Source G-b.]
Catholic Encyclopaedia.
2:7-8. [Source D-d.]
Cerminara, Dr Gina.
Many Mansions.
1:29. – 4:2.
The World Within.
3:20. [Source B-a.]
Chaffin, James L.
See *Proceedings of the Society for Psychical Research.*
Cochran, Lin.
Edgar Cayce on Secrets of the Universe.
3:23.
Cooper, Wendy; Dr Smith, Tom.
Beyond our Limits.
9:19.

Crookall, Dr Robert.

The Study and Practice of Astral Projection.

8:30.

What Happens When You Die.

9:3.

Cummins, Geraldine.

Beyond Human Personality.

7:15. – 8:26; 53. – 11:5; 14; 33; 37. – [Source J-d.]

The Road to Immortality.

9:26-27. – 11:6; 35. – [Source J-d.]

Swan on a Black Sea.

9:28. – 11:10; 32. – [Source J-d.]

They Survive.

9:29. [Source J-d.]

David-Neel, Lama Alexandra.

Magic and Mystery in Tibet.

4:26. [Source B-c.]

Descartes, René.

The Philosophical Works of Descartes.

1:4-5.

Douglas, Alfred.

Extra Sensory Powers.

8:40.

Dowding, Lord Air Chief Marshall.

Many Mansions.

10:5; 8.

Dowding, Private. – See Pole.

'E.K.' – See Sherwood.

Eliot, George.

Silas Marner.

8:1.

Euripedes. – See Lorimer.

Evans-Wentz, Dr W.Y.
The Tibetan Book of the Dead.
2:29. – 8:36. – 10:7; 11; 20. – 11:2. –[Source B-b.]
Fiore, Dr Edith.
The Unquiet Dead.
3:1. – 7:7-8; 10-11; 18-19; 27-29. – [Source J-g.]
You have been here Before.
10:4.
Flynn, Charles P.
After the Beyond.
9:16; 20-23.
Fox, Emmet.
Power Through Constructive Thinking.
2:37. – 3:9. – 4:21. – 8:21. – 11:11.
Fox, Oliver. – See Green.
Greaves, Helen. (Frances Banks.)
Testimony of Light.
9:31-32. – 10:13-14; 21; 40-41. – [Source K-a.]
11:3; 7; 18; 20; 23; 29-31. – [Source K-a.]
Green, Celia.
Lucid Dreams.
8:3.
Guirdham, Dr Arthur.
The Cathars and Reincarnation.
2:20-27.
Haich, Elisabeth.
Initiation.
F.2. – 1:31. – 4:36. – 12:2; 18.
Harding, Dr Rosamond E.M.
An Anatomy of Inspiration.
5:26; 28.
Hardinge, Emma.
Modern American Spiritualism.
6:5-7; 9. – 7:2.

Head, Joseph and Cranston, Sylvia L.
Reincarnation: The Pheonix Fire Mystery.
1:20. [Source F-a.]
2:6; 9. – [Source D-e.]
Heindel, Max.
The Rosicrucian Cosmo-Conception.
4:20; 34. – 10:28-29. – 11:16; 36. – [Source H-b.]
12:27-29. [Source H-b.]
4:34. [Source J-f.]
The Rosicrucian Mysteries.
8:28. [Source H-b.]
Holy Bible.
Old Testament.
1:21. – 6:2-3. – [Source D-a.]
Gospels.
2:3-5. – 7:22-23. – 8:54. – [Source D-b.]
Epistles.
8:16; 50. – [Source D-c.]
Holy Quran. – Koran.
Surah IV. v.157.
8:48. [Source E-a.]
Iverson, Jeffrey.
In Search of the Dead.
2:18. – . 9:7.
James, Prof. William.
The Varieties of Religious Experience.
5:2; 22.
Johnson, Dr Raynor C.
A Religious Outlook for Modern Man.
4:14; 24; 27. – 10:1.
Judge, William Q.
The Ocean of Theosophy.
1:10. – 3:6; 12; 17. – 9:11. – 12:21. – [Source I-a.]

Jung, Dr Carl G.

Memories, Dreams, Reflections.

2:33-34. – 5:8; 29. – 8:34.

Jurriaanse, Aart.

Bridges.

12:13-14; 24-26. – [Source I-d.]

Kardec, Allan.

Experimental Spiritism: The Mediums' Book.

5:6-7; 19-21; 27; 31. – 6:1; 13-14; 17-18; 23; 27. – [Source J-b.]

7:4-5; 20-21. – 8:2; 18-20 – [Source J-b.]

Khan, Hazrat Inayat.

The Sufi Message. Vol.5.

1:14-15; 17-18. – 10:34-36. – 12:22-23. – [Source E-b.]

Kübler-Ross, Dr Elisabeth.

On Children and Death.

4:30-32. – 5:10-11. – 8:43-44. –. 9:24-25.

Kung, Hans, van Ess, von Stietencron and Bechert.

Christianity and the World Religions.

3:5. – 12:5-6; 8-9; 20. – [Source A-e.]

Langley, Noel.

Edgar Cayce on Reincarnation.

3:10; 18.

Lingg, Ann M.

Mozart, Genius of Harmony.

4:22.

London College of Psychic Studies.

5:34. [Source K-d.]

Lorimer, David.

Survival?

p.1:27. – 8:12-13.

p.2:28 [Source F-e.]

Whole in One.

9:5-6; 14-15. – 10:33; 37-38.

Maclaine, Shirley.
Dancing in the Light.
3:31.
Going Within.
12:12.
Out on a Limb.
1:32. –. 2:1. – 5:30.
McTaggart, John Ellis.
Human Immortality and Pre-Existence.
2:30.
The Nature of Existence.
3:4.
Marshall Hall, Sir Edward, K.C.
– See Wingfield.
Masefield, John.
The Collected Poems.
2:12. – 3:7.
Maynard Smith, Canon H.
Frank, Bishop of Zanzibar.
7:24-25. [Source F-c.]
Moody, Prof. Raymond A.
Life After Life.
8:23-24. – 9:9-10.
Reflections on Life After Life.
9:8; 12; 17.
Muldoon, Sylvan; Carrington, H.
The Phenomena of Astral Projection.
8:11; 22.
Myers, F.W.H. – See Cummins.
Okri, Ben.
The Famished Road.
3:39. – 4:3. – [Source F-d.]
Olcott, Henry S.
The Buddhist Catechism.
2:16. [Source I-b.]

Ortzen Tony (ed.).
Silver Birch Companion.
1:26. – 6:12; 24; 28. – 8:7. – 11:4.
Oxford Book of English Verse.
Wordsworth, William.
4:1.
Brontë, Emily.
12:37.
Perry, Archdeacon Michael.
Psychic Studies: A Christian's View
Pre:2. – 1:7 – 7:3 – 9:18.
Plato.
The Last Days of Socrates.
Pre:1. [Source C-a.]
Protagoras and Meno.
4:15-17. [Source C-a.]
Playfair, Guy Lyon.
The Indefinite Boundary.
2:2; 10-11. – 6:10-11; 15.
4:23.[Source H-a]
Plotinus.
The Enneads. IV.
8:17. [Source C-b.]
Five Books of Plotinus.
1:24–25. [Source C-b.]
Pole, Major Wellesley Tudor. (Dowding, Private.)
Private Dowding.
11:27.
Proceedings of the Society for Psychical Research. Vol. 6.
5:9; 12-15. – 8:38. – [Source K-c.]
Puryear, Herbert B.
The Edgar Cayce Primer.
1:23.

Rahula, Dr Walpola.
What the Buddha Taught.
2:15 – 3:13-14. – [Source B-a.]
Randall, Neville.
Life After Death.
10:6; 9-10.
Rawlings, Dr Maurice. – See Cooper.
Ritchie, Dr George G.
Return from Tomorrow.
7:17. – 9:1–2. – 11:21.
Roberts, Jane.
Seth Speaks.
1:13. – 3:24-26; 28-29. – 4:4. – 5:5. – 6:26. –
8:27; 37; 45. – 10:2-3 – 11:9; 15; 17; 19; 22. – 12:3.
Rudolph, Kurt.
Gnosis.
8:46-47; 49. – [Source D-f.]
Said-Ruete, Emily.
Memoirs of an Arabian Princess.
5:3-4. – 7:26. – [Source F-b.]
Salter, Helen. – See Cummins.
Schweitzer, Dr. Albert.
My Life and Thought.
1:1-3.
Scott, G.F. – See Sherwood.
Seth. – See Roberts.
Seton, Ernest Thompson.
The Gospel of the Redman.
1:22. [Source G-a.]
Shankara, Acharya.
The Crest Jewel of Wisdom.
1:11-12. – 12:4. – [Source A-c.]

Sherwood, Jane.
The Country Beyond.
10:15; 17; 24.
Sigstedt, Cyriel Odhner.
The Swedenborg Epic.
5:17-18. [Source J-a.]
Silver Birch. – See Ortzen.
Songs of Praise.
No.501. Horae B.V. Maria.
12:40.
Stainton Moses, Rev. William.
Spirit Teachings.
6:20; 29. – 7:16. – 11:12; 24; 28. – [Source J-c.]
Stead, W.T.
Letters from Julia.
5:25. – 7:1. – 9:30. – 10:23.
Stevenson, Dr Ian.
Twenty Cases Suggestive of Reincarnation.
2:19. – 7:13-14.
Stietencron, H, von. - See Kung, et al.
Strindberg, Johan August.
Legends.
8:39. – 9:13.
Sunday Times Magazine.
London. 8 November 1992.
8:42.
Swedenborg, Emanuel.
Arcana Caelestia, Vol.1.
5:16. [Source J-a.]
Heaven and Hell.
1:8-9. – 5:23-24. – 7:12. – 8:14-15. – [Source J-a.]
9:4; – 10:26. – 11:8; 13; 25-26. – [Source J-a.]
The Minor Spiritual Diary.
10:19. [Source J-a.]

Taylor, Allegra.

I Fly Out with Bright Feathers.

2:36. – 6:25. – 8:35.

Taylor, Gordon Rattray.

The Natural History of the Mind.

7:9. – 8:31.

Teresa of Ávila, Saint.

The Life of Saint Teresa by Herself.

4:29.

Thomas, Rev. Charles Drayton.

Life Beyond Death with Evidence.

10:16.

The Times, London.

14 July 1992.

4:18-19.

4 April 1992.

4:35. [Source J-f.]

Tovey, Sir Donald. – See Brown.

Travis, W. – See Watson.

Van der Post, Laurens.

The Lost World of the Kalahari.

5:1. [Source F-e.]

Wambach, Dr Helen.

Life before Life.

3:32-38 – 4:5-13.

Reliving Past Lives.

8:32.

Watson, Dr Lyall.

Beyond Supernature.

8:41.

Weed, Joseph J.

Wisdom of the Mystic Masters.

8:29; 33.

Whitton, Dr Joel; Fisher, Joe.
Life Between Life.
3:2-3; 27; 30.
Willett, Winifred. – See Cummins.
Wilmot, S.R. – *See Proceedings of the Society for Psychical Research.*
Wilson, Colin.
Afterlife.
6:8.
Wingfield, K.
Guidance from Beyond.
6:16; 21-22; 30-31.
More Guidance from Beyond.
8:4-6. – 10:12.
Winner, Elaine. – See Flynn.
Wright, Dean N.T.
Jesus and the Victory of God.
8:51-52.
Yeats, William Butler.
The Collected Poems of W.B. Yeats.
1:28.
Zeilik, Michael and Gaustad, John.
Astronomy, The Cosmic Perspective.
12:35.
Zukav, Gary.
Dancing Wu Li Masters.
12:15-16.

Bibliography

Asch, Sholem: *The Nazarene,* Trans. Maurice Samuel, Routledge, London, 1939.

Barker, Elsa: *Letters from a Living Dead Man,* [1914], Rider, London, 1918.

Barrett, Sir William, FRS: *Death-Bed Visions,* [1926], The Aquarian Press, Wellingborough, Northamptonshire, 1986.

Beard, Paul: *Living On: A Study of Altering Consciousness After Death,* George Allen & Unwin, London, 1980.

Beard, Paul: *Survival of Death: For and Against,* [1966], Psychic Press, London, 1972.

Bhagavad Gita: The Song of God, Trans. Prabhavananda & Isherwood, [1946], Phoenix House, London, 1947.

Bible: See *Holy Bible.*

Blavatsky, H.P: *The Key to Theosophy,* Theosophical Pub., London, 1889.

Blofeld, John: *The Wheel of Life: The Autobiography of a Western Buddhist,* [1959], Rider, Century Hutchinson, London, 1987.

Bragdon, Claude: *Merely Players,* Alfred A. Knopf, New York, 1929.

Brihadaranyaka Upanishad, Trans. Madhavananda Vireswarananda, Advaita Ashrama, Almora, Himalayas, 1935.

Brown, Rosemary: *Immortals at my Elbow,* Bachman & Turner, London, 1974.

Brunton, Dr Paul: *The Wisdom of the Overself,* [1943], Rider, Hutchinson, London, Pocket Edn, 1983.

Butler, Rev. Alban: *Lives of the Saints,* Ed. Herbert Thurston and Norah Leeson, Vol.IV, [1779], Burns Oates & Washbourne,

London, 1933.

Campbell, Joseph and Moyers, Bill: *The Power of Myth,* Ed. Betty Sue Flowers, Doubleday, New York, 1988.

Catholic Encyclopaedia, Vols. 4, 11. Robert Appleton, New York, 1908, 1911.

Cerminara, Dr Gina: *Many Mansions,* [1967], Neville Spearman, London, 1983.

Cerminara, Dr Gina: *The World Within,* [1957], William Sloane, New York, 1968.

Cochran, Lin: *Edgar Cayce on Secrets of the Universe,* Ed. Charles Thomas Cayce, [1989], Aquarian Press/Thorsons, HarperCollins, London, 1990.

Cooper, Wendy and Smith, Dr Tom: *Beyond our Limits,* Stein & Day, New York, 1982.

Crookall, Dr Robert: *The Study and Practice of Astral Projection,* [1960], Aquarian Press, London, 1961.

Crookall, Dr Robert: *What Happens When You Die,* Colin Smythe, Gerrards Cross, Bucks, UK, 1978.

Cummins, Geraldine: *Beyond Human Personality,* Ivor Nicholson & Watson, London, 1935.

Cummins, Geraldine: *The Road to Immortality,* [1932], The Aquarian Press, London, 1955.

Cummins, Geraldine: *Swan on a Black Sea,* [1965], Pelegrin Trust, Pilgrim Books, Tasburgh, Norwich, England, 1986.

Cummins, Geraldine: *They Survive,* Ed. E.B. Gibbes, Rider, London, 1946.

David-Neel, Alexandra: *Magic and Mystery in Tibet,* [1967], Unwin Paperbacks, London, 1986.

Descartes, René: *The Philosophical Works of Descartes.,*Vol 1.

(See Haldane and Ross.)

Douglas, Alfred: *Extra Sensory Powers: A Century of Psychical Research,* The Overlook Press, New York, 1977.

Dowding, Lord Air Chief Marshall: *Many Mansions,* Rider, London, 1943.

Eliot, George: *Silas Marner,* [1861], The Classics Book Club, London, 1940.

Evans-Wentz, Dr W.Y: *The Tibetan Book of the Dead,* [1927], Oxford University Press, Oxford, 1960.

Fiore, Dr Edith: *The Unquiet Dead,* Doubleday, New York, 1987.

Fiore, Dr Edith: *You have been here Before,* Random House, New York, 1979.

Flynn, Charles P: *After the Beyond: Human Transformation and the Near-Death Experience,* Prentice Hall Press, New York, 1987.

Fox, Emmet: *Power Through Constructive Thinking,* [1932], Harper & Bros, New York, 1940.

Greaves, Helen: *Testimony of Light,* [1969], Neville Spearman, England, 1988.

Green, Celia: *Lucid Dreams: Proceedings of the Institute of Psychophysical Research,* Vol.1, Institute of Psychophysical Research, Oxford, 1968.

Guirdham, Dr Arthur: *The Cathars and Reincarnation,* Neville Spearman, London, 1970.

Haich, Elisabeth: *Initiation,* Trans. John Robertson, [1960], George Allen & Unwin, London, 1965.

Haldane, Elizabeth S. and Ross, G.R.T: (Trans.) *The Philosophical Works of Descartes,* Vol.1, University Press, Cambridge, 1911.

Harding, Dr Rosamond E.M: *An Anatomy of Inspiration,* Heffer & Sons, Cambridge, 1940.

Hardinge, Emma: *Modern American Spiritualism,* Pub. Author, New York Printing Co., New York, 1870.

Head, Joseph and Cranston, Sylvia: *Reincarnation: The Phoenix Fire Mystery,* Julian Press, Crown, New York, 1986.

Heindel, Max: *The Rosicrucian Cosmo-Conception, or Mystic Christianity,* [1909], Rosicrucian Fellowship, Oceanside, California, 23rd Ed, 1956.

Heindel, Max: *The Rosicrucian Mysteries,* Rosicrucian Fellowship Press, Ocean Park, California, 1911.

Holy Bible, Authorized King James Version, The Religious Tract Society, London.

*Holy Quaran,*Trans. Mohammed Marmaduke Pickthall, [1930], Quran Council of Pakistan, Karachi, 1st Edn, 1974.

Iverson, Jeffrey: *In Search of the Dead,* BBC Books,BBC Enterprises, London, 1992.

James, Prof. William: *The Varieties of Religious Experience: A Study in Human Nature,* [1902], Penguin Classics, Middlesex, 1986.

Johnson, Dr Raynor C: *A Religious Outlook for Modern Man,* Hodder & Stoughton, London, 1963.

Judge, William Q: *The Ocean of Theosophy,* The Theosophy Co., New York, 2nd Edn, 1893.

Jung, Dr. Carl G: *Memories, Dreams, Reflections,* (Ed.) Aniela Jaffé, [1961], Collins, and Routledge & Kegan Paul, London, 1963.

Jurriaanse, Aart: *Bridges,* [1978], Sun Centre, School of Esoteric Philosophy, South Africa, 1985.

Kardec, Allan: *Experimental Spiritism: The Mediums Book,* (Trans.) Anna Blackwell, [1861], Trübner, Ludgate Hill, London, 1876.

Khan, Hazrat Inayat: *The Sufi Message,* Vol.5, [1962], International Headquarters of the Sufi Movement, Geneva, Barrie & Jenkins, London, 1973.

Koran: See Holy Quran.

Kübler-Ross, Dr Elisabeth: *On Children and Death,* Collier Books, Macmillan, New York, 1985.

Kung, Hans; van Ess, Josef; von Stietencron, Heinrich and Bechert, Heinz: *Christianity and the World Religions,* Trans. Peter Heinegg [1987], Collins, London, 1987.

Langley, Noel: *Edgar Cayce on Reincarnation,* (Ed.) Hugh Lynn Cayce, [1967], Aquarian/Thorsons, HarperCollins, London, 1989.

Lingg, Ann M: *Mozart, Genius of Harmony,* Henry Holt, New York, 1946.

Lorimer, David: *Survival? Body, Mind and Death in the Light of Psychic Experience,* Routledge & Kegan Paul, London, 1984.

Lorimer, David: *Whole in One,* Arkana, Penguin Group, London, 1990.

Maclaine, Shirley: *Dancing in the Light,* Bantam Press, Transworld, London, 1986.

Maclaine, Shirley: *Going Within,* Bantam Press, Transworld, London, 1989.

Maclaine, Shirley: *Out on a Limb*, Elm Tree Books, Hamish Hamilton, London, 1983.

McTaggart, John Ellis: *Human Immortality and Pre-Existence*, Edward Arnold, London, 1915.

McTaggart, John Ellis: *The Nature of Existence*, Vol.II, Cambridge University Press, Cambridge, 1927.

Masefield, John: *The Collected Poems of John Masefield*, [1923], William Heinemann, London, 1932.

Maynard Smith, Canon H: *Frank, Bishop of Zanzibar*, Macmillan, New York and Toronto, 1926.

Moody Dr Raymond A.: *Life After Life: The investigation of a phenomenon – survival of bodily death*, [1975], Bantam Books, Mockingbird, New York, 1976.

Moody Dr Raymond A. *Reflections on Life After Life*, Corgi Books, Transworld Publishers, London, 1978.

Muldoon, Sylvan and Carrington, Hereward: *The Phenomena of Astral Projection*, [1951], Rider, London, 1969.

Okri, Ben: *The Famished Road*, [1991], Vintage, London, 1992.

Olcott, Henry S: *The Buddhist Catechism*, [1881], Theosophical Pub. Soc., London, 33rd Edn, 1897.

Ortzen, Tony, (ed.): *Silver Birch Companion*, [1986], Psychic Press, London, 2nd Edn, 1988.

Oxford Book of English Verse, Ed. Sir Arthur Quiller-Couch, [1900], Clarendon Press, Oxford, [New Edn, 1939], 1949.

Perry, Archdeacon Michael: *Psychic Studies: A Christian's View*, Aquarian Press, Thorsons Publishing Group, 1984.

Plato: *The Last Days of Socrates*, Trans. Hugh Tredennic, [1954], Penguin, Middlesex, 1964.

Plato: *Protagoras and Meno*, Trans. W.K.C. Guthrie, Penguin, Middlesex, London, 1956.

Playfair, Guy Lyon: *The Indefinite Boundary: An Investigation into the Relationship between Matter and Spirit*, Souvenir Press, London, 1976.

Plotinus: *The Enneads*, Trans. Stephen MacKenna, [1917], Faber & Faber, London, 4th Edn, 1969.

Plotinus: *Five Books of Plotinus,* Trans. Thomas Taylor, Edward Jeffrey, Pall Mall, London, 1794.

Pole, Wellesley Tudor: *Private Dowding,* [1917], Pilgrims Book Services, Tasburgh, Norwich, UK, 1984.

Proceedings of the Society for Psychical Research, Vol.6, 1889–90; Vol.7, 1891–92; Vol.36, 1928, The Society for Psychical Research, Kensington, London.

Puryear, Herbert B: *The Edgar Cayce Primer,* Bantam Books, New York, 1982.

Quran: See Holy Quran.

Rahula, Dr Walpola: *What the Buddha Taught,* [1959], Grove Press, New York, 2nd Edn, 1974.

Randall, Neville: *Life after Death,* Robert Hale, London, 1974.

Ritchie, Dr George: *Return from Tomorrow,* Spire Books, Fleming H. Revell, New Jersey, 1978.

Roberts, Jane: *Seth Speaks: The Eternal Validity of the Soul,* [1972], Prentice Hall, Simon & Schuster, New York, 1987.

Rudolph, Kurt: *Gnosis: The Nature and History of Gnosticism,* Trans. and Ed. Robert McLachlan Wilson, [1983], T.&T. Clark, Edinburgh, 1998.

Said-Ruete, Emily: *Memoirs of an Arabian Princess,* D. Appleton and Co., New York, 1888.

Schweitzer, Dr Albert: *My Life and Thought,* Trans. C.T. Campion, [1931], George Allen & Unwin, London, 1933.

Seton, Ernest Thompson: *The Gospel of the Redman: An Indian Bible,* [1937], Psychic Press, London, New Edn, 1970.

Shankara, Acharya: *The Crest Jewel of Wisdom: Vivekachudamani,* Trans. Charles Johnston, [1925], John Watkins, London, 1964.

Sherwood, Jane: *The Country Beyond – and The Psychic Bridge,* [1944], Neville Spearman, London, 1969.

Sigstedt, Cyriel Odhner: *The Swedenborg Epic: The Life and Works of Emanuel Swedenborg,* Swedenborg Society, London, 1981.

Songs of Praise, [1936], Oxford University Press, London, Melody 23rd Edn. 1972.

Smart, Ninian: *The Religious Experiences of Mankind,* Collins Fount Paperbacks, London, 1986.

Stainton Moses, Rev. William: *Spirit Teachings,* The Psychological Press Association, London, 1883.

Stead, W.T. *Letters from Julia,* Grant Richards, London, 1898.

Stevenson, Dr. Ian, MD: *Twenty Cases Suggestive of Reincarnation,* [1966], University Press of Virginia, Charlottesville, 2nd Edn. 1988.

Strindberg, Johan August: *Legends,* Andrew Melrose, London, 1912.

Sunday Times Magazine,(London), 8 November 1992.

Swedenborg, Emanuel: *Arcana Caelestia,* Vol.1, Trans. John Elliott, [1749], Swedenborg Society, London, 1983.

Swedenborg, Emanuel: *Heaven and Hell: From Things Heard and Seen,* [1758], Trans. Rev. J.C. Ager [1958], Swedenborg Society, London, 1966.

Swedenborg, Emanuel: *The Minor Spiritual Diary,* Vol.5, *c.* 1751. Held at the Swedenborg Society, London.

Taylor, Allegra: *I Fly Out with Bright Feathers. The Quest of a Novice Healer,* [1987], C.W. Daniel, England, 1992.

Taylor, Gordon Rattray: *The Natural History of the Mind,* [1979], Granada, London, 1981.

Teresa Of Ávila: *The Life of Saint Teresa by Herself,* [1562], Trans. J.M. Cohen, Penguin, London, 1957.

Thomas, Rev. Charles Drayton: *Life Beyond Death with Evidence,* W. Collins, London, 1928.

The Times (London), 14 July 1992 and 4 April 1992.

Van der Post, Laurens: *The Lost World of the Kalahari,* Hogarth Press, London, 1958.

Wambach, Dr Helen: *Life before Life,* Bantam Books, New York, 1979.

Wambach, Dr Helen: *Reliving Past Lives,* [1978], Hutchinson, London, 1979.

Watson, Dr Lyall: *Beyond Supernature: A New Natural History of the Supernatural,* Hodder & Stoughton, London, 1986.

Weed, Joseph J: *Wisdom of the Mystic Masters* [1968], A. Thomas & Co., Northants., 1978.

Whitton, Dr Joel L. and Fisher, Joe: *Life Between Life: Scientific Explorations into the Void Separating One Incarnation from the Next.* [1986], Warner, New York, 1988.

Wilson, Colin: *Afterlife,* [1985], Dolphin, Doubleday, New York, 1987.

Wingfield, K: *Guidance from Beyond,* Philip Allan, London, 1923.

Wingfield, K: *More Guidance from Beyond,* Philip Allan, London, 1925.

Wright, N.T: *Jesus and the Victory of God,* Vol.2, of Christian Origins and the Question of God, Society for Promoting Christian Knowledge, London, 1996.

Yeats, William Butler: *The Collected Poems of W.B. Yeats,*[1933], Macmillan, London, 1950.

Zeilik, Michael and Gaustad, John: *Astronomy: The Cosmic Perspective,* Harper & Row, New York, 1983.

Zukav, Gary: *Dancing Wu Li Masters: An Overview of the New Physics,* [1979], Bantam Doubleday Dell Group, New York, Bantam Edn, 1980.

Acknowledgements to Authors and Publishers

Excerpt from *The Wheel of Life: The Autobiography of a Western Buddhist* by John Blofield, published by Rider. Reprinted by permission of The Random House Group Ltd.

Excerpt from *The Tibetan Book of the Dead* by W.Y Evans-Wentz, published by OUP. Reprinted with permission from Oxford University Press.

Excerpt from *Life Between Life* by Joel L. Whitton and Joe Fisher, first published by Doubleday and Company. Copyright © 1986.

Excerpt from *Power Through Constructive Thinking* by Emmett Fox, published by HarperCollins. Reprinted with permission from HarperCollins. ©

Excerpt from *The Cathars and Reincarnation* by Dr Arthur Guirdham, published by Neville Spearman. Reprinted by permission from The Random House Group Ltd.

Excerpt from *The Testimony of Light* by Helen Greaves, published by Neville Spearman. Reprinted with permission from The Random House Group Ltd.

Excerpt from *Life After Life* by Raymond Moody, published by Rider. Reprinted with permission from The Random House Group Ltd.

Excerpt from *The Lost World of the Kalahari* by Laurens van der Post, published by Hogarth Press. Reprinted with permission from The Random House Group.

Excerpt from *What the Buddha Taught* by Walpola Rahula, published by Grove/Atlantic, Inc. Reprinted with permission from Grove Atlantic, Inc © 1959, 1974.

Excerpt from *Life After Death* by Neville Randall ©, first published by Robert Hale Ltd, 1974. Reprinted with permission from Robert Hale Ltd.

Excerpt from *The Natural History of the Mind* by Gordon Rattray Taylor © 1979, published by Harold Matson Co, Inc. Reprinted with permission from Harold Matson Co, Inc.

Excerpt from *I Fly Out With Bright Feathers* by Allegra Taylor, published by C W Daniel. Reprinted by permission of The Random House Group Ltd.

Excerpt from *Dancing Wu Li Masters* by Gary Zukav, published by Rider/Hutchinson. Reprinted with permission from The Random House group Ltd.